APEC and the RISE of CHINA

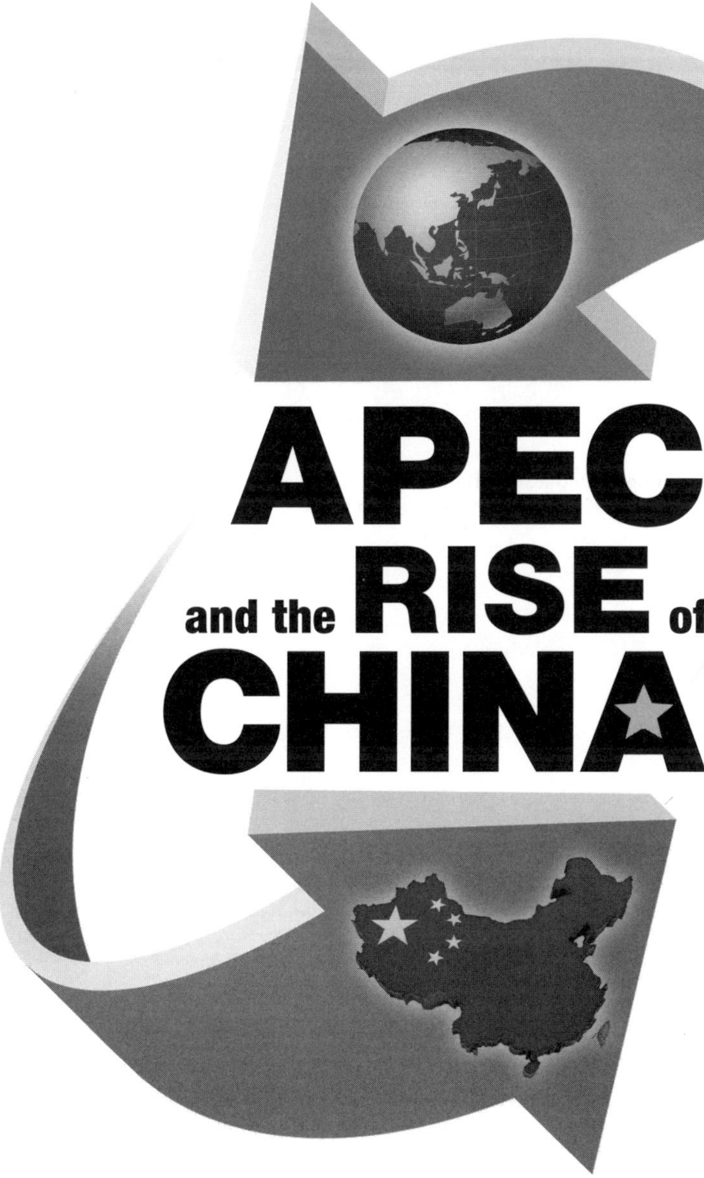

APEC and the RISE of CHINA

Editors

Lok Sang HO

Lingnan University, Hong Kong

John WONG

East Asian Institute, National University of Singapore, Singapore

World Scientific

NEW JERSEY • LONDON • SINGAPORE • BEIJING • SHANGHAI • HONG KONG • TAIPEI • CHENNAI

Published by

World Scientific Publishing Co. Pte. Ltd.

5 Toh Tuck Link, Singapore 596224

USA office: 27 Warren Street, Suite 401-402, Hackensack, NJ 07601

UK office: 57 Shelton Street, Covent Garden, London WC2H 9HE

British Library Cataloguing-in-Publication Data
A catalogue record for this book is available from the British Library.

APEC AND THE RISE OF CHINA

ISBN-13 978-981-4329-40-8
ISBN-10 981-4329-40-1

Typeset by Stallion Press
Email: enquiries@stallionpress.com

Printed in Singapore by World Scientific Printers.

Foreword

The first decade of the 2000s has just drawn to an end: the year when China became the world's second largest economy, ten years after her 2001 accession to the World Trade Organization and three decades since embarking on the path of economic reform, changing profoundly the region and the world in the process. China — her industrial output continuing to expand by over 60 percent since 2007 while most major mature economies' have shrunk — is now commonly dubbed the "factory of the world", and will increasingly be seen as a major "market of the world", as her leaders boost demand on the back of rising productivity and incomes in the country and region and against the backdrop of continuing weak growth in most mature economies. In parallel with this process, almost presciently, APEC was created in the early years of this period of change, twenty-one years ago. As the pre-eminent economic organisation of the region, charged with promoting trade and prosperity in Asia-Pacific, APEC is a first-line participant in the fundamental re-accommodation of the world economy to the phenomenal rise of China and the economies of the region.

Lingnan University was therefore pleased to convene a conference on APEC at 20 and the Rise of China, held in February 2010 with the help of the East Asia Institute of Singapore. The collection of nine chapters contained in this book grows out of the contributions presented at this conference and, we believe, represents a timely contribution to an important subject: an assessment of the achievements, promises and future of APEC upon completion of two decades in operation. Comprising only nine but very informative tight chapters, this volume addresses a range of subjects of great importance. First, how the region's evolving institutional architecture may best serve its interest, and whether and how greater integration of its economies can be achieved. Second, several chapters touch upon the global dimension, concerning the need for China to play a bigger role in global affairs, and the scope and need for better global governance. Several chapters also point to the importance of sustainable development: a continuing theme which both China and other countries in the region need to address.

I thank all participants at the conference and co-authors of this volume for their valuable contributions. In particular, I am grateful to Professor John Wong, Director of the East Asia Institute at the time, for his co-hosting the referred conference with us and for his help in facilitating the publication of this volume. I am also grateful to my colleague Professor Ho Lok-Sang for taking up my invitation to organise this event and for the fine results Professor Wong and he jointly delivered.

I hope this volume will serve as a useful reference for a number of years to come.

Jesús Seade
Director, Hong Kong APEC Study Centre
Vice President
Sydney S. W. Leong Chair Professor of Economics
Lingnan University, Hong Kong
January 2011

Contents

List of Contributors

Chien-peng CHUNG received his PhD in political science at the University of Southern California. He has published articles in journals such as the *Korean Journal of Defense Analysis, Problems of Post-Communism, China Quarterly, Pacific Affairs, China Report, Issues & Studies, Asian Affairs: An American Review, Harvard International Review*, and *Foreign Affairs*. He has also published two books, *Domestic Politics, International Bargaining, and China's Territorial Disputes*, and *China's Multilateral Cooperation in Asia and the Pacific: Institutionalizing Beijing's Good Neighborhood Policy*, with Routledge.

Lok Sang HO holds a doctorate in Economics from the University of Toronto. He was President of the Hong Kong Economic Association for 8 years up to 2007. He is currently Professor of Economics and Director of the Centre for Public Policy Studies, Lingnan University, Hong Kong. He has published over 90 academic papers in journals and book chapters, including *Journal of Housing Economics, Journal of Real Estate Finance and Economics, Contemporary Economic Policy, Policy Sciences, Urban Studies, Regional Studies, Social Science and Medicine, World Economy, Journal of International Economics, Pacific Economic Review, Journal of Asian Economics*, and *Industrial and Labor Relations Review*. He is the author of *Principles of Public Policy Practice* (2001) and *Health Care Financing and Delivery*: A *Model for Reform* (1997), and a joint editor of several books, including *Public Governance in Asia and the Limits of Electoral Democracy* (Edward Elgar, 2010), *China, Hong Kong, and the World Economy* (Palgrave-Macmillan, 2006), *Happiness and Public Policy* (Palgrave Macmillan, 2006).

Xiuping HUA obtained her PhD degree in Finance from the University of Sheffield Management School (UK). She joined the University of Nottingham Ningbo, China in September 2010. Prior to joining the University of Nottingham, she had worked as a research fellow at a prestigious Chinese non-governmental think tank in Economics and Finance, China Finance 40 Forum. Her current research interests include option returns and volatility, China's economic policy and financial market, international finance.

Yiping HUANG is Professor of Economics at the China Macroeconomic Research Center at the Peking University. He is also an adjunct professor at the Crawford School of Economics and Government of the Australian National University. Before moving back to academia in 2009, He was a managing director and chief Asia economist for Citigroup, General Mills International Professor at the Columbia University, director of the China Economy Program at the Australian National University and policy analyst at the Research Center for Rural Development of the State Council. He has published numerous papers in academic journals and four academic books. He received his PhD in Economics from the Australian National University and Master of Economics from the Renmin University of China.

Lionel Wei-Li LIONG is Project Research Officer at the Institute of China Studies, University of Malaya, Malaysia. Lionel is currently pursuing his postgraduate studies at the University of Cambridge, United Kingdom.

Rafael LEAL-ARCAS is Senior Lecturer in International Economic Law and European Union Law, and Deputy Director of Graduate Studies, Queen Mary University of London (Centre for Commercial Law Studies), United Kingdom. He is author of more than 60 publications on international trade law, WTO law, international investment law, international environmental law, and EU law. Among his publications are the books *International Trade and Investment Law:*

Multilateral, Regional and Bilateral Governance (Edward Elgar, 2010) and *Theory and Practice of EC External Trade Law and Policy* (Cameron May, 2008). For electronic access to some of his publications, see http://papers.ssrn.com/sol3/cf_dev/AbsByAuth.cfm?per_id=327976. A member of the Madrid Bar, he is a 2011 Global Research Fellow at NYU Law School and at the World Trade Institute in Bern. He has been a Visiting Scholar at Georgetown University Law Center, Fellow at Georgetown's Institute of International Economic Law, Fellow at the American Society of International Law, Visiting Researcher at Harvard Law School, Visiting Researcher at New York University School of Law, Fellow at the Australian National University, and Visiting Scholar at the University of Wisconsin-Madison Law School. He completed his graduate legal education at Stanford, Columbia, the London School of Economics, and the European University Institute, Florence, Italy.

Zhongying PANG is Professor of International Relations, School of International Studies, Renmin University of China. He obtained his PhD in International Politics from Peking University. He has been writing on regional and global affairs. His Chinese publications include *China and Asia* (Shanghai Academy of Social Sciences Press, 2004), *Global Governance: Views from China* (ed., Hong Kong Peace Books, 2006) and *Global Governance and China* (Peking University Press, 2011). His English published papers include "Globalisation and China: China's Response to the Asian Economic Crisis", "Assessing the Diplomatic Power of China", "Playing by Rules: China's Growing Global Role", "China in Africa", "China's Non-intervention Question". Pang was a political member of the Chinese Embassy in Jakarta, Indonesia and a Visiting Fellow at the Brookings Institution in Washington, US.

Khee Giap TAN is Chair of Singapore National Committee for Pacific Economic Cooperation (SINCPEC), Co-Director of Asia Competitiveness Institute of Lee Kuan Yew School of Public Policy, National University of Singapore.

John WONG is Professorial Fellow of the East Asian Institute of the National University of Singapore (NUS). He was formerly Research Director of EAI and Director of the Institute of East Asian Political Economy, Singapore (1990–1996). Prior to this, he taught Economics at the University of Hong Kong (1966–1971) and then the NUS (1971–1990). He also taught briefly at Florida State University as a Fulbright Visiting Professor in 1979. He had visiting appointments with Harvard's Fairbank Centre, Yale's Economic Growth Centre, Oxford's St. Antony College, and Stanford University. In 1996, he held the Chair of ASEAN Studies at the University of Toronto. He has done consultancy work for the Singapore government and many international organisations, including UN ESCAP, ADB, UNIDO, and APO. He serves on the editorial board of many learned journals on Asian studies and economic development. He has written and edited 28 books, and published over 400 articles and papers on the development of China and other East Asian economies, including ASEAN. He obtained his PhD in Economics from London in 1966.

Emile Kok-Kheng YEOH is Director and Associate Professor of the Institute of China Studies, University of Malaya, Malaysia. He graduated with a PhD from the University of Bradford, West Yorkshire, England (1998). His research interests include institutional economics, China studies, decentralisation and fiscal federalism, and socio-racial diversity and the role of the state in economic development. His works appeared in *The Copenhagen Journal of Asian Studies, GeoJournal: An International Journal on Human Geography and Environmental Sciences, International Journal of China Studies, Malaysian Journal of Economic Studies and the Copenhagen Discussion Paper Series,* among others, and his recent edited or authored books include *Ethnic Interaction and Segregation on Campus and at the Workplace* (2004), *Economic Kaleidoscope* (2005), *China and Malaysia in a Globalizing World* (2006), *Emerging Trading Nation in an Integrating World* (2007), *Facets of a Transforming China* (2008), *China in the World* (2008), *CJAS Special Issue* (26(2)): *Transforming China* (2008), *Regional Political Economy of China Ascendant* (2009), *China-ASEAN*

Relation (2009), *Towards Pax Sinica?* (2009), *IJCS Special Issue* (1(1)): *Changing China* (2010), *East Asian Regional Integration* (2010) and *IJCS Special Issue* (1(2)): *Social Change in the Age of Reform* (2010).

Im-Soo YOO is Professor Emeritus at the Department of Economics, Ewha Womans University, Seoul, Republic of Korea. He obtained his Bachelor of Arts and Master in Business Administration from Yonsei University, Korea, and holds a PhD in Economics from University of Cologne, Germany. Dr Yoo has been teaching for the past 30 years. He has served Visiting Professorship at various universities throughout Europe and Asia including University of Munich, University of Potsdam and University of Paris III. Dr Yoo served as Visiting Professor at the Faculty of Economics and Administration, University of Malaya, Kuala Lumpur, Malaysia, and currently he is a Senior Research Fellow at the Institute of China Studies, University of Malaya. Dr Yoo was advisor to the Board of Audit and Inspection of Korea and also several other government and corporate organizations. He was President of Korean Association for Contemporary European Studies and currently President of Asia-Europe Perspective Forum. His current research interests include international economics, trade, economic development and global finance especially for economic integration between European Union and East Asian community.

Bin ZHANG is Senior Research Fellow at Institute of World Economics and Politics (IWEP), Chinese Academy of Social Sciences. He is also managing editor of *Journal of World Economy* (Chinese). His research focuses on China's monetary policy, RMB exchange rate policy, regional financial cooperation in East Asia.

1

APEC and the Rise of China: an Introduction

Lok Sang Ho

Lingnan University

John Wong

East Asian Institute, National University of Singapore

THE APEC PROCESS

APEC (Asia Pacific Economic Cooperation) was created in 1989 by 12 members as a loose consultative forum, with no organisation structure and with only a limited programme for some broad sectoral cooperation. The original long-term concept was the formation of the Asia-Pacific Community, which was initially advocated by Australia's former Prime Minister Bob Hawke and Japan's former Prime Minister Masayoshi Ohira. Prior to this, the informal academic forum PAFTAD (Pacific Trade and Development), the independent Pacific business network PBEC (Pacific Basin Economic Council), and the tripartite organisation PECC (Pacific Economic Cooperation Council) had laid down some broad cooperative framework and helped drive and shape the official APEC process. The APEC process can facilitate regional cooperation largely because the annual gathering of APEC leaders provides a useful and convenient platform for members to exchange views and share ideas, and it also promotes various forms of bilateral and multilateral cooperation.

In November 2009, as the APEC leaders gathered in Singapore to celebrate its 20th birthday, the organisation had 21 economies as members. When APEC was first formed in 1989, its average tariff rate in the group of 12 was 16.9%. By 2004, it went down to 5.5%. In 1989, APEC's share of the world's exports was 58%. By 2008, its exports constituted 67% of the world's total (44% of the world trade). APEC today comprises 2.7 billion population or 40% of the world's total, and accounts for 55% of the world's total GDP in PPP (purchasing power parity) terms. APEC is politically and economically a formidable grouping indeed.

To speed up economic cooperation, the 1994 Bogor Declaration was a breakthrough as it set free and open trade and investment as the most important goal for APEC. Developed APEC economies were committed to eliminating obstacles to trade and investment by 2010, and developing APEC economies by 2020. Subsequently, various programmes or action plans such as the Osaka Action Agenda, Manila Action Plan, Shanghai Accord, Busan Roadmap had all provided further commitments to realising such goals. In the liberalisation and facilitation of trade and investment, APEC is supposed to follow the guiding principles of "comprehensiveness" (i.e. policy dialogues can target all forms of trade and investment barriers) and "open regionalism".

In terms of substantive economic cooperation, however, APEC has so far delivered very few tangible results and its overall pace of trade liberalisation process has achieved preciously little. This is partly due to its enormous diversity (in terms of geography, culture, political ideology as well as stages of economic development) and partly because of its emphasis on consensus and voluntarism for policy implementation — many agreements made within APEC are of non-binding nature. Operationally, when it comes to serious economic coopertion, its programmes are often frustrated by the so-called "spaghetti bowl effect", i.e. getting disrupted by numerous bilateral and sub-regional Free Trade Agreements (FTAs)/Economic Partnership Agreements (EPAs) that are already in existence in the region. APEC is, therefore, facing the challenge of how to reduce the negative interaction from the multilayers of FTAs/EPAs in the region.

Not surprisingly, APEC in recent years had run into a kind of "identity crisis" as well as "credibility crisis", particularly towards the end of the Bush Administration, which was quite luke-warm towards APEC activities. Though President Obama showed renewed US interest in APEC, the outbreak of the global financial crisis had soon diverted the attention of APEC leaders from regional cooperation to their own economic woes at home. After all, APEC as a loose grouping is simply not equipped to deal with global economic crises. If anything, the economic crisis had actually led to more trade protectionism and more serious global economic imbalances on the part of many members, which are not conducive to trade liberalisation and economic cooperation.

In fact, the global financial crisis had brought about considerable uncertainty to APEC's ongoing economic cooperation process, thereby further widening the gap between APEC's aspirations and their achievability. Worse still, the global economic crisis has also aggravated APEC's "identity crisis". It is understood that any progress towards economic cooperation will depend on the complete economic recovery of its members. And then what? Is there new direction for APEC? What will be the focus of its next phase of cooperation: security, climate change or others? Who will be the main driver?

THE RISE OF CHINA

Thanks to its success in economic reform and the open-door policy, China's economy has achieved spectacular growth at 9.7% for the period of 1978–2009. With its nominal GDP totaling about US$4.9 billion at the end of 2009 and continued strong growth in 2010, China has overtaken Japan as the world's second largest economy — though China has long been the world's second largest economy in PPP (purchasing power parity) terms. In 2009, China overtook Germany as the world's leading exporting country. Globally and regionally, China has been a top trade partner (No. 1 or No. 2) with many major economies. For years, China has also been the world's most favourite destination for foreign direct investment (FDI). Over 90% of the Fortune's 500 have set up business in China. On account of its persistent "twin surpluses" — surplus in both current and capital accounts, China's foreign exchange reserves in early 2010 swelled to US$2.45 trillion as the world's largest holding. In fact, China for many years has been capital surplus economy, with its outward FDI rapidly rising — US$48 billion in 2009. The economic rise of China along with its far-reaching global and regional impact in terms of trade and investment is indeed unmistakable.

Of even greater importance is the fact that China suffered the least during this global financial crisis as it ended 2009 with a hefty 8.7% growth, compared to negative rates of growth for most industrial economies. China had also led the global economy in recovery, pulling many regional economies out of their recession. Is China destined to play a more important and pivotal role in the future APEC process?

In 1991, APEC scored a great political feat as it successfully admitted to the grouping the "three components" of China — the "People's Republic of China" on the Mainland, Taiwan (officially, "Chinese Taipei") and Hong Kong (officially, "Hong Kong, China"). From the outset, China was keen to be part of the APEC process, not just because this facilitated China's accession to the WTO but also, some 60–70% of China's trade and FDI stemmed from the APEC region — 8 or 9 of China's top 10 trade partners are APEC members. This explains why China has all along actively participated in APEC's various activities. At the same time, China has been keeping a rather low profile and behaving cooperatively in various APEC negotiations.

However, it seems quite clear that China's role and function in APEC is about to shift in the post-financial-crisis years ahead. First, the rapid rise of China's economy along with its extensive external outreaches has enabled China to play the critical role of an important engine of economic growth for a great number of APEC member economies. Indeed, China has for years followed a trade pattern whereby it consistently incurs trade deficits with its Asian neighbours by importing (machinery and equipment, and high tech parts and components from Japan, Korea and Taiwan; and raw materials and natural resources from the Association of Southeast Asia Nations (ASEAN) and Australia, etc) from them more than China exports to these economies. In this way, China's neighbours have been making use of China's huge domestic market as a source of their own economic growth.

Second, thanks to its export-oriented pattern of economic growth, China has become a strong integrating force in the region. It is well known that almost 60% of China's trade is made up of processing trade. China has to import before it can export. Before exporting a massive amount of finished manufactured products to the world over, China has to import all sorts of parts and components as well as natural resource products from its Asia-Pacific neighbours. China is a critical link for all the major international supply chains. In other words, China is crucial in numerous regional and global production networks. China's economic growth, therefore, also serves as a catalyst for the market-driven form of economic integration.

In terms of institutional arrangements, China has also been instrumental in promoting the "formal" process of regional economic integration in East Asia. The China-ASEAN Free Trade Agreement, as the first ASEAN plus one initiative of its kind, went into effect in 2010. China's economic relations with its ASEAN neighbours to its south have thus been expanding rapidly, and China is now ASEAN's third largest trade partner. In Northeast Asia, China has already established very strong trade and investment links with Japan and South Korea (China being their No. 1 trade partner). Taking advantage of its warmer relations with Japan, China is recently very keen to strengthen existing tripartite cooperation arrangements with Japan and South Korea. In the middle, China has gone on seven rounds of supplementary agreements of Closer Economic Partnership Arrangements (CEPA) with Hong Kong and Macau, and is presently pursuing similar arrangements with Taiwan, know as ECFA (Economic Cooperation Framework Agreement).

In short, APEC's East Asian member economies, which are neighbouring China, have been drawn increasingly closer towards

China either by informal market forces or by formal cooperation arrangements. So far, China has yet to establish any formal economic cooperation arrangements with North American economies and Australia. But China has already established very strong economic symbiosis with these advanced economies through an extensive web of trade, investment and finance. China is therefore set to play a pivotal role in re-vitalising the future APEC process.

In geo-political terms, however, the picture is more complicated. China's political and economic relations with individual APEC members are still riddled with problems and misconceptions. Several chapters in this book, particularly that by **Pang** and that by **Leal-Arcas**, highlight some of the difficult geo-political issues that are accompanying the rise of China, the former from a mainlander's perspective, the latter from a western perspective. Each demonstrates the big gap between expectations and reality — a theme noted by **Chung** and others as well. Some of China's neighbours, as well as its distant ally and adversary — the United States, still view the rise of China with apprehension. The greater integration of China into the APEC economy will also not be an easy and smooth process. Politically and economically, the USA is still a predominant power in the region for the foreseeable future. Japan's economic presence also remains very strong. For its greater and smoother economic involvement in APEC, China needs to cultivate good relations with both USA and Japan — hence the importance of the APEC's "G3". In short, China's more active participation in the future APEC process will pose a big challenge to China as much as to other APEC members.

Two of the key themes that come out from this collection is that China is now really an economic giant. It is not only "the factory of the world", but is fast moving into the role of "the importer of the last resort". As **Huang** started his chapter, "On January 1, 2005, Chicago-based journalist Sara Bongiorni made a New Year's resolution: not to buy any made-in-China products for a year. The Bongiorni family experienced an eventful year finding consumer goods that are not made in China, from candles for birthday cakes to shoes for sport activities. Sometimes they were able to find goods made in Japan or Korea or even the US, but prices were 20–50% higher. Even worse, they could not tell if these products contained any parts made in China (Bongiorni 2007)." This shows how much the world depends on China for its needs. But China has also emerged as the strongest importer when all the other markets weaken. Today American households are in need of rebuilding their asset base and are increasing their savings. It is generally recognised that the US will therefore import less relative to the earlier projected trajectory in the years to come. Huang acknowledged that the sustained growth of the Chinese economy at nearly 10% per year is possible, but may require a serious effort on the part of the Chinese authorities to reform its factor markets and in particular to render true costs more transparent, and thus to reconstruct incentives so that China's economic growth can be more sustainable. Against the background of a rapidly growing China, **Yeoh, Yoo and Liong** examined the new intra-regional trade relations within the Asia Pacific region, and particularly within the ASEAN+1 nations, noting that "China has started forming FTAs with many Asian nations and is in the process of playing an even more important role in the Association of Southeast Asian Nations (ASEAN) and ASEAN Free Trade Area (AFTA)". The authors noted that the Asia-Pacific region, unlike the EU and America, have always lacked a strong leadership. APEC, which was formed more than 20 years ago, is an attempt to promote economic partnership within the region under one leadership, so far without much success. The stakes are high and China has an important part to play in promoting mutually beneficial trade relations within the region.

Another theme that comes out from this volume, one that is echoed just recently by an article in *China Daily* (June 17, 2010) by Jin Bosong, research fellow and vice-director of the Department of Chinese Trade Research at the Chinese Academy of International Trade and Economic Cooperation, is that China should play a bigger role in global affairs and particularly global economic affairs. According to **Leal-Arcas**, "China should therefore play a more prominent multilateral role, not only at the WTO, but also at the IMF and the World Bank as well as in international economic governance". According to Leal-Arcas, China meets all the three criteria that Fred Bergsten listed to be required of a global power. He cited Robert Zoellick and Justin Lin, the President and The Chief

Economist of the World Bank respectively, in arguing that China and the US must cooperate and become the engine for the G20, "Without a strong G-2, the G-20 will disappoint". In recent years, China indeed has become much more vocal about international issues. Zhou Xiaochuan's March 23, 2009 essay on the website of the People's Bank of China is a case in point, as he called for the replacement of the US dollar as the dominant world currency by an alternative "international reserve currency that is disconnected from individual nations and is able to remain stable in the long run".

One key subject related to China as an importer is the RMB exchange rate. As is widely known, the RMB has come under tremendous pressures to appreciate, and in July 2005 China did allow the RMB–US exchange rate to gradually appreciate relative to the US dollar. But the pace of appreciation was regarded as grossly inadequate. Views among economists fall into opposite camps. At one extreme, Nobel Laureate Paul Krugman argued in *New York Times* that the RMB should appreciate significantly, saying that China was hurting the recovery of the world economy by not appreciating its currency fast enough. At the other extreme, Robert Mundell, another Nobel Laureate, along with Justin Lin, warned against rapid RMB appreciation, saying that this would not help the US to promote its exports, but would hurt American interests. The experience of Japan does lend credence to the latter view, as Japan lost its role as an engine of growth for Asian economies and as a major importer. Its stagnant economy has already added many more "lost years" to the "lost decade".

Reflecting these divergent views are two contributions in this volume. One, by **Zhang**, argued in favour of a 10% appreciation against the US dollar under a scheme that he called "a middle ground solution". The other, by **Ho**, argued in favour of the RMB pegging against a basket of currencies each weighted by their respective GDP's (lagged two years), saying this would increase the flexibility of the exchange rate without risk of destabilizing the system. He argued that many of the other Asian economies may also find a similar regime for their own currencies beneficial as well. This proposal is similar to that made by some Japanese scholars, and is pertinent to the subject of integration in that by pegging to such a basket individually, the currencies that do so will effectively become a currency block, with mutual exchange rates stabilised. He argued that the exchange rate for each currency vis-à-vis this basket should be pitched at such a level that is consistent with internal balance i.e., balanced fiscal budget at full employment. On the other hand, Zhang argues that the one-off 10% RMB appreciation against the US dollar should go hand in hand with an annual ±3% band against the US dollar, and that now is a very good time for implementing the trade-off solution to the RMB exchange rate reform.

APEC was born in 1989, and more than two decades has gone since. The fact is that it is still alive, and that countries are still waiting to join the club. According to Shiro Armstrong, writing in East Asia Forum (June 2, 2008), "India is on the doorstep, wanting to join APEC and there is potential for leverage to be used positively to reach an agreement with India ('come into line with APEC developing countries on Doha and we'll let you in our club'). It was American frustration at Indian posture in the Doha negotiations that kept the door closed to India in Sydney last September (i.e. 2007)". Logic suggests that an organisation should not survive if its members do not find it serving a useful purpose, and that it cannot be dysfunctional when others still seek membership. As **Chung** pointed out, APEC adopted an "evolutionary approach" of being a loose forum, "where commitments are voluntary with emphasis on arriving at consensus unhurriedly through personal diplomacy and informal discussions has come to dominate the *modus operandi* of the forum". As such, it is not easy to count items quantitatively as evidence of its success. First of all, there is little consensus to speak of beyond the basic principles of freer trade and greater intra-regional cooperation. Chung described the evolutionary process, and laid out the two possible competing designs, namely the "Western/American/Structured" vs. the "Asian/Chinese/Process-oriented" design, and offered glimpses into how politics interfered with economics in reality. One incident worth mentioning is that at a time when domestic politics required Japan to keep tariffs on imported rice, wheat and other cereals at the range of 300–500%, it also realised that moving closer to the Asian position on the non-binding, voluntary, consensual and non-discriminatory nature of APEC's functioning may garner it the support of Asian countries in deflecting US pressure on trade liberalisation.

"Disappointed with the 'flexibility' already demonstrated by APEC member economies at Bogor, US President Clinton skipped Osaka (1995) altogether". Chung noted the apparent failure of APEC, for example, when it quietly dropped its own goal of creating a free trade and investment zone among its developed member economies by 2010. But he nevertheless considered it quite successful, in terms of bringing nations across the Pacific together to discuss trade, investment, and other issues at a high level.

Pang painted a less sanguine picture for the future of APEC. While he acknowledged China's reaffirmation of open regionalism and welcomed the US as an APEC member, he was wary of American domination and suspicious of the possible damaging effect of US interference. In particular, he saw a possible Trans-Pacific Partnership between Japan and US as detrimental to existing East Asian processes. At the same time he recognised the concrete achievements at the subregional level, such as the agreement between China and ASEAN (CAFTA) as well as monetary and financial multilateral cooperation/governance — wider currency swap arrangements like Chiang Mai Initiative (CMI) and Asian Bond Market Initiative (ABMI). However, to him, these achievements appeared to overshadow what APEC can do and indeed call into question the meaningfulness of the very existence of APEC.

Our concluding chapter, written by **Tan and Chiang,** looked at APEC and the rise of China from a more global perspective. They touched upon most of the issues discussed in the chapters throughout the book. The central message that they wanted to convey, and one that reflected sentiments expressed by **Huang**, whose chapter was devoted to an analysis of the sustainability of the rapid development of mainland China, was that the governments of developing countries in Asia have to invest more in social infrastructure and social capital, as these nations confront the consequences of globalisation on the environment and on the social fabric, particularly the widely observed increase in income disparity. As **Huang** pointed out, many companies are currently shirking their social responsibilities. "If companies strictly follow policies on social welfare contributions, commonly their payrolls would have to rise by at least 35–40%, including contributions to pensions (20% of payroll), medical insurance (6%), employment benefit (2%), work injury insurance (1%), maternity benefit (0.8%) and housing entitlement (5–10%).[1] By contributing less than required, especially for migrant workers, companies essentially reduce their cost of labour". Similarly, APEC has to rise to the challenge of promoting sustainable development through better governance and public education to ensure that development is compatible with a healthy environment and ecological balance, and through working out a comprehensive social safety net, an affordable healthcare system and affordable public housing to mitigate the increasing income disparity, in order to avoid possible social instability that could arise along with globalisation.

Mirroring what was expressed in an earlier chapter by **Pang, Tan and Chiang** noted that a matter that is of some concern to China and to ASEAN members is the role of the United States in an Asia Pacific community that includes the US and India as proposed by former Australian Prime Minister Kevin Rudd. The worry is that the US might dominate, eventually dictating the agenda that will come under discussion in the name of economic cooperation and integration. But Tan and Chiang looks at this matter more positively. The original spirit of APEC is open regionalism, and that means no country should be excluded. In order to prevent the domination of any single country by virtue of its sheer size or influence, all that APEC needs to do is to establish more formal rules that will guard against such domination. From this perspective, then, informality and open regionalism may not be compatible over the longer term, and the evolution of APEC is probably best seen to be in the direction of establishing more formal rules of governance that ensure fairness and equal participation.

Lok Sang Ho and John Wong
January 2011

NOTES

1. These were estimates provided in person by former Ministry of Finance official Zhai Fan in 2001.

Part I

Overview of Issues

2

Designing Asia-Pacific Economic Cooperation

Chien-peng Chung*

Lingnan University

ABSTRACT

This is a study of competing visions or designs of trans-Pacific economic cooperation, and attempts to unify, or retain, the differences that have evolved, in the organization and objectives of the multilateral Asia — Pacific Economic Cooperation (APEC) forum. This analysis also demonstrates the challenges faced by groups of countries with very different political-economy structures and values as they attempt to constitute an arrangement to gain trade advantages. Differences over how best to reach APEC's goals of trade liberalization, the extent to which APEC should be institutionalized, and the items to be put on the agenda of the annual conferences are at times so deep that the effective functioning of the forum itself gets questioned. There has been no shortage of meetings or reports within APEC, except that they typically lead to extremely few concrete proposals that all parties could agree on to implement and evaluate together, and even fewer results.

The contention in designing alternative visions for APEC may be seen as a reflection of opposing interests on liberalization and institutionalization within the forum between the United States, developed or industrialized countries and open export-oriented market economies on the one hand, and China and developing or industrializing countries on the other hand, with Japan having moved from the predominantly "Western" "camp" to the mostly "Asian" one. Fundamentally, while adherents of the "Western" design would like to promote economic competition and perpetuate the advantages that they enjoy with trade and investment liberalization, advocates of the "Asian" vision still believe to some extent in preserving the business-political nexus and industrial policies that have brought a respectable measure of political stability, material prosperity and diplomatic influence to countries like Japan, South Korea, Taiwan and Singapore. These two roadmaps reflect differences of interest and value, and are not easily reconcilable.

Keywords: APEC; design; trade; investment; liberalization; institutionalization.

INTRODUCTION

This is a study of competing visions or designs of trans-Pacific economic cooperation, and attempts to unify, or retain, the differences that have evolved, in the organisation and objectives of the multilateral Asia-Pacific Economic Cooperation (APEC) forum.[1] This analysis also demonstrates the challenges faced by groups of countries with very different political-economy structures and values as they attempt to constitute an arrangement to gain trade advantages. The means and goals of regulating and advancing trans-Pacific economic cooperation are important for us to care about because this macro-region encompasses half of world trade and investment.

APEC was formed in 1989 on the urgings of the governments of Japan and Australia with 12 founding countries gathering for its first meeting of government ministers on economic matters.[2] It was built upon a sense of shared interests and mutual trust derived through the efforts of the Pacific Economic Cooperation Council (PECC), a quasi-governmental regional institution where government officials from the countries that eventually launched APEC have been participating and interacting in a private capacity since 1980.[3] Twenty years have passed since APEC was established, and the forum now consists of 21 members. Countries coming together to craft a transnational forum implies a joint search for some common purpose. However, doing so also means that the medium would reflect the confluence or divergence of the national interests and underlying values of the constituent members, particularly that of the larger economies, as defined by their governing elites.

To the United States, the usefulness of APEC depended on its ability to accelerate the process of trade liberalisation within the grouping, particularly in improving US access to East Asian markets in areas where the US is competitive, such as aircraft, telecommunications, banking and insurance, and in strengthening America's hands in trade negotiations with the European Union (EU). A major consideration of both Japan and Australia in helping to bring about APEC was their attempt to thwart protectionist impulses on the part of the Europeans and Americans, through influencing the development of an open or non-discriminatory trans-Pacific trade liberalising economic arrangement. Japan had also hoped APEC would play to its strength as a major economic power and provide a stage for it to claim a leadership role in the Asian half of the forum through its trade with, investment in, technological transfers to, and financial institutions operating in other Asian countries.

China's vision for APEC was that of a consultative forum where decisions should be made gradually and through consensus, and economic and technical cooperation should be carried out on an equal footing with the reduction of trade barriers.[4] China had hoped that APEC could assuage US unilateralism in trade relations, enhance its prospects of gaining admission into the World Trade Organization (WTO), and legitimise its expanding influence in the Asia-Pacific region.[5] As for the countries of the Association of Southeast Asian Nations (ASEAN), while fully cognizant of APEC's usefulness in keeping the US market open in the face of increasing American protectionist sentiments, they were worried that joining APEC would mean diluting the salient position of ASEAN as a bloc in managing Southeast Asian affairs for themselves. At a ministerial conference at Kuching, Malaysia, in 1990, the ASEAN countries came to a consensus that participation in APEC must not come at the expense of ASEAN unity and cohesion, that APEC should not evolve from a forum for discussion into an arena for economic bargaining or negotiation, and that APEC ought not be transformed into a formal, structured institution.[6]

As APEC evolved, an "evolutionary approach" generally favoured by the Asian, Chinese and developing member governments or economies loosely organised around a forum where commitments are voluntary with emphasis on arriving at consensus unhurriedly through personal diplomacy and informal discussions has come to dominate the *modus operandi* of the forum; this has often been contrasted with a "legalistic and institutional approach" championed by the United States, and supported by Canada, Australia and New Zealand, which was to focus on building APEC up as a formal and structured organisation where the primary function of structured negotiations is to produce binding contracts and agreements.[7] In the former case, the appeal and stress is on the contribution to national development and domestic security through technical and economic cooperation — the subsuming of markets to the political logic of security and order,[8] while in the latter case, the construction of a trans-Pacific market is conceived primarily in terms of maximising individual choice by locking in the liberalisation of trade and associated economic processes through binding, comprehensive targets.

Reflecting two major organisational modes of economic regionalism, this division in the fundamental outlook for the forum has led to differences over how best to reach APEC's goals of trade liberalisation, the extent to which APEC should be institutionalised, and the items to be put on the agenda of the annual meetings, differences that are at times so deep that the effective functioning of the forum itself gets questioned. These divergent approaches almost guarantee that, although there is broad agreement among APEC member economies on the principles of economic cooperation and liberalisation of trade and investment, consensus on any concrete issue will typically be hard to achieve.

ONE "WESTERN/AMERICAN/STRUCTURAL" DESIGN (1989–1993)

The earliest "Western/American/Structured" (shortened to"Western") vision or design for APEC was what the US, major Western countries like Australia, New Zealand and Canada, and Japan had in mind as far back as the occasion of its inaugural meeting, then only at the level of ministers concerned with foreign and economic matters, in Canberra, Australia, in November 1989. Such a design would have accorded well with the structured and bureaucratised representative democratic systems of governance that policy makers in these countries embrace. The US was initially not too enthusiastic about APEC, and still trying to figure out its exact purpose. However, when an expert body of economic advisors, known as the Eminent Persons' Group, was constituted by the forum at its 1992 meeting, and soon took on the task of advocating - across-the-board trade liberalisation, Washington's interest in the grouping was greatly raised.

The high point of the "Western" design was reached at the first APEC Heads-of-State Meeting or Leaders' Summit at Blake Island off Seattle in the US in November 1993, when the host, US President Bill Clinton, suggested renaming and structuralising the Asia-Pacific Economic Cooperation as the Asia-Pacific Economic Community, along the lines of the European Economic Community, precursor of the EU. President Clinton had pointed out that US strategic policy in the Asia-Pacific region would henceforth be based on three elements: (1) Comprehensive US involvement in Asia-Pacific economic cooperation, (2) Realisation of an Asia-Pacific multilateral security mechanism under US leadership, and (3) Promoting democratisation in Asia-Pacific countries.[9] The American vision for APEC was clearly not just for the forum to push for a structured Asia-Pacific-wide free trade area, but also for the body to turn into a multilateral security arrangement under the direction of the US, and realise its objective of spreading political pluralism.

As primarily an economic forum, trade liberalisation, in the "Western" vision, was to be APEC's principal objective, as it was that of the US, which organised, led and dominated the Seattle Meeting. At least until 1995, the US economic policy stance on APEC could be summarised as follows: (1) Transform APEC as soon as possible into an Asia-Pacific free trade area through negotiations and agreements, (2) Liberalise trade in all economic sectors to avoid delay and allowing member economies to make strategic choices of "pick and choose", (3) Adopt the principle of discrimination between member and non-member economies to avoid non-member economies "free riding" on APEC's trade liberalisation efforts, and (4) Push for a structured forum with legally binding commitments through collective agreement.[10] As outlined in 1992 by the Australian government, there were four steps for APEC to take to advance its trade liberalisation objectives: reduce uncertainties in the regional market, address physical impediments to trade, harmonise national regulations and standards, and improve market access.[11]

The English-speaking industrialised economies saw traditional business practices elsewhere, particularly in the East and Southeast Asian countries, as manifesting widespread collusion, between firms, across industries, and among the political and economic elites, based on patronage and close personal ties, and these entrenched customs and domestic interest networks were what they wished to sweep away with the promotion and institutionalisation of trade liberalisation within APEC. Debates over free trade, and the attendant principle of discrimination, would become the major bones of contention between the US and industrialised Western economies on the one hand, and China and the developing Asian economies on the other.

China was obviously too large an Asian-Pacific economy to be left out of the forum, but its membership has proven to be problematic right from the beginning. The US has argued that, since China was not a market economy, it should not be allowed to join APEC. However, since the People's Republic of China claims Taiwan as part of its territory and was about to "resume" sovereignty over Hong Kong from Britain, diplomatic realities dictated that the exclusion of China would also mean the exclusion of the vibrant market economies of Hong Kong and Taiwan. This quandary was resolved when, as the 1991 Seoul ministerial meeting approached, Taiwan agreed to attend APEC meetings as "Chinese Taipei", together with China and Hong Kong.[12] China accepted this arrangement reluctantly, as long as all APEC members were designated as "economies" and not "states", which reflected its diplomatic weakness and isolation in the wake of the June 1989 Tiananmen Incident and its concern not to be left out of an emerging inter-governmental regional economic process, particularly since about 75% of China's trade and 80% of its foreign capital in the early 1990s involved other APEC members.[13] APEC governments then agreed that China would have an effective veto over who would represent Taiwan at the leaders' and other meetings.

The major institutional advancements for APEC took place between the 1992 ministerial meeting in Singapore and 1994 leaders' meeting in Bogor, Indonesia. A small secretariat with a very limited budget, autonomy and research capability was established at the Singapore meeting to facilitate and coordinate APEC activities. The APEC Secretariat is led by an Executive Director seconded from the member economy which is the annual host of the APEC process, and usually aided by one official each seconded from the foreign affairs or trade ministries of member economies for two to three years, and a proximate number of locally recruited administrative support staff.[14] Aside from the Secretariat, an Eminent Persons' Group (EPG) was also established at the 1992 meeting, the majority of whose members were economists under the chairmanship of American economist C. Fred Bergsten, and saw the task of the EPG as devising a roadmap for APEC to set itself on the path of trade, investment and later even financial liberalisation.

It was at the Seattle Leaders' Meeting in 1993 that arrangements were made for the two arguably most important APEC standing policy committees, the Committee on Trade and Investment (CTI) and the Budget and Management Committee (BMC) to be established in 1994 and meet twice a year. The Economic Committee, established at the 4th APEC Ministerial Meeting in 1994, has a mandate to promote structural, regulatory and legal reform in member economies, but this committee has been extremely hesitant, and one may even say, almost powerless, to drive any changes within the forum, except by organising seminars and workshops on strengthening economic and legal infrastructure.[15] By 1994, institutionally, there were in place five levels of organisational activities, from top to bottom: APEC Informal Leaders' Meeting, Ministerial Meeting, Sectoral Ministerial Meeting, Senior Officers' Meeting (SOM), and committee or working group, plus the Secretariat. Typically, the APEC Informal Leaders' Meeting takes place at the second half of every year, coinciding with concurrent meetings of foreign ministers, ministers of economics and trade, and business leaders. These ministerial meetings, which approve the budget and set policy directions for the forum in the following year, build on the ministerial meetings of economic sectors held occasionally throughout the year, all of which are supported by the SOMs, which are held four times a year, and serve as a coordinating body for the committees and working groups.[16]

TWO COMPETING DESIGNS: "WESTERN/AMERICAN/STRUCTURED" VS. "ASIAN/CHINESE/PROCESS-ORIENTED" (1994–1995)

Japan's Ministry of International Trade and Industry (MITI) had disseminated a proposal to Asia-Pacific countries in mid-1988 for an annual series of regional economic ministers' meetings, and the Australian government of Prime Minister Bob Hawke then expressed strong interest in MITI's idea, which led to coordination between Japan and Australia to carry out the APEC initiative.[17] The "Asia-Pacific" regional concept was an indication that Asian countries were ripe for recognition as a core group in regional economic cooperation and targets for trade liberalisation efforts, as a result of their decades of substantial growth.

Even so, as a regional trade grouping, APEC had a competitor almost right from its birth that refuses to go away. Worries about emerging trade blocs and protectionism in Europe and North America led Malaysia in December 1990 to propose an East Asian Economic Group (EAEG) that excluded the US, Canada, Australia and New Zealand. US officials opposed the proposal for "drawing a line down the Pacific", and under pressure from Washington, Tokyo was non-committal about EAEG.[18] As decided at the ASEAN finance ministers' meeting in October 1991, EAEG was renamed EAEC, grouping the ASEAN states with China, Japan and South Korea into an "East Asian Economic Caucus" within APEC to discuss issues of common concern to East Asian economies, despite US opposition.[19] Except for the open, industrialised and heavily export-oriented economies of Hong Kong and Singapore, which are unsurprisingly ardent free-trade advocates, the EAEC would become, for the "Western" design, a viper in APEC's womb, and an altogether self-standing ASEAN+3 conclave by December 1997.

As a large and expanding economy, the role of China in APEC is obviously important in determining the goals and direction of the forum. When China joined APEC, some Chinese had feared that the developed economies, led by the US and Japan, might dominate APEC. However, they were soon reassured by the presence of other countries also concerned about the potential dominance of larger powers. APEC membership included the ASEAN collective, which like China, remained highly committed to the norm of upholding sovereignty in the conduct of international relations, and very cautious in making sure that APEC's institutional development would not constrain members to a course of action that they have no wish to pursue. In the run-up to hosting the Bogor summit, President Suharto of Indonesia was convinced by the US and Australia to press the cause for trade liberalisation within APEC, at least to set a timetable to that effect.[20] Although Suharto seemed to have lost interest in this cause when his country was no longer the host of

APEC, the dominant theme at Bogor would continue to be the free trade push championed by the US and other Western countries. However, China and ASEAN managed to set aside US President Clinton's prior proposals at Seattle for "securitising" APEC or institutionalising it to any meaningful extent.

One of China's main objectives in APEC is to strengthen its relationship with ASEAN.[21] Within APEC, China has unfailingly supported ASEAN's 1990 "Kuching Consensus", based on the "ASEAN Way", which has evolved through decades of interaction among ASEAN member states and is characterised by the norms of decision-making based on consensus, gradualism, and voluntarism.[22] China shares the belief with ASEAN and other developing countries within APEC that, because the economic starting point of members are different, their abilities to sustain market opening efforts are also different, and hence the principle of non-binding unilateral action after consultation should apply with respect to effecting trade liberalisation measures. China and other developing countries in APEC were successful in making their case at Bogor for a deadline of 2010 for developed countries to carry out free trade and investment within the forum while developing countries will have up till 2020 to meet these goals. This 1994 Bogor Declaration would prove to be the high-water mark in the operationalisation of APEC, as few tangible results have been achieved since then, with the advent of the "Asian/Chinese/Process-oriented" (shortened to "Asian") design for the forum, championed by China, South Korea, and most countries of ASEAN.

Although Malaysia rejected outright Bogor's liberalisation timetable, ASEAN and China has achieved broad agreement by the time of that summit on what should be their preferred form of cooperation within APEC, which are to be based on the norms or principles of voluntary and unilateral action, consensus, "open regionalism" through non-discriminatory trade and investment liberalisation, equal attention to both liberalisation and inter-state economic and technical cooperation, and retaining APEC as an official forum for discussion and not negotiation.[23] By the end of 1994, ASEAN governments have come to an agreement to negate any notion of embracing binding investment principles or adopting dispute settlement mechanisms, both recommended by the EPG. To quote Feinberg, "member governments purposefully eschewed creation of a powerful international bureaucracy that might develop a mind of its own... whose relative autonomy might give it the power and the will to drive policy".[24] In rejecting "Western" bargaining methods with specific goals, APEC fell back practically by default on the less structured and more informal "Asian" approach characterised by unilateral and voluntary measures that appear to reflect and withstand better the sensitive sovereignty concerns, powerful domestic political — economic interests, diverse political beliefs, different levels of economic development, and occasionally difficult foreign relations of countries, or economies, in the broad Asia-Pacific region. ASEAN governments then successfully asked for the EPG's mandate to be terminated at the 1995 Leaders' Meeting in Osaka, to be replaced by an APEC Business Advisory Council (ABAC) for the diffused business community to serve as the forum's peak advisory body. Although ABAC sends a representative to APEC Ministerial Meetings and business groups played an important role in pushing for the liberalisation of both intra-Asian and trans-Pacific information technology (IT) and telecommunications trade, replacing EPG with ABAC cannot be considered progress in the institutionalisation of APEC.

Since how liberalised trade should be has become a contentious issue within the forum, as most developing member economies did not seem to want free trade to be thrust upon them, Bogor did not determine any final standards for trade liberalisation. That is, it never defined whether tariff should be eliminated entirely or reduced to a low figure of, say, 3% or 5%. Consequently, when leaders to the APEC summit in 1995 in Osaka, Japan, met to finalise the Osaka Action Agenda, where member economies undertook to "gradually reduce tariffs and non-tariff measures", no quantitative or joint targets were set. While the US, Australia and other major agriculture exporting countries were in favour of trade liberalisation in all areas, South Korea and Japan in particular argued for the exclusion of agriculture and other areas that they considered to be politically sensitive from such consideration,[25] given the strength of the farmers' lobby in their electoral processes. Malaysia and Thailand both have domestic automobile and automobile parts industries that they wished to protect. Osaka also failed to resolve the issue of "non-discrimination", whereby any trade or investment privileges given by one APEC member economy to another will automatically be extended to non-APEC members. This failure was primarily due to the fact that the US was afraid that, if the principle of "non-discrimination" were adopted, then Most Favoured Nation (MFN) status will have to be automatically and unconditionally extended to a major economy like China that was as yet not a member of GATT/WTO; thus after heated debate, the Osaka Action Agenda managed only to urge APEC member economies to exert their best effort to realise the "non-discrimination" principle.[26] Although tariff barriers were by then very low for the US as compared to other APEC economies, there were still quite a few items from its non-tariff menu that it could have chosen from to reduce import barriers but did not,[27] therefore undermining what the US has exhorted other APEC members to do.

The major benefit for China and developing countries in Asia is the "flexibility" as arrived at through the artful waffling and compromises by APEC members at the Osaka meeting. Considering the great diversity in the stages of economic development and sociopolitical systems among member economies, a "flexible" approach in settling down to a consensual and non-binding style of policy cooperation is perhaps necessary to overcome mutual distrust and initiate and implement actions. Since China is a large developing country with low per capita income, on the difficult road from reforming a planned economic system into a market-oriented one, it wanted APEC to move gradually, and consensually, which means giving every member an effective veto over any proposal that, in its opinion, may have an adverse effect on it if implemented. For the developing countries, the free trade objective, if pursued too fast and too furiously, risks exposing many of their manufacturing and service industries to competitive pressures which they could not withstand.[28] Japan was determined to keep tariffs on imported rice, wheat and other cereals at the range of 300% to 500%,[29] to protect its politically-influential agricultural sector, and began to realise that moving closer to the Asian position on the non-binding, voluntary, consensual and non-discriminatory nature of APEC's functioning may garner it the support of Asian countries in deflecting US pressure on trade liberalisation.[30] Disappointed with the "flexibility" already demonstrated by APEC member economies at Bogor, US President Clinton skipped Osaka altogether.

After 1995, the lofty goals of trade and investment liberalisation have in reality been replaced by that of business facilitation in focusing on simplifying custom and other procedures, reducing the costs of business transactions and promoting the exchange of trade information. At the 2001 APEC summit in China's Shanghai, the US tried to revise the Osaka Action Agenda, by introducing proposals such as the liberalisation of tariffs until they reached zero, reduction of all non-tariff measures to the maximum possible extent, and elimination of all such measures counter to WTO stipulations, but it did not manage to have any of these suggestions included in the final declaration,[31] which reflected the degree of disagreement among APEC participants.

ONE "ASIAN/CHINESE/PROCESS-ORIENTED" DESIGN (1996–2000)

ASEAN and Chinese officials have always insisted that economic and technical cooperation should receive at least equal priority with trade and investment liberalisation on APEC's agenda.[32] During the leaders' meeting at Manila in 1996, both the Chinese President and Foreign Minister came out strongly in favour of strengthening economic and technical cooperation within APEC. At the close of the meeting, under the aegis of host Philippines, an "APEC Framework Declaration on the Principles of Economic and Technical Cooperation" was adopted, which reflected the importance attached to economic and technical cooperation by developing members of APEC, more so than to trade and financial liberalisation, which was the preference of the forum's more industrialised members.

The Manila Action Plan, arrived at through the 1996 APEC Manila ministerial meeting, outlined 6 areas for economic and technical cooperation: developing human capital, fostering sound and efficient capital markets, strengthening economic infrastructure, harnessing technologies of the future, promoting environmentally-sustainable growth, and encouraging the growth of small and medium-sized enterprises.[33] Thus "Ecotech" aims to develop human capital through technical training, build state or institutional capacity as a foundation for economic growth, and reduce economic disparities amongst APEC member economies. Developing countries see "Ecotech" as a foundation for promoting national economic development and poverty reduction, which would in turn serve as a basis for accepting trade and investment liberalisation in the indefinite future.

As written into the Manila Action Plan, APEC's main vehicle for advancing toward the Bogor goal of "free and open trade and investment" is the Individual Action Plans (IAPs) submitted by member economies. The reporting of IAPs are based on activities to meet the goals of free and open trade and investment in such issues areas like tariffs, non-tariff measures, investment, services, customs procedures, standards, intellectual property, competition policy, government procurement, deregulation, rules of origin, and dispute mediation.[34] In addition, Collective Action Plans (CAPs) assist economic integration through the forum's provision of databases, promotion of transparency, studies of best practices and policy initiatives, and business facilitation.[35] Neither commitments to the targets outlined in the IAPs nor those in the CAPs are binding. Even though APEC has instituted peer review of member economies' IAPs,[36] under the principle of voluntarism, countries approach the Bogor targets at their own pace, which cannot guarantee faithful and effective enforcement.

Criteria for membership could not be agreed upon at the 1997 summit in Vancouver, Canada, so a ten year moratorium on new membership was then instituted, although Vietnam, Peru and Russia as Pacific Rim countries were allowed to join APEC the following year on an extemporised basis. Concerning APEC's concerted Early Voluntary Sectoral Liberalisation (EVSL) scheme, introduced at the Vancouver summit, it was clear that Japan, which by then was firmly in the economic doldrums, would not liberalise its agriculture, forestry and fisheries sectors to trade, given their politically powerful lobbies, despite intense pressure from the US.[37] Since the failure of EVSL negotiations in 1998, torpedoed by Japan, with support from other Asian countries, in order to protect narrow domestic interests, US efforts to push for more rapid trade liberalisation within APEC have been largely stymied. Since the 1998 summit in Kuala Lumpur, Malaysia, and the 1999 summit in Auckland, New Zealand, whatever remains of liberalisation efforts within APEC was left to individual member economies to put in place on a sectoral basis unilaterally.[38] APEC lost considerable credibility when it proved unable to come up with any concrete measures to assist Asian member economies ravaged by the financial crisis then raging through the region.

With the Asian financial crisis in 1997–1999, US pressure on affected countries to adopt liberal economic reforms were dramatically increased, with loans from the International Monetary Fund (IMF) and the World Bank to South Korea, Thailand, and Indonesia made conditional on establishing new regulatory, bankruptcy and accounting procedures, liberalisation of capital markets, privatisation of public enterprises and the breaking up of cartels.[39] The overall approach taken by the US through the IMF and World Bank reflected their collective perspective that Japan's economic problems and the Asian crisis flowed from the inefficiencies and distortions of the various state-centred approaches to capitalist development which prevailed in East Asia. The Asian financial crisis did afford a chance for the deepening of economic liberalism in East Asia, particularly in the countries that suffered the most, but it also led to crisis of faith in international economic institutions led by the US, and the unpopularity of the American position within APEC with regional countries.

Up till the time of its joining the WTO, Beijing has sought to use APEC as a shield to resist external pressure for the rapid dismantling of trade barriers, and was altogether opposed to adding capital market liberalisation to the APEC agenda, by arguing that financial liberalisation was none of APEC's business.[40] To many in the Chinese officialdom, APEC remains one aspect of US strategy to enhance its national economic competitiveness through breaking down the trade and financial entry barriers of member economies to its penetration. Thus when ASEAN suggested abolishing the EPG, headed by the fervent American free trade advocate C. Fred Bergsten, this stance was supported by China to curb what it perceived to be US influence and free trade crusading in APEC.

Given the by then dominant "Asian" approach in APEC, the success that the US had in 2000 in convincing member economies to support significant reductions in tariffs for integrated circuits, semiconductors, computer software and other IT products, of which the US is the world's biggest exporter, albeit on an individual and voluntary basis, should be considered no mean feat. The Americans have since been persuaded by other Asia-Pacific countries to be less confrontational toward China and more accommodating toward a much slower pace of realising regional and global free trade than what the US would prefer. For Japan, putting the breaks on any concerted APEC push for trade liberalisation has the advantage of aligning it more closely with Chinese and ASEAN interests and perceptions.[41] Over the years, all players have agreed, reluctantly or otherwise, that APEC would essentially be a non-formal or minimally institutionalised forum for consultations and discussions among high-level representatives of member economies on matters of common interest and concern, particularly in the economic realm. Hence leaders' meetings are customarily prefixed with the term "informal", and all rules and principles adopted by APEC are labelled as "non-binding".[42]

ONE ("ECONOMIC") AND A HALF ("SECURITY") DESIGN (SINCE 2001)

China and the ASEAN collectivity have always emphasised that regional cooperation, in both economic and security spheres, must take into account the principles of national sovereignty and non-intervention in the domestic affairs of states. Heterogeneity of political systems, sovereignty claims, border disputes, secessionist actions, security tensions and mutual suspicions among members have caused APEC meetings to exclude security and political issues from their agenda. However, since the APEC summit of 2001, it was agreed that such issues could be discussed, but only if they pertain directly to the economic security of member economies.

Meeting in China's Shanghai just one month after the 9–11 attacks, APEC leaders at their 2001 summit promised to cooperate with the US to counter all forms of terrorism, acknowledging that terrorist activities will endanger the security and prosperity of the whole world. The harmful effects of terrorism on tourism were threatening a significant source of many member countries' economic development. The resultants "APEC Leaders' Statement on Counter-Terrorism" directed members' finance and transportation ministries to, respectively, freeze the funds of terrorist organisations and improve air and maritime security. This Statement was the first political-cum-security declaration by APEC since its formation. Under an arrangement made by China as the host of the summit, no representatives from Taiwan (Chinese Taipei) or Hong Kong were allowed to attend the discussions pertaining to terrorism, since they were regarded by the Chinese as only non-sovereign economies.[43]

Following the terrorist bombing in Bali in October 2002, at the APEC leaders' meeting at Los Lobos, Mexico, the US led a drive to cooperate in notifying immigration authorities of suspicious travellers by member governments and increase customs security in monitoring shipping containers from high-risk points of origin. Measures such as requiring biometric technology on exit and entry documents, as well as standardised passenger and baggage screening, were all part of the US proposal.[44]

At the 2003 APEC meeting in Bangkok, Thailand, the US managed to persuade fellow APEC members to set up a Counter-Terrorism Task Force to study the issue of terrorist threats at that meeting. APEC's 2004 summit meetings in Santiago de Chile, and the 2005 meeting in Busan, South Korea, have continued to provide occasions for world leaders to confer on major issues such as North

Korea's nuclear intentions and emphasise the need to pursue counterterrorism measures. The 2006 APEC meeting in Hanoi, Vietnam, further pledged to improve aviation security and encourage member economies to develop strategies and share best practices to defend food supply from deliberate contamination. At the 2007 APEC meeting in Sydney, Australia, the host country, together with the US, brokered a draft for forum leaders to adopt that would reduce energy intensity by 25% and increase forest cover by at least 50 million acres in APEC member economies by 2030; however, true to APEC practices, the draft also stipulated that both goals are non-binding.[45] The 2008 APEC meeting in Lima, Peru, merely called on member economies not to adopt trade protectionist measures during trying economic times. Confounding wide expectations, disagreements at the 2009 APEC meeting in Singapore precluded the adoption of a target for reducing global greenhouse gas emissions in the summit's Final Statement.[46] Although APEC was not set up as a confidence-building mechanism, the annual summitry does provide for the leaders of member economies more than a "photo opportunity"; it offers an effective channel to meet and exchange views on one another's position on important affairs affecting the world.

There is no sign that the institutionalisation of the forum has somehow progressed beyond allowing it to remain principally a discussion group, albeit a high-level one, for economic and related security interests. This is because there are few common and concrete purposes for members to work on. APEC members do not have a universal enemy, terrorist or otherwise, that threatens them all in the same way or to the same degree.

As a multilateral forum with many meetings, seminars, workshops, projects, reports and organs, APEC is not particularly well-endowed financially, with its Secretariat's annual operating budget, including building rent and staff's salaries, totaling a mere US$4 million.[47] This is in accord with the structural minimisation approach for APEC favoured by its developing country members. As for projects funded by APEC, there are currently 251 with US$18.5 million in funding, at an average of less than US$74,000 for each project,[48] with very few allocated up to the per project limit of

US$300,000 ever.[49] Yet even with financing a small survey, conference, or database construction, any APEC member economy can veto it through an action of indefinite delay by one of its representatives in the meetings of the BMC, senior officials or ministers as it moves up the endorsement process.[50]

To allow some APEC members to move faster on specific liberalisation measures, APEC encourages "Pathfinder Initiatives".[51] However, since APEC commitments are not legal but rather political in adhering to the by now paramount "Asian+" design, there can be no sanctions to punish laggards or defectors. Peer pressure from fellow economies to get an APEC agenda adopted works only to the extent that it is in the interest of a member to accept that pressure. Decisions made at the APEC summits and ministerial meetings, if there any, are non-binding, and left to individual members to execute. The goal of maintaining a tranquil atmosphere at APEC meetings is overriding.[52] As such, most APEC activities still remain at the stage of promoting dialogue, exchanging information, holding seminars and publishing reports.

WHAT FUTURE FOR APEC?

By putting out serious proposals for free trade and investment in expectation of its non-execution, notwithstanding the supposed role of peer pressure or concern with diffused reputation, APEC seems to have settled on an uneasy, and perhaps institutionalised, game of compromise between the preferences of the go-getting Westerners and the foot-dragging Asians.

The crux of the contention in designing alternative visions for APEC may be seen as a reflection of opposing interests on liberalisation and institutionalisation within the forum between the US, its allies, developed or industrialised countries and newly-industrialised economies on the one hand, and China and developing or industrialising countries on the other hand, with Japan moving from the "Western" "camp" to the "Asian" one some time between 1994 and 1995. Adherents of the "Western" design see a positive correlation between openness to the global economy and nations' Gross

Domestic Product growth rates, and would like to promote and perpetuate the advantages that, as competitive economies, they enjoy or would do so with trade and investment liberalisation. Advocates of the "Asian" vision, despite suffering through the adverse impact that the Asian financial crisis had in varying degrees on their economies, and conceding that the attendant vested interests, bureaucratic red-tape and corruption do inhibit economic competition, still believe to some extent in preserving the business-political nexus and sovereignty-upholding industrial policies that have brought a respectable measure of political stability, material prosperity and diplomatic influence to countries like Japan, South Korea, Taiwan and Singapore. These two roadmaps reflect differences of belief and interest and are not easily reconcilable. Indeed, such divergent approaches have been mirrored in the constant tussle and occasional compromises between liberal and protectionist sentiments often exhibited among representatives of countries in a larger economic deliberating forum — the current Doha Round of WTO trade talks.

The 1993 inaugural APEC Leaders' Summit at Seattle was significant to the extent that the profile of the forum was henceforth heightened. By 1995, the institutional or organizational structure of APEC that exists today has been put in place, but it was also at the Osaka Summit that the last major joint effort to push for comprehensive trade and investment liberalisation clearly failed, and where members decided that an autonomous structure for the forum was not in the offing by abolishing the EPG. By the end of 1997, technical and developmental issues have clearly dominated forum deliberations, and APEC's EAEC sub-grouping had become formalised as a self-standing ASEAN+3, grouping leaders of ASEAN, Japan, China and South Korea together in annual conclaves that are independent of APEC but adopt, naturally it would seem, the forum's "Asian" design as a working ethos. As Asian economies have fully recovered to strong economic growth from the devastating financial crisis of last century's end and the debilitating Severe Acute Respiratory Syndrome (SARS) in 2003, and amid the swift economic rise of China, the "Asian" design for APEC, with its emphasis on voluntary action, political commitment, open regionalism and broad economic cooperation, is likely to continue dominating the forum's enterprise at the expense of the "Western" one, based on negotiated agreement, legal obligation, specific reciprocity and sharply focused agenda.[53] Although India had expressed its desire to join APEC, the forum decided at its 2007 summit that India's case will not be discussed before 2010. Some western economies in APEC had apparently delayed India's application because of worries that, as a large developing Asian economy, its joining would increase Asia's weight in APEC,[54] and move the forum even further away from the "Western" design.

Given its important economic and security roles in the Asia-Pacific region, the US has preferred, and still prefers, to deal with regional polities on a bilateral basis. Having secured an FTA with Singapore by the end of 2002, the US voiced interest in exploring similar deals with Malaysia, the Philippines and Thailand.[55] The spirited pursuit of bilateral FTAs reflects Washington's ambivalence about the continuing prospects of a regional economic forum that is seemingly ineffective, at least from the point of view of securing definite commitments from East Asian governments to liberalise US imports into regional economies. Even on crucial matters such as the reduction of the more than US$200 billion trade deficit with China, accompanied by charges of dumping, high tariffs, inconsistent application of laws and regulations, and intellectual property rights violation, the US has not sought to use APEC to any extent as an arena to exert pressure on Beijing, preferring instead to do so at bilateral meetings with Chinese government officials. Although an APEC led by the US would not have been welcomed by every member economy, an absentee or absent-minded role on its part, or protectionist measures adopted by the US government to save domestic manufacturing jobs in the global economic recession which began in mid-2008, would put the continuing effectiveness of the forum into very serious doubts.

Coming out of more than a decade of sluggish growth, industrial closures, lost jobs, contraction in bank lending and frequent loan recalls,[56] Japan concluded FTAs with Singapore and Mexico to spur its economy. Doubtful of the success of the WTO's Doha Round on trade liberalisation and the efficacy of APEC, Singapore completed similar agreements with Australia, New Zealand, the US, and the European Free Trade Association countries.[57]

Since joining APEC, China has used it to improve and develop its diplomatic profile and economic relations with countries in the Asia-Pacific that are important to it. APEC is now far from being the only regional forum in which China is a member; nonetheless, taking part in the activities of APEC has the important consequence of raising the confidence and reducing the suspicion of the Chinese leadership and foreign policy community in interacting with foreign officials and diplomats. At the same time that the US is widely viewed as backing down from the multilateral approach, and Japan is seen as engaging in more protectionist economic policies, China is increasingly stressing a more pro-active foreign policy and liberal economic agenda, in endorsing multilateral structures, supporting freer trade, and sponsoring security arrangements.[58] China has become keen to promote regional institutions where the US and its allies are excluded, such as the Shanghai Cooperative Organisation, ASEAN+3 and ASEAN+China, under the rubric of which ASEAN states and China signed the Framework Agreement on Comprehensive Economic Cooperation in 2002 to begin negotiations to realise an ASEAN-China Free Trade Area between China and all ASEAN states by 2015. China's participation in APEC can be expected to continue at some perfunctory level, but the flow of real diplomatic energy would swing toward the realm of bilateral relations and multilateral organisations where China feels not only more comfortable, but also more economically powerful.

The "concerted unilateral liberalisation" touted in APEC's IAP scheme has been displaced by "concerted bilateral liberalisation",[59] in the sense that bilateral trade agreements have emerged as the preferred mechanism for APEC member economies to realise reciprocal market access, despite complex rules of origin documentation and the possibility of trade diversion, consequently making APEC itself virtually redundant as a forum to advance overall freer trade.

In 2007, APEC accepted a proposal by Australia and Japan to add to the Secretariat a small Policy Support Unit, to be funded by voluntary contributions, to provide expert analysis, prepare policy papers for APEC committees, and design and implement capacity-building programmes.[60] Given the apparent failure of the Doha Round, the US has also agreed to consider seriously the idea of a Free Trade Area for the Asia Pacific (FTAAP) put forth by ABAC.[61] If the Policy Support Unit proves effective and the FTAAP comes to fruition, the *modus operandi* of APEC may move, at least part ways, back to the "Western" design, but given the existing culture of the forum, these are long shots. APEC's trade ministers, meeting in Singapore from 22 to 23 July 2009 in preparation for the forum's summit scheduled for later that year, could only make vague references to the need for member economies to fight protectionism and revive the Doha Round in the existing trying economic times.[62] Even APEC's own goal of creating a free trade and investment zone among its developed member economies by 2010 has been quietly dropped.

Yet, despite its many limitations and unfulfilled promises as a multilateral decision-making process for trade and investment policy issues, APEC has brought together the leaders of most economies of any size on both sides of the Pacific Ocean to discuss trade, investment, and of late, economic security and even environmental concerns; provided the US with a platform to demonstrate to the world a greater degree of economic multilateralism than before; and proven to be a useful vehicle in "socialising" China into becoming a more accepted and committed member of the international system. We may be asking too much of it in asking for more.

NOTES

* Associate Professor, Department of Political Science, Lingnan University. Email: cp2chung@LN.edu.hk

1. A revised version of this essay will be published as Chapter 3, "China's Approaches to APEC," of my forthcoming book, *China's Multilateral Co-operation in Asia and the Pacific: Institutionalising Beijing's "Good Neighbor Policy."* London and New York: Routledge, 2010.

2. The 12 founding members that formed APEC on 6–7 November 1989 were Australia, Brunei Darussalam, Canada, Indonesia, Japan, South Korea, Malaysia, New Zealand, Philippines, Singapore, Thailand and the United States. Economies that subsequently joined the forum were the People's Republic of China, Hong Kong and Chinese Taipei (Taiwan) on 12–14 November 1991, Mexico and Papua New Guinea on 17–19 November 1993, Chile on 11–12 November 1994, and Peru, Russia and Vietnam on 14–15 November 1998.
3. Terada, T. (2007). "Japan and the Evolution of Asian Regionalism." In H. Dieter (Ed.), *Evolution of Regionalism in Asia.* London and New York: Routledge, pp. 61–62.
4. Camilleri, J. A. (2003). *Regionalism in the New Asia-Pacific Order: The Political Economy of the Asia-Pacific Region,* Volume II. Cheltenham & Northampton: Edward Elgar, p. 161.
5. *Ibid.*
6. Lu, J. (1997). "Dongmeng guojia de APEC zhengce (ASEAN Countries' APEC Policies)." In J. Lu (Ed.), *Yatai Jinghe Zuzhi yu Zhongguo* (*APEC and China*). Beijing: Jingji Guanli Chubanshe, 1997 (Economic Management Press, 1997), p. 103.
7. Camilleri, *Regionalism,* p. 144; Liu, W. (1997). "Meiguo de APEC Zhengce (America's APEC Policy)." In J. Lu (Ed.), *Yatai Jinghe Zuzhi yu Zhongguo* (*APEC and China*). Beijing: Jingji Guanli Chubanshe, 1997 (Economic Management Press, 1997), p. 81.
8. Beeson M. and Jayasuriya, K. (1998). "The Political Rationalities of Regionalism: APEC and the EU in Comparative Perspective." *The Pacific Review,* 11, 3 p. 316.
9. Liang, Y. and X. Wang (2000). "Zhongguo de APEC zhengce jiqi dui dongya guoji guanxi de yingxiang (China's APEC Policy and its Influence on East Asian International Relations)." *Zhongguo Zhengzhi Yanjiu* (*Chinese Political Studies*), 3 p. 57; and Shen, J. (2003). "Zhongguo yu APEC de huxiang shiying ji APEC de weilai (Mutual Accommodation between China and APEC and the Future of APEC)." In Wang Y. (Ed.), *Construction in Contradiction: A Multiple Insight into Relationship between China and Key International Organizations.* Beijing:

Zhongguo fanzhan chubanshe, 2003 (China Development Press, 2003), p. 137.

10. Liu, J. "Meiguo de APEC Zhengce (America's APEC Policy)." p. 83; and Shen, "Zhongguo yu APEC de huxiang shiying ji APEC de weilai (Mutual Accommodation between China and APEC and the Future of APEC)." p. 141.
11. Camilleri, *Regionalism*, pp. 147–148.
12. Walsh, J. R. (1993). "A Pillar of the Community: The Role of APEC in US Policy." *The Journal of East Asian Affairs,* 7, 2 pp. 551, 554.
13. Morrison, C. E. (2002). "APEC in Sino-American Relations: A Vehicle for System Integration." In J. Ruland, E. Manste and W. Draguhl (Eds.), *Asia-Pacific Economic Cooperation (APEC): The First Decade.* London and New York: Routledge Curzon, pp. 127–128.
14. Goodings, S. (2003). "The APEC Secretariat: A Management Perspective." In R. E. Feinberg (Ed.), *APEC as an Institution: Multilateral Governance in the Asia-Pacific.* Singapore: Institute of Southeast Asian Studies, p. 68.
15. http://www.apec.org/content/apec/apec_groups/committees/economic_committee.html, accessed 31 July 2008. This and subsequent internet references beginning with <http://www.apec.org/content/apec/> or <http://www.apec.org/apec/> refer to the official website of the Asia Pacific Economic Cooperation (APEC).
16. Bodde, W. Jr. (1994). *View from the 19th Floor: Reflections of the First APEC Executive Director.* Singapore: Institute of Southeast Asian Studies, p. 67.
17. Terada, T. "Japan and the Evolution of Asian Regionalism." pp. 62–63.
18. Munakata, N. (2006). *Transforming East Asia.* Tokyo: Research Institute of Economy, Trade and Industry, and Washington D.C.: Brookings Institution Press, p. 74.
19. Shi, M. (1997). "Yatai Jinghe Zuzhi dansheng de lishi Beijing (The Historical Background of the Birth of APEC)." In J. Lu (Ed.), *Yatai Jinghe Zuzhi yu Zhongguo* (*APEC and China*). Beijing: Jingji Guanli Chubanshe (Economic Management Press, 1997), p. 11; and Lu, "Dongmeng guojia de APEC zhengce (ASEAN Countries' APEC Policies)." pp. 104–105.

20. Ravenhill, J. (2001). *APEC and the Construction of Pacific Rim Regionalism.* Cambridge: Cambridge University Press, pp. 106–108.
21. Moore, T. G. and Yang, D. (1999). "China, APEC and Economic Regionalism in the Asia Pacific." *The Journal of East Asian Affairs,* 13, 1 p. 392.
22. See Acharya, A. (2000). "The Evolution of ASEAN Norms and the Emergence of the ASEAN Way." In *Constructing a Security Community in Southeast Asia: ASEAN and the Problem of Regional Order.* London: Routledge, pp. 47–79.
23. Shen, J. "Zhongguo yu APEC de huxiang shiying ji APEC de weilai (Mutual Accommodation between China and APEC and the Future of APEC)." p. 143.
24. Feinberg, R. E. (2001). "Regional Trade and Security Arrangements in the Asia Pacific and the Western Hemisphere in Comparative Perspective." In J. C. Hsiung (Ed.), *Twenty-First Century World Order and the Asia Pacific: Value Change, Exigencies, and Power Realignment.* New York and Basingstoke: Palgrave, p. 195.
25. Wei, M. (1996). "Yatai Jinghe Zuzhi fazhan lichengzhong de rougan wenti he woguo zhanlue yu zhengce sikao (Several Problems on APEC's Development Path and Thoughts on our National Strategy and Policy)." *Zhongguo Zhengzhi Yanjiu* (*Chinese Political Studies*), 4 p. 54.
26. *Ibid.*
27. Lu, J. and Zhang, Y. (1996). "Yatai Jinghe Zuzhi fazhan zhong de jige guanxi ji qianjing (Several Relationships and the Future of APEC's Development)." *Dangdai Yatai* (*Contemporary Asia-Pacific*), 5 p. 8.
28. Camilleri, *Regionalism,* p. 143.
29. Zhao, J. "Riben de APEC Zhengce (Japan's APEC Policy)." In J. Lu (Ed.), *Yatai Jinghe Zuzhi yu Zhongguo* (*APEC and China*). Beijing: Jingji Guanli Chubanshe (Economic Management Press, 1997), p. 95.
30. Shen, J. "Zhongguo yu APEC de huxiang shiying ji APEC de weilai (Mutual Accommodation between China and APEC and the Future of APEC)." p. 145.
31. Lu, J. (2002). "APEC: Shanghai huiyi de chengguo ji jinhou fazhan sikao (APEC: The Fruits of the Shanghai Meeting and Thoughts on its Future Development)," *Zhongguo Waijiao* (*China's Foreign Affairs*), 5, p. 50.

32. "China, APEC and Economic Regionalism in the Asia Pacific." Moore and Yang, op. cit., p. 388.
33. Feinberg, "Regional Trade and Security Arrangements in the Asia Pacific and the Western Hemisphere in Comparative Perspective." p. 202.
34. http://www.apec.org/content/apec/about_apec/how_apec_operates/action_plans_.html, accessed 31 July 2008.
35. Feinberg, "Regional Trade and Security Arrangements in the Asia Pacific and the Western Hemisphere in Comparative Perspective." p. 202.
36. Zhong, W. (2003). "APEC tongxing shencha ji woguo de celue (APEC Peer Review and our National Policy)." *Dangdai Yatai* (*Contemporary Asia-Pacific*), 5, p. 56.
37. Damond, J. M. (2003). "The APEC Decision-Making Process for Trade Policy Issues: The Experience and Lessons of 1994–2001." In R. E. Feinberg (Ed.), *APEC as an Institution: Multilateral Governance in the Asia-Pacific*, Singapore: Institute of Southeast Asian Studies, p. 96; and Dent, C. M. (2003). "The Asia-Pacific's New Economic Bilateralism and Regional Political Economy." In C. M. Dent (Ed.), *Asia-Pacific Economic and Security Cooperation.* New York and Basingstoke: Palgrave, p. 78.
38. Zhou, J. (2001). "Cong APEC de dutexing kan tade fanzhan qianjing (Looking at APEC's Future Development from its Special Features)." *Guoji Zhengzhi* (*International Politics*), 11, p. 70.
39. Berger, M. T. (2002). "Anglo-American Liberalism and East Asian Capitalism after the Cold War." In C. J. W.-L. Wee (Ed.), *Local Cultures and the "New Asia".* Singapore: Institute of Southeast Asian Studies, p. 91.
40. "China, APEC and Economic Regionalism in the Asia Pacific." Moore and Yang, op. cit., pp. 400–402.
41. Ravenhill, *APEC*, pp. 99–103.
42. Zhang, J. (2000). "The Functions of APEC and Implications for China: A Critical Review." In P. Drysdale, Y. Zhang and L. Song (Eds.), *APEC and Liberalisation of the Chinese Economy.* Canberra: Asia Pacific Press at the Australian National University, p. 32.
43. Lu, J. (2004). "The Five Big Challenges to APEC in Coming Years." 10 November. http://www.iaps.cass.cn/english/Articles/showcontent.asp?id=692, accessed 27 February 2007.

44. Aggarwal, V. K. and Kwei, E. (2006). "Asia-Pacific Economic Cooperation (APEC): Transregionalism with a New Cause?" In H. Hanggi, R. Roloff and J. Ruland (Eds.), *Interregionalism and International Relations.* London and New York: Routledge, p. 78.
45. http://www.cnn.com/2007/POLITICS/09/08/apec.ap/index.html?iref=newssearch, accessed 31 July 2008. This is the CNN website.
46. Baroud, R. (2009). "Apec Leaders will not Commit to Specifics on Environment." *Brunei Times,* 15 November. http://www.bt.com.bn/en/apec/2009/11/15/disappointment-ahead-copenhagen-apec-leaders-will-not-commit-specifics-environment, accessed 31 January 2010.
47. Estimated figure by APIAN (APEC International Assessment Network), *Remaking APEC as an Institution: The Third APIAN Policy Report.* Singapore: Singapore APEC Study Center for APIAN, 2002.
48. Feinberg, R. E. (2008). "Voluntary Multilateralism and Institutional Modification: The First Two Decades of Asia Pacific Economic Cooperation (APEC)." *Review of International Organizations,* 3, p. 253.
49. Feinberg, R. E. and Lawrence, J. (2006). *Improving APEC's Coherence — Preliminary Conference for APEC 2007, "Reshaping APEC for the Asian Pacific Century — Priorities and Strategies."* 11–12 December 2006, Melbourne, Australia, pp. 2–3.
50. Feinberg, R. E. (2003). "Project Selection and Evaluation: APEC's Budget and Management Committee and the Secretariat." In R. E. Feinberg (Ed.), *APEC as an Institution: Multilateral Governance in the Asia-Pacific.* Singapore: Institute of Southeast Asian Studies, pp. 74, 77.
51. http://www.apec.org/content/apec/apec_groups/committees/economic_on_trade.html, accessed 31 July 2008.
52. Damond, J. M. "The APEC Decision-Making Process for Trade Policy Issues." p. 102.
53. Morrison, "APEC in Sino-American Relations." p. 131.
54. *Malaysian Sun,* 9 September 2007, A1.
55. Dent, "The Asia-Pacific's New Economic Bilateralism and Regional Political Economy." p. 80.
56. MacIntyre, A. and Naughton, B. (2005). "The Decline of a Japan-Led Model of the East Asian Economy." In T. J. Pempel (Ed.), *Remapping*

East Asia: The Construction of a Region. Ithaca, NY and London, UK: Cornell University Press, pp. 85–86.

57. Aggarwal V. K. and Kwei, E. "Asia-Pacific Economic Cooperation (APEC)." p. 83.
58. Chow, M. E. (2006). "ASEAN-China F.T.A.: Trade or Tribute?" *The Singapore Yearbook of International Law,* 10, p. 261.
59. Dent, C. M. "The Asia-Pacific's New Economic Bilateralism and Regional Political Economy." p. 79.
60. APEC, Joint Ministerial Statement, 13th Meeting of APEC Ministers Responsible for Trade, Cairns, Australia, 5–6 July 2007.
61. Morrison, C. and Pedrosa, E. (2007). *An APEC Trade Agenda? The Political Economic of a Free Trade Area for the Asia Pacific.* Singapore: Institute of Southeast Asian Studies.
62. Xinhua, "APEC to Fight Protectionism Through Concrete Plans." http://news.xinhuanet.com/english/2009-07/23/content_11755848.htm, accessed 1 July 2009.

3

Rebalancing Relations between East Asian and trans-Pacific Institutions: Evolving Regional Architectural Features

Zhongying Pang

Renmin University of China

ABSTRACT

Various forms of multilateral regional institutions have evolved since the birth of APEC. APEC is now coming under increasing scrutiny for its very reason of existence, as more and more formal sub-regional or bilateral FTAs emerged. China and Japan continue to push forward East Asian cooperation monetarily, financially and in trade. APEC could be replaced or reformed by introducing new trans-Pacific arrangements such as an ongoing trans-Pacific trade program. Big regional players like China, Japan, and the US and their regional interactions will determine the future of the co-existence of multilateral-institutions. Relations between East Asian and trans-Pacific institutions should be rebalanced for mutual accommodation rather than mutual competition.

Keywords: Asia Pacific Institutions; China; East Asian Regional Institutions; regional architecture; US.

INTRODUCTION

The "East Asia Community" or "Asia-Pacific Community" exists only on paper. Even the ASEAN, which constitutionally goes toward "ASEAN Community", is also not a Southeast Asian version of an EU-like regional integration. There is still not a unified multilateral framework of coordination within Asia-Pacific. But, the issue of the regional architecture remains a central issue of debate. Not only to big powers like China, Japan and the US, but also to smaller nations like many ASEAN countries, the stake are high whether Asia-Pacific can operate cooperatively as a region.

In 1990s, as the number one trans-Pacific forum, APEC's initial progress with euphoria and rhetoric about trade and investment liberalisation was suddenly undermined by the Asian financial crisis. A consequence of that crisis was the well-known birth of experimental regional integration in East Asia for the first time. Before this regional practice, East Asia/Asia has had a one-century-long history of both "pan-Asianism" and regionalism. Different from trade liberalisation motivated by APEC, "ASEAN+3" (Southeast Asian nations, now ten countries, plus Northeast Asian nations, firstly China, Japan and South Korea) set a historic goal that goes beyond trade integration and moved a step towards an East Asia Community (or, more modestly and politically, an East Asia community).

Since the emergence of "ASEAN+3" process, there have been a number of regional arrangements including bilateral and multilateral ones. Different from APEC's relative informality and even partial ineffectuality, and despite a lack of "concrete vision of the eventual architecture of institutional economic integration",[1] these Asian regional institutions have made a number of breakthroughs, including trade integration, such as the agreement between China and ASEAN (CAFTA) as well as monetary and financial multilateral cooperation/governance — wider currency swap arrangements

Chiang Mai Initiative (CMI) and Asian Bond Market Initiative (ABMI).

There is a background to this issue: many people in the world do believe the regional economic and strategic weight has shifted/moved from America to Asia (or, a strategic trend: relatively, China is rising, the US is declining), but many in China still think China has neither the political intention nor the capability (including the regional institutional one) to be a sustainable challenger to the US hegemony. In discussing current trans-Pacific relations among big powers, it is extremely important to take note of this widening gap.

However, to the US, which has maintained a strategy of preventing any other power from challenging US global and regional domination, leadership, and primacy, a decade long boom of ASEAN-led regional institutions (although they are definitely in their nascent stages) really serves as a geo-strategic "wake-up call". During the Bush administration, particularly its second term (2004–08), Washington began to perceive East Asian regional cooperation as a big challenge to the US. But, as Washington's foreign policy was preoccupied by other agendas and was over confident to its effectiveness and centrality of regional bilateral alliance system, it failed to come up with a new approach to Asia, still sticking to the "'hub and spokes' approach to Asia — with the United States as the hub, bilateral alliances as the spokes, and multilateral institutions largely at the margins of American policy".[2] The Obama administration has to change America's policy and approach to East Asian institutions. Through visits and speeches, US political leaders are elaborating its renewed "principles of engagement in the Asia-Pacific". In a high profile manner, the US came "back" to Southeast Asia and beyond.[3]

This article briefly discusses APEC's transformation in the past two decades since its beginning, with special attention to both APEC's variants and counterparts in East Asia and its current and potential alternatives. It emphasises the relationship between Asian/East Asian and Asia-Pacific (trans-Pacific) institutions. This chapter addresses the roles played by big players, particularly the US, Japan, and China, in such regional institutions.

APEC IS NOT AN ASIA-PACIFIC ECONOMIC COMMUNITY

There are two alternative assessments on APEC's strengthens and weaknesses, achievements and failures in the past 20 years.

One is a view of applause. Those who see success in APEC's performance cite the annual APEC "Economic Leaders Meeting" (the APEC Summit) as a signal of the importance of the trans-Pacific economic forum. There is little doubt that these meetings really helped boost the host country's self-image and perhaps even the economy. APEC is like a big regional Expo. Considering the huge size of APEC region, each hosting country was excited to host the event and to seize the opportunity to befriend with other members.

APEC is certainly not useless. According to APEC's secretariat, "an independent research" finds that "APEC members trade with each other more than they do with other free trading agreement partners and much more with trading partners who are both members of APEC and members of the World Trade Organization. This demonstrates the high level of *de facto* integration between members of APEC, even under non-binding arrangements".[4]

On the other hand, many have been critical of APEC. To them, "APEC is a perfect excuse for chat"; "It is not a serious regional institution-building"; "The Economic Leaders' Meetings, are better remembered for the attire of the leaders than for its substantive pronouncements".[5] APEC is too informal or too non-binding to be effective. It has over-emphasised "open regionalism". It is the largest trans-regional body in the world. Gradually, its rules and forms are too old to "bottle" the new "wine" such as the rise of China and East Asian institutions. It is too American dominated to be balanced across the Pacific.[6]

To be fair, APEC encouraged economies in Asia, particularly economies still not fully opened (China) or highly managed (Malaysia) to unconditionally/unilaterally open up or to deregulate in order to let global market/financial forces prevail. To some APEC economies, the over-openness of their markets was dangerous not only economically but politically. Therefore, after the 1997 financial crisis broke out, such economies had to keep distance with APEC's "unilateral liberalisation" and turned to the "necessary evil" of more regulation and control by the state. As a result, to a large extent, APEC's central doctrine "liberalisation" in 1990s actually was paused or interrupted.

This chapter is neither for praising nor for criticising. I agree that APEC has been useful and valuable commercially or diplomatically. But the good times are over: APEC has been marginalised by various truly regional (although imperfect and premature) East Asian regionalism/cooperation initiatives. The decline — if temporary — of American hegemony is a latest blow to APEC. Within APEC, both the US and its allies have to seek a more effective alternative to APEC.

In a sense, APEC is at the same time effective and ineffective in pursuing multilateralism. Its initial effectiveness mainly existed in its first decade — its successful China absorption/integration strengthened its legitimacy as a most inclusive trans-regional body and its setting of ambitious trans-Pacific deadlines to liberalise trade and investment were attractive to all. During this period, both the US and ASEAN political leaders played leading roles. But, APEC's indifference and inaction to respond to the "Asian financial crisis" created its first Waterloo. After that, there was continuing doubt over its relevance to East Asian members.

The start of East Asian cooperation marked the theory of East Asian regionalism was translated into practice for the first time. With the support and push from Japan and China, the ASEAN had brought to the fore a number of "East Asia" processes. The birth of these East Asian regionalist projects further reduced the demand for APEC. In APEC's second decade in the 2000s, it had to co-exist with "ASEAN-led" East Asian economic cooperation.

Of course, at the same time, both ASEAN and its partners in Northeast Asia, China, Japan and South Korea, continued to play critical roles in APEC. China hosted APEC in 2001 just after the September 11 terrorist attack. In 2005, some ASEAN members in APEC established the early foundation of the Trans-Pacific Partnership (TPP) Agreement, an Asia-Pacific trade agreement involving East Asian institutions' future competitor and, at the same time, possibly the need to APEC's future alternative.

MULTILATERAL INSTITUTIONS

Regional institutions (the existing and the proposed) in Asia and the Pacific fall within four categories. These categories are natuarlly overlapping and not mutually exclusive. The four categories are: the "Southeast Asian", the "Pacific", the "East Asian", and some "in between the East Asian and the Pacific". They include:

- "ASEAN Community": When ASEAN relatively recovered from the financial crisis in 1997, in the late 2000s, its temporary emphasis on the importance of "East Asia" cooperation during the crisis gradually faded. Asia's first relatively fledged sub-regional integration strengthened its status by going integration: "The ASEAN Community is comprised of three pillars, namely the ASEAN Political-Security Community, ASEAN Economic Community, ASEAN Socio-Cultural Community".[7] Its regional charter began on 15 December 2008 and it not only "serves as a firm foundation in achieving the ASEAN Community" but perhaps has the spill-over effect in other parts of Asia. The charter secures ASEAN's leadership position in East Asia.
- "ASEAN+1": The majority of Asian regional institutions are based in ASEAN. Now, ASEAN has concluded FTAs with all six non-ASEAN members of the East Asia Summit, a mini-APEC.[8] Furthermore, ASEAN expands the "ASEAN+1" to forge a new ASEAN-US ties, the most important "ASEAN+1" arrives.
- Asian monetary cooperation: This multilateral monetary facility is a result from the Chiang Mai Initiative (CMI), which East Asian economies first initiated in 2003. Originally about a currency swapping mechanism to protect the region from increasing risks in financial globalisation, the plan has grown larger. Of the reserve, China and Japan take the co-leadership.[9]
- Shanghai Cooperation Organization (SCO): From geo-political perspectives, this organisation deserves to be mentioned in

discussing APEC-related issues. Because China and Russia, SCO's organisers, are both APEC members. The SCO originated in Central Asia, which was formerly part of the Soviet Union, but it covers the majority of Eurasia and the continental East Asia. As a great nation located in between the Pacific Asia and Eurasia, China wisely seeks balanced regional relations. Considering China's unstable western parts (two "X"s: Xizang/Tibet and Xinjiang in particular) and the US's continuing intervention in the two "X"s, China fully knows the strategic importance of the SCO region.

- A Northeast Asia Peace and Security Mechanism (NEAPSM): In its joint statements, particularly the 19 September 2005 Joint Statement, a multilateral process called the Six-Party Talks has proposed the NEAPSM. According to China-US Joint Statement issued in 17 November 2009 in Beijing, this will be a "permanent peace regime" in this sub-region in Asia-Pacific. The nature of the NEAPSM is trans-Pacific. It offers a regional approach to deal with international issues like the nuclear weapons proliferation, with a view to lasting regional security through effective multilateral regional cooperation.
- TPP: Many Chinese analysts did not know what TPP stands for before the 2009 APEC Singapore Summit. The Trans-Pacific Partnership suddenly emerges as both a trade agreement and a strategic alliance. TPP is called a "high quality" arrangement of Asia-Pacific economic cooperation. In contrast, APEC is really a low quality trans-regional grouping. There are some interesting questions: Is TPP an inevitable answer to APEC's growing marginalisation and irrelevance? Is TPP a way to "restore America leadership" in the region? Several key ASEAN nations not only Singapore but also Vietnam (2010 ASEAN chair and the US's new regional partner) are keen to promote the TPP for engaging the US; the US current administration finds a strategic value of the TPP and quickly decided to enter into negotiations of the agreement.[10] Other APEC members which are excluded by East Asian institutions such as Taiwan tries to join the TPP.[11]

- "Asia-Pacific Community" (APC): Australia had played a leading role in forging APEC. It wants to play a leading role again in proposing a single Asia-Pacific institution. Australia's Kevin Rudd, coined and sent the idea of APC in recent years. His APC policy team organised a big Asia-Pacific conference in Sydney from 3–5 December 2009.[12]
- "East Asia Community" (EAC): In principle, optionally, "ASEAN+3" wants to be an East Asian Community. But, in recent years, leaders from both Southeast Asia and Northeast Asia decreasingly talked about the future of "ASEAN+3" as the base of EAC. Since 2005, the East Asia Summit (EAS) has made EAC more impossible rather than possible. Suddenly, in Tokyo, the ruling JDP represented by the Prime Minister Yukio Hatoyama proposed a Japanese edition of EAC. The proposal is based on the exiting framework of EAS, but maybe different from any Asia-Pacific institution if the US joins the EAS. In other words, today's Japan seeks a regional institution in between the existing ASEAN-led East Asian institutions and trans-Pacific institutions.

Critics in the US of the growing regional cooperation in East Asia have charged that the East Asian institutions and trans-Pacific institutions are mutually competitive and exclusive. Some of them have argued that the theory and practice of East Asian regionalism are a catastrophe to "open regionalism" — APEC's core principle. They have always seen that East Asian processes without the US are not good for existing regional order but are good for alternatives such as Japan or China-centred ones. In conclusion, such worries simply see East Asian processes as not compatible with the APEC and other trans-Pacific processes.

Perhaps a fundamental reason of the new trans-Pacific initiatives and efforts made by either Australia or America is the deeply ingrained worry about competition. It can be interpreted as a number of new attempts by the Western players to unify/integrate multi-institutions — a wide diversity of regional architecture.

Each institution has its mission and enjoys its legitimacy. There is little likelihood that they would be amalgamated into one ultimate framework for the entire broad region. As the inventor of "reformist phrase" and "multi-multilateralism", Francis Fukuyama, labeled as a conservative scholar, thinks from the regional governance perspective, these various institutions reflect the diversity and complexity of the region. As he argues, even "a truly liberal principle would argue not for a single, overarching, enforceable liberal order but rather for a diversity of institutions and institutional forms to provide governance across a range of security, economic, environmental, and other issues".[13]

CHINA'S ATTITUDE

Over the past 20 years China's attitude to regional institutions has evolved into a stable and predictable regional multilateral policy.

Firstly, China sees itself as a part of the regional system. China's interests are well-served by an inclusive regional grouping and a freer trading environment.

At least from 1949 to the end of the Cold War in 1989, the People's Republic of China was not an indispensible part of the world economy. Prior to 1979 when it officially opened itself to the world, it did not even engage in international/regional trade except with Hong Kong and a handful of friendly countries. Since the late 1970s, especially the accession to the WTO in 2001, China has established itself as a major trading nation.

To the US, APEC facilitated China's integration into the America-dominated "global economy". In the 1990s, APEC was one of China's main channels to link with outside economies. The experience in APEC helped China's accession to the WTO.[14] Then APEC also provided a much needed diplomatic channel for nurturing China-US ties.

A result of China's WTO membership was that China and the US turned their relations into an unprecedented largest bilateral economic interdependence in world economic history.[15] Both Beijing and Washington have known the relations are good for both sides if they could manage their differences. If a trade war happened, both would become losers — the worst scenario.

Should the bilateral relations break down, the results would be disastrous. "During the Cold War, we spoke of 'mutually assured destruction', in which the United States and the Soviet Union had so many nuclear weapons that one side could not destroy the other without destroying itself. Swap 'mutually' for 'monetarily' and you get the new MAD — 'monetarily assured destruction' — which exists between China and the United States. One consequence of the financialization of the US economy was that we managed to get China to swap real goods for paper, and a terrible rate of return on holding the paper, for more than 20 years, in the course of which the Chinese (and other East Asian economies) built up astonishingly large trade and current account surpluses".[16]

Secondly, the engagement and participation in regional institutions is a key part of China's strategic/realistic embrace of multilateralism.

After a temporary doubt and reluctance in the early 1990s, China began to firmly adhere to the principle of multilateralism. China's leaders have conducted their high profile global and regional summitries without any disconnection. Multilateral diplomacy helped ease the pressures and tensions that China faced in the region. China has been facing a number of dilemmas in the region:

- Political dilemma: Generally, China's fine economic/business relations with others helped improve its political relations. But, the economic relations have their limits in bringing about better political relations. From 1998 to 2006, China-Japan relationship was once summarised by a general saying: "hot economics but cold politics". Many of the bilateral and even multilateral interactions between China and the others can be described in the same way. China's close economic relations with the US have not changed the nature of China-US political relations.
- Economics dilemma: In the past China had doubted deeply and resisted strongly the theory and practice of free trade. But, as a trading nation and the "world's factory", today's China heavily depends on the sustainability of the free trade system and it has become a major force against protectionism in trade and invest-

ment. But, while taking advantage of China's opening up, others complain China's openness is quite problematic, especially and clearly the political openness. The tension between the company Google and China is being classified by the US government as a part of bilateral trade frictions: China's internet censorship is considered as a new "trade barrier".

- Security dilemma: The economically booming Asia-Pacific is also dynamic and energetic in the arms race. The US continues to strengthen its regional military alliances. Many countries in the region are already strong military powers in their own right. South Korea is strong enough to initiate preemptive war against North Korea — the 9th nuclear weapon power.[17] At the same time, reactively and defensively, China has to modernise/revolutionise its military in order to not only deal with the worst scenario triggered by the arms race but also protect China's growing "overseas interests". Objectively, a growth-oriented China perhaps has benefited greatly from the Pax Americana (American Peace), but it is never a part of the America-led alliance system. The US and other regional powers justify their strengthened military alliances by addressing China's military build-up.

Thirdly, as China's surrounding environment is so complex geostrategically, China's approach to Asia is to be a good neighbour.

China-ASEAN is an example of this and shows China's great care in handling relations with its neighbours. Regional institutions helped improve China's relations with ASEAN. China has been eagerly showing good will to ASEAN by accepting the "ASEAN way" and regional rules produced by ASEAN. China is the first external player which acceded to ASEAN's Treaty of Amity and Cooperation (TAC) in 2003.[18] China supports ASEAN's leading role in regional institutions. China continues to look to the "ASEAN+3" as a "main channel" to achieve greater economic integration.

Fourthly, China endorses the concept of "open regionalism". Reflecting this, China finally and formally acknowledges the US's "indispensable" role in Pacific Asia. The China-US Joint Statement in 2009 states: "China welcomes the United States as an Asia-Pacific nation that contributes to peace, stability and prosperity in the region". "The two sides stressed that they share broad common interests in the Asia-Pacific region and support the development and improvement of an open and inclusive regional cooperation framework that is beneficial to all. The two sides will work to encourage APEC to play a more effective role in promoting regional trade and investment liberalisation and economic and technical cooperation and for the ASEAN Regional Forum to play a more effective role in strengthening regional security cooperation".[19]

Some has long supposed that an enduringly rising China would pursue regional hegemony.[20] But Chinese leaders and diplomats have repeatedly reassured the region that China would never seek Chinese dominance. Interestingly, to avoid international misunderstanding, China has even not pursued international leadership (Deng Xiaoping: "Bu Dai Tou" — not take the lead) because leadership always means hegemony.

Finally, China is in no hurry to promote a single, integrated regional institution such as TPP and APC. The emergence of multi-institutions may be an indication of an inevitable multi-polar world in the 21st century. But China has to respond to such policy challenges posed by the US and Australia. China could encourage and support closer and effective interaction of existing regional cooperation and integration initiatives to establish a de facto network of coordination among different regional institutions. China's membership in TPP will be considered and sought seriously if most of ASEAN members and Japan finally joins it. China will continue to pay attention to Australia' APC idea but has refrained from endorsing or opposing it.

Deng Xiaoping said China is both a big and a small power.[21] This is true not just today. In the past, China was such a complex and contradictory power. In the future, as many developments indicate, Deng's sober argument is likely to continue to hold. As a big power, China needs to accommodate the demands from small powers, especially its Asian fellows. A best way to accommodate is the provision of regional public goods. As a small power, China needs to be accommodating with the big powers, especially the US and Japan in the same region. A rising China with growing regional stakes seeks a regionalist approach to be a key contributor to the regional order. This would not only better serve China's interest but also others; as well it would not only bring regional peace but also contribute to global peace.

ASEAN'S CENTRE STATUS IS GUARANTEED BY US'S NEW ASIA-PACIFIC STRATEGY

ASEAN strategically straddles East Asia and the Pacific. As a group of small and medium powers, ASEAN has resisted the domination of big powers. They have managed to play a unique role in between big powers. Now, ASEAN has enjoyed improved relations with all big powers including the US, Japan, India and China. These powers need ASEAN and tolerate its usual balancing acts.

The US rediscovers the strategic importance of ASEAN in the formation of US centred Asia-Pacific "regional architecture". According to US Secretary of State Hillary Clinton,[22]

- Washington highly values ASEAN as "an important success story"; "A strong, integrated ASEAN will serve broader regional interests";
- Washington continues to support ASEAN by enhancing the US-ASEAN Enhanced Partnership and the economic-focused US-ASEAN Trade and Investment Framework Agreement;
- Washington applauds ASEAN's decision to establish a new Intergovernmental Commission on Human Rights;
- Washington is eager to strengthen the ASEAN Regional Forum (ARF);
- Washington establishes an ambassadorial post to ASEAN in Jakarta;
- The United States might play a role in the East Asia Summit (EAS).

In the foreseeable future, ASEAN appears able to keep good relations with both China and the US. ASEAN is unlikely to choose between China and the US. Instead, for its own balance of power diplomacy, it promotes a deep regional presence of the US. Some ASEAN leaders have managed to advise that the US should realise the strategic importance of the APEC region. Singapore's Lee Kuan Yew warns: "America will lose economic ground to China and find itself excluded from the economic dynamism of East Asia if Congress continues to resist FTAs. During the next two to three decades, the region will grow in economic weight and the balance of power in the world will shift to Asia and the Pacific region". "China's competitive advantage is in the economic arena, with its huge, well-qualified manpower pool and its growing consumer market". "The contest of this century will take place in the Pacific between the US and China, and it will be economic, not military. America cannot retain its position as the leading global power if it loses influence in the Pacific".[23]

THE TRAJECTORY OF THE REGIONAL POLICY OF CHINA AND JAPAN AND THEIR INTERACTIONS IS A KEY

Currently, in China-US economic disputes, the US accuses China as causing the global (economic) imbalance (read: US-China economic ties). But, actually, the imbalance was very much a result of America's own making. As mentioned before, after Japan, China has been linked or integrated by the US as part of the US-centered global economy. "For decades, the United States has relied on a tortuous financial arrangement that knits together its economy with those of China and Japan. This informal system has allowed Asian countries to run huge export surpluses with the United States, while permitting the United States to run huge budget deficits without having to raise interest rates or taxes, and to run huge trade deficits without abruptly depreciating its currency".[24]

China and Japan have enormous potential to develop their mutual economic relations. The two have common experience and perception of gains and pains from the economic relations with the US. They can develop a common stand to improve the East Asia-US imbalance or the America-dominated regional order in East Asia in order to reduce the future risks of financial collapse.

Japan's timid new efforts on an East Asia community show that it fully knows its economic dilemma resulting from its long economic integration with the US. Japan really wants to achieve a new relations with the US on "equal footing". China has formally rejected the US's unofficial proposal of a "G2". The refusal to form a G2 should be good for China-US to rebalance their imbalanced interdependence. It is also good for East Asian cooperation/integration. China's relations with the US are indeed vital, but more important to China is not forming a G2, but diversifying its foreign relations and not neglecting the other powers in Asia and elsewhere. In either "Strategic Economic Dialogue" (2006–08) or ongoing "Strategic and Economic Dialogue", China expressed its worry on US budget policy and China's US-dollar assets. The challenges and risks posed by both Japan-US and China-US economic relations give China and Japan the incentive to work together in dealing with the US. But, due to many strategic reasons and various other considerations, both China and Japan are reluctant to formally make an economic alliance for a shared truly regional East Asian Community.

The Obama administration seeks to restore America's domination in Pacific Asia, but, paradoxically, due to the large trade deficit with China and Japan, the US president says East Asia could no longer rely on the US market but their own domestic consumption.[25] Washington also repeatedly says that "the US alone can't solve the world's problems". The aim of this is for others to share the US's burden in a crisis time. But, this US position can be interpreted as a self-declaration of the beginning of the end of the US hegemony. "After hegemony",[26] it is more imperative and necessary to establish regional accords and frameworks. For having cooperation from the region, the US needs regional multilateral arrangements. At the same time, regional multilateral arrangements can bind the US's unilateral actions. A historic turning point for rebalanced East Asia-US relations is coming. A fundamental reason for Japan's economic success after its defeat in the World War II is that the US provided a market for Japan. Similarly, China's economic achievement was also because of such a US market effect.

Now, things have changed. At least for a while (global economic recovering period, maybe for several years), America's current economic crisis has reduced the importance of the US market to export-driven East Asian economies. Objectively, many key economic challenges and problems the US faces will not be easily overcome in the foreseeable future. As a consequence, East Asians have no better choices than to seek East Asian cooperation. China and Japan are the largest trading partners in the region. Although both China and Japan still very much dependent on the US market, but the era of absolute reliance is over. If the two can overcome the politics and security dilemmas between themselves, the possibility of a China-Japan-driven East Asia community is high. China-Japan economic ties will be strengthened as China continues to grow and Japan relies on China's market to solve its own economic and social problems. That is why the Japanese new vision on East Asia community has its real rationales and why China-Japan relations have been improving in the time of global crisis.

CONCLUDING REMARKS

The coexistance of East Asian regional institutions and Asian Pacific regional institutions does not imply "drawing a line down in the middle of the Pacific".[27] A second Cold War — a Cold War between China and the US is highly unlikely. While China has benefited from a growing, open and cooperative regional environment, China has been constrained and regulated by the existing Asia-Pacific multilateral order. So, although tensions and frictions between China and the US always occur, both Washington and Beijing realise that "it is in the interest of both the US and China to continue forging a wider and genuine strategic relationship".[28] East Asian institutions and trans-Pacific institutions have converged. But, on the other hand, their paths and objectives have diverged. As the Japanese leaders described, the East Asia community will be a European Union-like body. The EU does not include the US. The East Asia community also should not include the US. The ultimate framework of East Asia is very much dependent on the policy stance of China and Japan. If they really want to build balanced and equal footing based relations with the US (if they do not want to continue to live in an unequal, hegemonic/America-centred regional environment), a commonly pursued East Asia community is a necessary and legitimate choice with clearly far-reaching significance.

Such an East Asia community should not be exclusive and should be open. The EU and the US achieve coordination through trans-Atlantic institutions such as the NATO. Like the EU, a proposed East Asia Community could and will have better cooperation and coordination through a number of trans-Pacific institutions.

However, the future of multilateral institutions in Asia and the Pacific is still uncertain. East Asian institutions may be short-lived because America attempts to resume its regional multilateral domination. Japan hosted the APEC in 2010. The US will host APEC in 2011. Washington is viewing this Japanese APEC leadership as an opportunity to sell its core Asia-Pacific agenda — TPP, which may deconstruct East Asian cooperation and reconstruct Asia-Pacific cooperation: "The United States and Japan should work closely to move the process forward in 2010 and perhaps bring it to a successful conclusion: a signing of the Trans-Pacific Partnership at the Honolulu Summit in the fall of 2011".[29] If Japan decided to join TPP, the expanded TPP would deal a hard blow to existing East Asian processes.

NOTES

1. Munakata, N. (2010). "The US, China and Japan in an integrating East Asia." Washington: Brookings Northeast Asia Commentary, Number 35, January 14.
2. See Feigenbaum, E. A. and Manning, R. A. (2010). *The United States in the New Asia.* New York: Council on Foreign Relations.
3. US Secretary of State Hillary Clinton repeatedly said in several key policy remarks in Asia and the US that "the United States is back" to Asia.

4. APEC Secretariat, "APEC Members Enjoy De Facto Integration, Analysis Reveals." See, http://www.apec.org/apec/news_media/media_releases/200911_9_tradecreation.html.
5. Quoted from Desker, B. "Apec at 20: Old Promises, New Challenges." See http://www.rsis.edu.sg/publications/Perspective/RSIS1112009.pdf.
6. On the role of America's hegemony in regional institutions in Asia-Pacific, see Beeson, M. (2009). "East Asian Regionalism and the End of the Asia-Pacific: After American Hegemony." *The Asia-Pacific Journal*, 2-2-09.
7. Overview on ASEAN, see http://www.aseansec.org/64.htm.
8. Munakata, N. "The US, China and Japan in an Integrating East Asia."
9. "Asia's IMF." *China Daily*, 30 December 2009.
10. US President Obama announced to APEC leaders in November 2009 in Singapore.
11. "Taiwan Seeks to Join P4 Trade Group." See http://www.chinapost.com.tw/business/asia/b-taiwan/2010/01/30/242892/Taiwan-seeks.htm.
12. See http://www.apc2009conference.org/site/.
13. Fukuyama, F. (2007). *America at the Crossroads: Democracy, Power, and the Neoconservative Legacy*. New Haven, Conn.: Yale University Press. Quote from Wright, T. (2009). "Toward Effective Multilateralism: Why Bigger May Not Be Better." *The Washington Quarterly*, July, p. 164.
14. Desker, B. "APEC at 20: Old Promises, New Challenges."
15. US President Obama said at the 1st US-China Strategic and Economic Dialogue in Washington DC: "U.S.-China Relations to Shape 21st Century," 27 July 2009.
16. Blyth, M. "The End of American Capitalism? Mark Twain, Lake Wobegon, and the Current Crisis." See http://www.america.gov/st/business-english/2009/May/20090513104454wrybakcuh0.4169995.html.
17. Bandow, D. "Letting Go." The American Spectator. See http://spectator.org/archives/2010/01/25/letting-go.
18. The US signed the TAC in 2009.
19. From Chinese Foreign Ministry and US White House websites.
20. For example, Gries, P. H. (2005). "China Eyes the Hegemon." *Orbis*, 49, 3, pp. 401–412.

21. Deng Xiaoping (1994). *Selected Works*, Volume 3. Beijing: People's Press, p. 105.
22. US Secretary of State Hillary Clinton Remarks on Regional Architecture in Asia at the East-West Center in Honolulu, Hawaii on 12 January 2010.
23. Lee Kuan Yew (2010). "The Importance of APEC to the US." *Straits Times*, 11 January.
24. Judis, J. B. "Debt Man Walking." ejoural USA, p. 9. See: http://www.america.gov/media/pdf/ejs/0509.pdf#popup.
25. "Remarks by President Barack Obama at Suntory Hall." Tokyo, Japan, 14 November 2009.
26. Quoted from Keohane, R. O. (1984). *After Hegemony: Cooperation and Discord in the World Political Economy*. Princeton University Press.
27. James Baker (former US Secretary of State) words, quote from Bergsten's speech.
28. Dr. Zbigniew Brzezinski replied in an email interview with the author, 28 January 2010.
29. Bergsten C. F. (2009). "The Future of APEC and Its Core Agenda: Keynote Speech to the APEC 2010 Symposium." Tokyo, December 9.

Part II

Role of China

4

Will China Become an Engine of Growth for the Region?

Yiping Huang

Peking University

ABSTRACT

China has become the second largest economy of the world. It plays an increasingly more important role in the global market economy. But can China be a new engine of growth for Asia? Quantitative assessment suggests that a one percentage point increase in Chinese growth often leads to acceleration of Asian growth by an average of 0.5 percentage point. Although this is still only half of the impact of changes in US growth, China is already an important driver of regional economic growth. Whether or not China can become a growth engine for the region depends critically on sustainability of its own growth. And the biggest challenge for China is to transform the development pattern, through reduction in investment share of GDP, strengthening of consumption, and improvement in income equality. This paper highlights the key to reduction of structural risks facing the Chinese economy: completing liberalisation of the factor markets and removing distortions to factor costs.

Keywords: China; Chang, Gordon; Lin, Justin; China: WTO accession; Pei, Minxin; cyclical synchronization; factor market distortions; structural imbalances; Wen, Jiabao; RMB exchange rate.

INTRODUCTION

On 1 January 2005, Chicago-based journalist Sara Bongiorni made a New Year's resolution: not to buy any made-in-China products for a year. The Bongiorni family experienced an eventful year finding consumer goods that are not made in China, from candles for birthday cakes to shoes for sport activities. Sometimes they were able to find goods made in Japan or Korea or even the US, but prices were 20–50% higher. Even worse, they could not tell if these products contained any parts made in China (Bongiorni, 2007).

The Bongiorni family's experience was a unique example of life in a globalised world. And China's economic influences can be felt anywhere in the world, let alone in the region. Today, China produces about 12% of the world's manufacturing products. Its shares in the consumer goods markets, especially labour-intensive products such as garments, toys and travel goods, are even greater. China accounts for close to one-tenth of the world's total exports and nearly one-fifth of the world's labour-intensive exports.

Since the end of the Second World War, many of the Asian economies have been closely linked to the US economy. The US was the most important export market for most Asian economies and regional exchange rate policies were often tied to the US dollar. But the importance of these ties began to decline during the past decade. Following China's WTO accession at the end of 2001, its regional influences grew rapidly. China not only emerged quickly as the global manufacturing center but also became the largest export markets for some Asian economies, including Korea and Taiwan.

In a way, China is already driving growth in the region. China was the first major economy to escape growth recession during the 2008–09 global financial crisis, pulling along with it some neighbouring economies. But some questions about China's regional roles remain unanswered. One central issue is sustainability of China's rapid growth, which has been a controversial issue for the entire reform period.

When China's economic reforms began, economists were generally cautious about their prospects. This was understandable because China was navigating unknown waters without a map. However, some scholars showed their confidence in China's ability to achieve strong growth relatively early. In the early 1980s, Dwight Perkins predicted at least 6–7% annual growth in the coming decades (Perkins, 1986). Slightly later, Ross Garnaut argued that ascendancy of the Chinese economy would be the most important global economic event in the following two decades (Garnaut, 1989).[1]

Another economist in the optimistic camp is Justin Lin. Lin and his co-authors were the first to describe the Chinese economic success as the "China Miracle" (Lin *et al.*, 1995). Later, he and his followers made efforts trying to generalise China's successful reform experience. His ideas are summarised in his Marshall Lecture book, *Economic Development and Transition* (Lin, 2009).

But the world is never in short supply of pessimistic scholars. The best known China bear is probably Gordon Chang. Chang's central thesis is that economic reforms deliver both strong growth and social conflicts. Further opening of the economy will eventually lead to collapse of the Chinese economy (Chang, 2001). And, unlike Lin, Minxin Pei is quite skeptical about China's gradual reform approach, as it not only delays but also amplifies many of the problems. Pei believes that gradualism is bound to fail (Pei, 2006).

In this chapter, we attempt to explore the issue of China's regional economic roles by asking three related questions. First, what are China's current impacts on Asian economies? Second, is China's rapid growth sustainable? And, three, how will the Chinese economy evolve in the coming decade? Answers to these questions should lay the foundation of our understanding of the future dynamics between the Chinese and regional economies.

CHINA'S CURRENT REGIONAL ECONOMIC ROLES

Before the 2008–09 global financial crisis, the "decoupling thesis" was once very popular among some Asian investors and policymakers. The central argument of the thesis was that Asian growth was no longer dependent on the US economy. If Asian economies could rely on each others' supports, then they could achieve rapid growth regardless of growth performance of the US economy. The hope of decoupling, however, collapsed quickly as the US crisis dragged almost every Asian economy into growth recession.

In reality, while the decoupling thesis was a little too early, complete synchronisation was not accurate for describing economic relations between Asia and the US. Perhaps the "Kawai hypothesis" provides a more accurate description of the relationship: synchronised in terms of economic cycles but divergent in terms of growth trends.[2] Indeed, quarterly data show increasing convergence of growth rates in China and the US (Figure 1).

This increasing cyclical synchronisation is consistent with the trend of globalisation during the past decades. China's share of exports in GDP rose from less than 10% at the beginning of economic reform to 37% in 2007. This means external demand, especially demand from the US became increasingly more important. Such growing relations were behind cyclical synchronisation. A collapse of the US economy, like what happened in 2008–09, was bound to have significant impact on the Chinese growth.

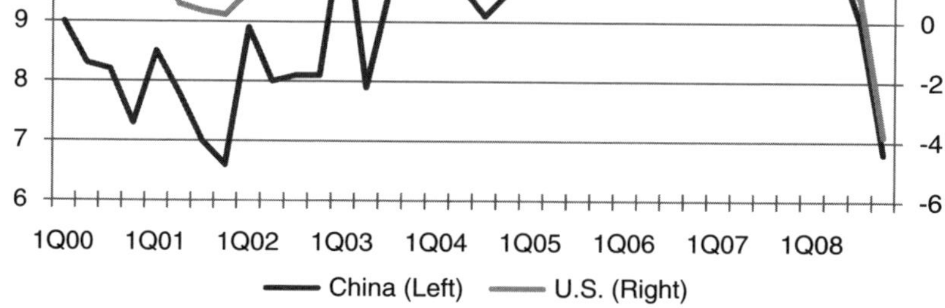

Figure 1. Quarterly GDP Growth in China and US, 1Q 2000–4Q 2010 (% year/year)
Source: CEIC Data Company and National Bureau of Statistics

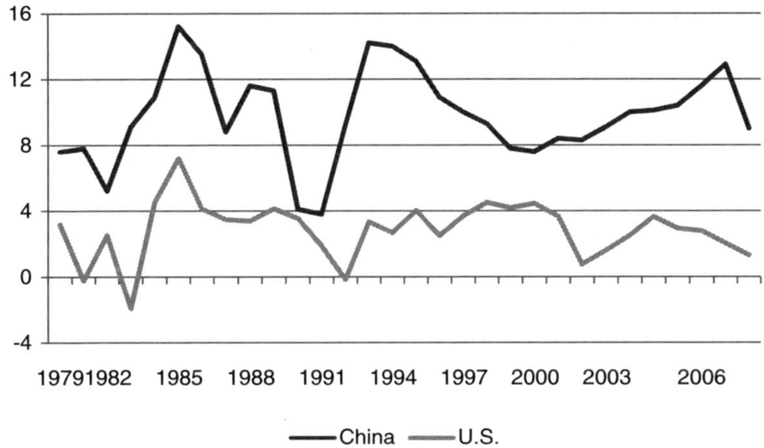

Figure 2. Annual GDP Growth in China and the US, 1979–2008 (%)
Source: CEIC Data Company and National Bureau of Statistics

The annual data, however, present a different picture (Figure 2). Trends of GDP growth in China and US actually showed very clear signs of divergence. Such divergence can be explained by at least two factors. As a middle-income and dynamic economy, China still enjoys much higher growth potential than the US. And, two, even in face of external shocks, China enjoys much greater policy flexibility in supporting growth. Eventually, increases in the degree of divergence will determine China's ability driving regional growth.

One factor often behind the "decoupling thesis" was the rapidly growing intraregional trade. Clearly China's emergence as the global manufacturing center is crucial for the shift of supply chain and for the rise of intraregional trade in the region. If growth of intraregional trade continues, then it is possible that Asian economies would become less dependent on external markets. In other words, Asian markets might be able to support growth within the region.

The disaggregated data, however, provide a slightly different picture: increases in intraregional trade during the past decade in Asia did not necessarily mean growing importance of final demand within the region. Instead, growth of intraregional trade was mainly driven by movements of intermediate goods. As the assemblers increasingly moved to China, for instance, the rest of the region exported more and more intermediate products to China for processing and re-exports.

Data on trade in finished goods confirm that, before the global financial crisis, still about 60% of them went to the US, Europe and Japan, about 20% went to the other regions and the remaining 20% stayed within the region. China absorbed a total of 6% of Asia's exports of finished goods. So China is important but is not as important as either the US or Japan in this regard. But of course, this relativity is changing very rapidly as China continues to grow much faster than any of the industrial economies.

China's international economic influences are probably best illustrated by its roles in the global commodity markets. Today, China accounts for about 6% of world GDP and 21% of world population. But it is already a dominant player in global commodity markets. China consumes more than half of the world's iron ore and more than 30% of world's aluminum and zinc (see Figure 3). In fact, China's strong demand was the driving force behind the so-called "super-cycle thesis" for the global commodity markets.

Perhaps one more mysterious area where China has an important role is Asian exchange rate policy. Asia used to be a dollar-block, i.e., Asian currencies were more or less tied to the US dollar. But this has been changing. According to some empirical estimation, Chinese yuan already plays a similar role of (in cases of Indonesian rupiah and Malaysian ringgit) or even more important roles (in case of Singapore dollar) than the US dollar (Table 1). Some experts believe that a yuan-block is already in the making.

This is indeed puzzling simply because Chinese yuan is not yet convertible. Yuan's international is perhaps supported by China's massive foreign exchange reserves, which currently stand at more than $2.5 trillion. Therefore, currency confidence is not an issue. But more importantly, it must be closely related to economic relations between China and the rest of the region. Competitive relations, for instance, would make policymakers in other countries to monitor closely yuan exchange rate relative to their own currencies.

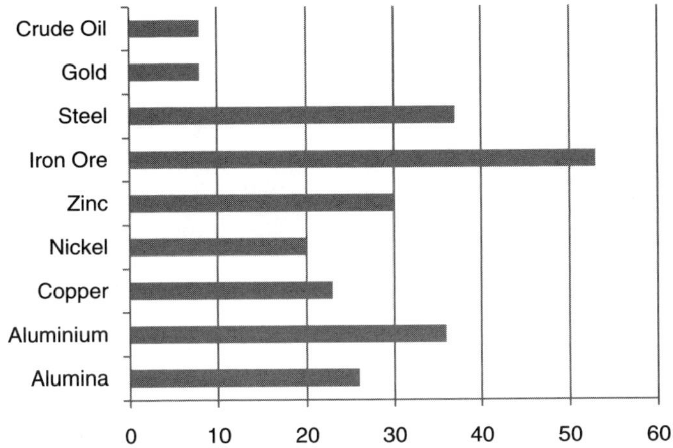

Figure 3. China's Shares of Global Commodity Consumption (%)
Source: Citi Investment Research

Table 1. Estimated Currency Basket Weights for Asian Currencies

	US dollar	Euro	Japanese yen	Chinese yuan
Indonesian rupiah	0.47	0.08	–0.01	0.46
Korean won	0.48	0.48	–0.24	0.28
Malaysian ringgit	0.45	0.15	–0.03	0.43
Philippine peso	0.73	0.16	–0.04	0.14
Singapore dollar	0.25	0.29	–0.03	0.49
Thailand baht	0.49	0.13	0.01	0.37
Vietnamese dong	1.04	0.00	0.00	–0.03
Indian rupee	0.56	0.12	–0.01	0.33

Source: Takatoshi Ito (2010)

So exactly how important is the Chinese growth for the regional economies? To answer this question, we apply the Oxford Economic Model (OEF) to run some simulations. We first implement an exogenous shock of 1% increase in the US growth in the model and then repeat the same exercise by raising the Chinese growth by 1%. A short summary of the finding is that a 1% increase in US growth

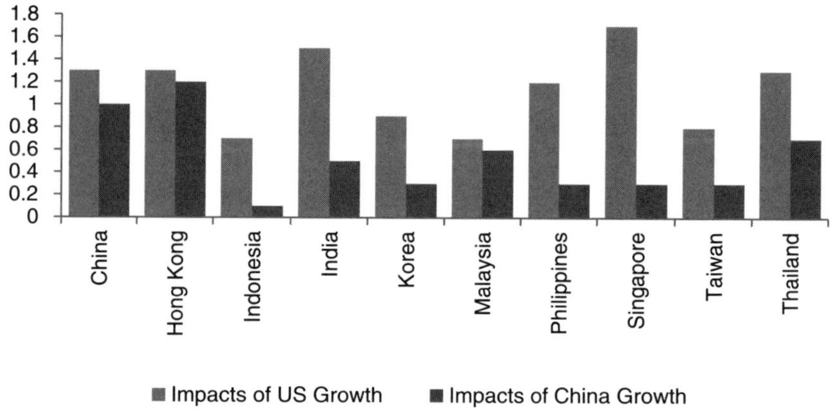

Figure 4. Impacts of Increase in US and Chinese Growth by 1 Percentage Point on Asian Growth (percentage point)

Source: Author's simulation results by applying the Oxford Economic Forecasting Model (www.oef.com)

raises Asian growth by an average of 1.1 percentage points, while a 1% increase in Chinese growth raises Asian growth by an average of 0.5 percentage point (Figure 4).

These suggest that change in China's growth performance is already a very critical factor for the regional economy. So far its impacts are roughly only about half of those of the US. But the economies of China and the US are moving forward at very different paces. If China can continue its rapid growth of the past decades, then its influences can one day exceed those of the US.

FACTOR MARKET DISTORTIONS AND STRONG ECONOMIC GROWTH

But sustainability of rapid growth is a strong assumption. When Wen Jiabao became the Premier in 2003, he said that the Chinese growth model had some major problems such as overinvestment, large external imbalances, inefficiency of resource uses, income inequality, pollution, etc. During the following years the government took various measures to correct these problems. But unfortunately the problems became bigger. In our view, the main reason was because the government relied mainly on administrative measures. But the fundamental cause lied in the incentive structure.

A unique feature of the Chinese reform, however, was the asymmetric approach toward market liberalisation: the government rapidly freed up product markets but was much more reluctant to remove distortions in factor markets. After 30 years of economic reform, transactions of almost all products today are undertaken within free markets. But the markets for labour, capital, land and resources remain highly regulated. And the pricing and costs of these factors are also significantly distorted (Huang, 2010).

Factor market distortions

Labour. During the pre-reform period, there was no labour mobility and wages were all set by the government, regardless of effort. This changed when surplus rural labour started to emerge following the HRS reform in the early 1980s. The underemployed rural workers found non-agricultural jobs, sometimes outside their villages. This was the beginning of China's labour market. In the early 1990s, restrictions on the urban economy loosened as the growth of the non-state sector gathered momentum. Reform of the SOEs, including laying off a massive number of redundant workers in the late 1990s, and a surge of foreign direct investment inflow facilitated labour market development in China. At the end of 2009, there were a total of about 150 million migrant workers across the country.

But operation of labour markets is still heavily distorted. And many workers, especially migrant workers, remain significantly underpaid. For instance, many companies often under-contribute to the social welfare benefits of their employees. If companies strictly follow policies on social welfare contributions, commonly their payrolls would have to rise by at least 35–40%, including for contributions to pensions (20% of payroll), medical insurance (6%), employment benefit (2%), work injury insurance (1%), maternity benefit (0.8%) and housing entitlement (5–10%).[3] By contributing less than required, especially for migrant workers, companies essentially reduce their cost of labour.

Again, the household registration system, which was a product of the central planning era, still restricts labour mobility and discriminates against farmers moving to work in the cities. According to this system, people cannot move legally unless it is approved by the government. When migrant workers find jobs in the cities, they are normally not entitled to pensions and medical care. Their children cannot attend local public schools. They cannot enjoy a housing subsidy. In short, they may be able to work in urban industries for years, but it is very difficult for them to settle down. For this reason, migrant workers' pay is sometimes only half of the pay of urban residents, even if they perform the same job functions.

The argument that institutional distortions repress labour costs is often strongly disputed by economists. Skepticism about repressed wage costs derives from the perception that labour should be cheap in any case, given China's massive surplus labour in the countryside. But this is not necessarily so. If social welfare policies were implemented properly and the household registration system was abolished, migrant workers would likely receive higher compensation. Many of them may choose to settle down in the cities. The real question is how much would such rise in labour compensation reduce labour demand and therefore lower migrant workers' total income. In an economy with surplus labour, the answer to this question depends mainly on wage elasticity of demand for labour.

Capital. Distortions to the cost of capital take at least two forms. One is the undervalued currency, and the other is generally repressed domestic interest rates. Currency undervaluation is better known since it has been the focus of some international policy debates. There are different approaches measuring equilibrium exchange rates based on purchasing power parity information, the structural characteristics of the economy or the imbalances. While most economists agree that the RMB is probably undervalued, they disagree on the magnitude of the undervaluation. The normal range of the undervaluation estimated for the RMB is between 5% and 50% (Clive and Williamson, 2008).

Under-estimation of the domestic cost of capital is underscored by existence of financial repression (Wang, 2010). Financial repression likely reduces capital efficiency and capital costs. A World Bank study suggests that financial liberalisation in emerging market economies would raise domestic interest rates by a couple of percentage points (Caprio *et al.*, 1994). This could be interpreted as financial repression reducing interest rates by a couple of percentage points.

Such distortion of capital costs can be confirmed by comparison of the GDP growth potential-government bond yield relationship across countries. In theory, nominal GDP growth potential indicates average return to investment. Therefore, the risk-free government bond yields should converge with this rate of return. In China, however, the gap is close to 10 percentage points — assuming nominal GDP growth at 11% and 5-year government bond yield at 3%. This is high compared with 6.5 percentage points in India, 6.2 percentage points in Thailand, 5.7 percentage points in Malaysia and 2.6 percentage points in Korea at the end of 2008. Clearly, capital is too cheap in China.

Land. Land is owned by collectives in the countryside and by the state in the cities. Until recently there was no market for land. Land transfer for non-agricultural uses has to be approved by the government. In the past, land fees were decided by local authorities, although users also had some bargaining power. But since all local governments were keen to attract more investment, they often provided concessions on land use fees. This was common when local governments competed with each other to attract investment projects by offering tax exemptions and lower land use fees.

In recent years, however, the governments turned to more market-oriented land transfer mechanisms, such as auctions and negotiations, to both improve transparency and boost local government revenues. This practice is more applicable in the case of property development. For industrial use it is still common for the government to apply land use fees. And on average the land use fees are only about 16% of the costs through auction. Manufacturers, therefore, receive implicit subsidies on land inputs.

Energy. Institutional distortions in domestic energy markets are widespread, although the magnitudes of cost distortions have varied wildly over the years. Of the different types of energy products, coal prices are the closest to market prices. Electricity tariffs are set by the authorities through public consultation. The most visible and sometimes also most volatile distortions are in areas of oil products.

In 1998, in an important step in oil price liberalisation, the State Council announced a formula linking domestic prices to the weighted average of prices in New York, Singapore and Rotterdam. NDRC would adjust domestic prices, with a couple of months' delay, if the international weighted average moves by more than 8%. In 2000, NDRC raised oil prices 7 times in order to bring domestic prices closer to the international levels.

However, when international prices moved violently, NDRC was reluctant to follow for fear of disrupting economic growth. For instance, when international crude prices reached their recent peak, at close to $150 per barrel in 2008, the equivalent domestic prices were only around $80 per barrel. Oil price distortions are highly volatile, given the State Council's formula and fluctuations in the international markets.

Environment. Environment is not a conventional factor of production. However, compensation for pollution should be counted as part of production costs. Over the past three decades, the Chinese authorities instituted a relatively complete set of environmental protection regulations and policies. The problem, however, is the big gap between the intent of these policies and their implementation. Local governments, especially those in underdeveloped areas, are often not willing to protect the environment at the expenses of income and GDP growth. Such lapses in policy implementation constitute an effective subsidy to producers.

The National Development and Reform Commission (NDRC) and the Ministry of Environmental Protection (MOEP) once estimated the net damage to environment at 3% of GDP in 2004. Pollution of air, water and soil not only affects economic productivity but also generates serious health problems. Environmental degradation in China contributed to global climate change, evidenced by rapid melting of the glaciers in the Himalayas. It has also led to regular drought in Northern China and frequent floods in Southern China (Woo and Huang, 2004).

Crude estimation of factor cost distortions

How serious are these distortions? In order to gauge the significance of these factor market distortions, we intend to make some crude quantitative estimates. Huang (2010) made one of the first attempts at the measurement of factor market distortions and found that it amounted to 2.1 trillion yuan in 2008, or about 7% of GDP. His estimation, however, was made only for one year. In a follow-up study, Huang and Tao (2010) refined some of the methods and extended the estimation to include nine years from 2000 to 2008. Based on those estimates they also made a preliminary attempt to gauge of the impact of factor market distortions in 2009 (see Table 2).[4] It should be noted that the estimates by Huang and Tao were somewhat higher than that by Huang.

It is useful to make clear the qualifications surrounding these estimates before drawing any implications. The task of estimating the distortions is quite difficult to say the least, as in most cases there is no information about undistorted factor prices. The purpose of the estimation was not to provide accurate estimates. Rather we hope to get some idea of the possible magnitude of the distortions and, more importantly, changes in their impact over time. We acknowledge that some of the assumptions we have to make are problematic and that, therefore, the estimates are subject to improvement once new information becomes available.

Despite potential problems, the estimation results reveal some important patterns. First, of all the distortions, capital market

Table 2. Estimated Cost Distortions in China, 2000–09 (% GDP)

	Labour	Capital	Land	Energy	Environ	Total
2000	0.1	4.1	0.5	0.0	3.8	8.5
2001	0.2	3.9	0.5	0.0	3.5	8.1
2002	0.8	3.9	0.4	0.0	3.3	8.4
2003	1.0	3.8	1.1	0.0	3.3	9.2
2004	2.0	3.1	0.9	0.6	3.0	9.5
2005	2.4	3.0	1.3	1.7	3.0	11.4
2006	2.7	3.1	2.0	1.6	2.8	12.2
2007	3.2	3.6	1.2	1.6	2.4	12.0
2008	3.6	3.4	1.0	0.7	1.9	10.6
2009*	2.7	3.5	0.9	0.7	1.8	9.6

Note: * Estimates for 2009 are very preliminary based on estimates for other years and available information for 2009 and are subject to major revision when new information is available
Source: Huang and Tao (2010), page 18

distortions are by far the most important. Capital cost distortions contribute about 40% of total cost distortions on average. This helps to explain the persistent problem of overinvestment in China and also rapid development of capital-intensive industries despite continued job market pressures.

Second, labour market distortions have actually grown in recent years, despite loosening policy controls and increasing rural-urban migration. This is a result of both the rising number of migrant workers and persistent, even widening, income gaps between migrant workers and urban workers. Indeed the statistics suggest that while labour demand has increased in recent years, migrant workers' pay did not keep pace with that of urban workers, especially when social welfare benefit contributions are considered.

Third, energy cost distortions fluctuated widely across years, reflecting volatilities in international oil prices and the varying response of Chinese authorities to these changes. China has already adopted a price mechanism which closely tracks changes in international energy prices. But the authorities hold down domestic prices when international prices surge rapidly. Therefore, energy cost distortions are sometimes asymmetric. When international prices are low, there is little distortion. When international prices are high, distortions increase rapidly.

Fourth, environmental cost distortion was the only item that showed consistent improvement. This is a very important result, assuming the estimates reflect actuality. Despite the perception of worsening in the environment, the pollution problem has probably reached a turning point. And this is attributable mainly to a stepping-up of policy efforts in recent years. The growing public awareness of the problem probably also helped.

And, finally, the aggregate estimates of cost distortions show significant increase in the years after 2004, consistent with the observation that structural imbalances worsened during the same period. The trend of continuous liberalisation and recent increases in total impact of cost distortions are not necessarily contradictory with one another. These contradictory trends could arise because of a slower rise in distorted prices than undistorted prices despite loosening controls. It could also arise because the quantity of factors grew rapidly even though unit distortions declined. The moderation of the impact of total distortions after 2006, however, may suggest that the worst of the imbalance problems are already behind us.

MACROECONOMIC CONSEQUENCES OF FACTOR MARKET DISTORTIONS

Why does China pursue this approach to liberalisation? In practice, only some of the factor market distortions were deliberately adopted by the government. An obvious example is price control for petroleum. The intention of policymakers was to adopt free market price mechanisms for oil and other energy products. However, when international prices rise significantly, they often fear that increases in domestic prices would hurt households and industries that are sensitive to energy price shocks. Distortions were introduced in order to minimise the shock.

Other distortions are legacies of the central planning system and are only transitional phenomena. For instance, the government clearly understands that the household registration system is discriminatory and inefficient in nature. But abolition of the system requires a number of other institutional conditions, such as social welfare systems for all rural residents. Also, while financial liberalisation is probably preferred, it is also conditional on effective improvement of the SOEs and state-owned financial institutions.

Yet China's adoption of this approach to reform was not accidental. Fundamentally, this provided an effective way of achieving the fastest growth possible. The rationale is perhaps best illustrated by Deng Xiaoping's two popular phrases:

> *White or black, a cat is a good cat as long as it catches mice*; and *Growth is a hard principle.*

In fact, the whole economic and political system was adapted for pursuing strong economic growth. The government functioned more like a business than a provider of public services (Yao, 2010). Rigourous statistical analyses confirm that GDP growth rate was the single most important variable determining the future of provincial governors and Party secretaries (Li and Zhou, 2005).

Repression of factor costs in order to achieve rapid growth is not unique in China. In fact, it is commonly seen in many other developing countries. Factor cost distortions were also observed in Japan and Korea during their early stages of economic development. By adopting such distortions, the governments of these countries probably shared the same goal of achieving faster economic growth (Lin, 2009).

China's pre-reform urban industrialisation strategy also contained some elements of factor cost distortions. The unified purchase and marketing system (UPMS) for agricultural products was specifically designed to ensure supply of food and agricultural materials to the urban sector. Since the state prices were normally below market prices, UPMS artificially lowered production costs for urban industries. This gave rise to extraordinary industrial profits, which were then re-invested in urban industries.

In essence, the pre-reform industrialisation policy subsidised urban industries by heavily taxing farmers, who were at that time the only possible source of funds. Song Guoqing was the first to unveil the underlying logic pre-reform agricultural policies, especially the UPMS (Song, 1994).[5] He argued that the UPMS was really a substitute for a land tax.

But clearly the pre-reform industrialisation policy failed in the end. This reinforces an important point that any distortions to market forces are likely inefficient and costly in the end. But why has the post-reform approach worked much better? In retrospect, the post-reform approach differs from the pre-reform strategy in at least two respects. One, in pre-reform China, there was no free market for products. Resource allocation was extremely inefficient. This was completely changed during the reform period.

And, two, in the pre-reform period, production teams, enterprises, and individuals did not have any decision-making autonomy. Often the plans did not suit local conditions. But more importantly, agricultural workers' efforts were not linked to their rewards. So there was no incentive to work hard. Again, this changed quickly during the reform period.

So how do cost distortions affect the economy during the reform period? At the simplest level, we may view the distortions as a production subsidy, that is, cost distortions in most of their guises are like producer subsidy equivalent (PSEs). Cost distortions boost profits from production. This was essentially why China quickly rose as a global manufacturing center within a few years following its WTO accession. There was no better place to produce than in China — labour was cheap; capital was cheap; land was cheap; energy was cheap; producers further enjoyed tax exemptions; and there was no real charge for pollution (Huang, 2010).

Low costs also stimulated investment. Most importantly, capital is cheap. According to our estimates, capital was by far the most important item in total cost distortion over the past ten years. Thus, it was almost impossible for the government to control the overinvestment problem. When potential investment returns are so high, any NDRC initiatives to slow investment were bound to fail. This explains why China moved into heavy industries so quickly in the early 21st century even though the government still hoped to create more jobs. As the investment share of GDP was close to 50%, it is easy to understand why China consumes such large volumes of raw materials. Perhaps it is also easy to understand why urban infrastructure was so advanced in a country where per capita GDP was only slightly above US$3,000.

Cost distortions make Chinese products a lot more competitive in international markets. This was behind the unusual growth in China's economic openness, with the export share of GDP rising from 8% in 1978 to 35% in 2008, an unusually high level for a large economy. This also explains why China's international influence is disproportionate to its income level and even its economic size. Close to 70% of Chinese GDP is externally-oriented (exports plus imports), compared with 20–30% for the US and Japan. This also explains why China exports so much capital. In fact, our factor cost distortion estimates provide a reasonably good fit with the current account balance during the past ten years.

While cost distortions were positive for production, investment and exports, at least in the short term, they were clearly negative for household income and consumption and welfare. While the national saving ratio rose steadily over the past 20 years, household saving as a share of GDP remained stable. Corporate saving rose from 11.7% of GDP in 1992 to 22.9% in 2007 (Figure 5).

More importantly, the share of labour compensation in national income dropped from 51.4% in 1995 to 40.6% in 2006, while the share of household income in national income declined from 66.8% in 1996 to 50.6% in 2007 (see Figure 6).

All these suggest that factor cost distortions were a fundamental force behind China's recent large external imbalances. This, in turn, contributed to the global imbalances through growing current account and capital account surpluses. Distortion of incentives significantly inflated investment and export activities. At the same time, as household income relative to GDP declined over time, consumption also weakened inevitably in relative terms. This further widened external imbalances.

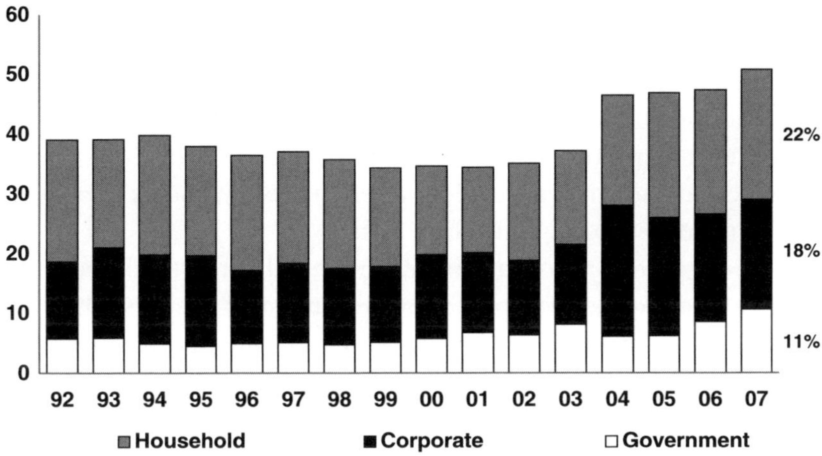

Figure 5. Composition of National Savings, 1992–2007 (% of GDP)

Source: Lin (2010)

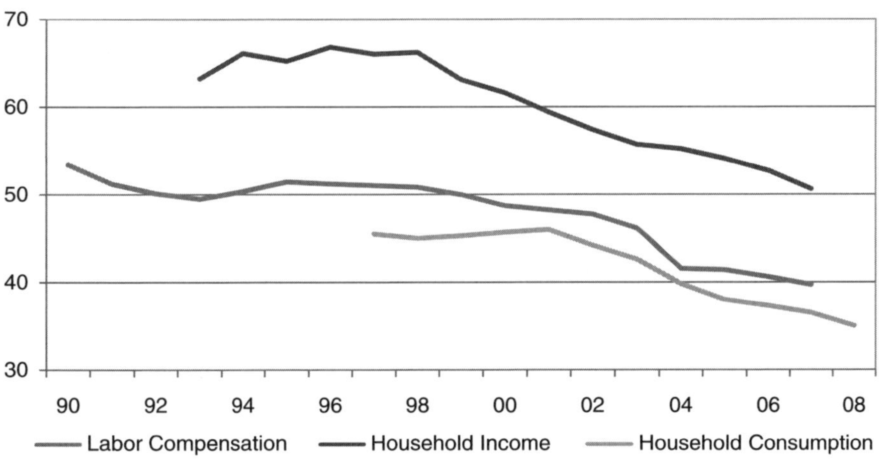

Figure 6. Shares of Labour Compensation, Household Income and Household Consumption in National Income, 1990–2007 (%)

Source: Bai and Qian (2009a and 2009b)

In explaining China's current account surpluses, the literature has proposed five possible factors: (1) measurement errors, which suggest "hot money" inflows disguised in forms of current account items due to stricter capital account controls; (2) saving and investment gap, which is really an identity definition of the current account; (3) industrial relocation, which points to transfer of trade surpluses to China alongside relocation of manufacturing factories to China; (4) policies promoting strong growth, which hints possibility of domestic production greater than domestic demand; and (5) exchange rate, which argues that an undervalued currency boosts exports but inhibits imports (Huang and Tao, 2010).

All these factors were important in contributing to China's trade surpluses and capital outflows. However, most of them, such as policies promoting strong growth and exchange rate, fail to account for the recent surge in current account surpluses. Others, such as saving and investment gap, do not offer actionable policy responses. Compared with these, factor cost distortions appear to provide a more reasonable explanation of recent fluctuations in current account surpluses with important policy implications.

While, in practice, factor cost distortions artificially lifted growth in China during the past years, it would be wrong to recommend this as a policy prescription for other developing countries. In fact, most developing countries adopted similar policies, including China in the pre-reform period, but did achieve similar performance. An extreme example of that strategy was the former Soviet Union, which mobilised all resources to support growth. Growth was strong for a while but the risks quickly took hold of the economy.

This is why we are seeing ever growing structural imbalances in China, which alongside other problems such as inefficient resource use, income inequality and pollution, could seriously affect China's ability to sustain its rapid growth. If these problems continue to cumulate, they would lead to disruption of China's growth path. This is probably also why there are always pessimists about China's growth outlook. And this is perhaps also why optimists like Wen Jiabao continues to lose sleep at night.

CONCLUDING REMARKS

China's experiences during its reform period were sometimes characterised as "economic miracle". The average growth rate of 10%

over a period of 30 years is indeed unprecedented. During that period, China was transformed from an agrarian, closed economy to a major global economic power. China is set to overtake Japan to become the world's second largest economy in 2010 and to even overtake the US to become the world's largest economy within the next decade or two.

Alongside rapid growing of China's own economic size, its influences on the regional economies also increased significantly. This is evidenced by China's central role in regional supply chains, in the commodity markets and in exchange rate policies. Most importantly, quantitative analyses suggest that a 1% increase in Chinese growth leads to increase by an average of 0.5 percentage point in Asian growth. Today, this is important but is still only half of the influences of the US. But the relative dynamism is likely to change quickly assuming China continues on its rapid growth path.

But the assumption of sustainability of rapid growth is a strong one. The government has been trying very hard for the past years in order to improve growth sustainability by transforming the growth model. Unfortunately that effort failed. In this chapter, we offer one hypothesis explaining why China's growth performance was so successful and why its growth model was so problematic.

We argue that it is closely related to China's unique approach to reform — asymmetric liberalisation of product and factor markets and price distortions for labour, capital, land, resources and the environment. In retrospect, some of these distortions, such as control of energy prices, were deliberately adopted, and others, such as the household registration system, are transitional phenomena. But they share common motivation: to achieve strongest possible economic growth.

Judging from the data, this approach to reform has been very successful in promoting economic growth. At the same time, it also underlies many growing imbalance problems. Cost distortions artificially increased profits from manufacturing production and quickly turned China into a global manufacturing center through supply of cheap labour, cheap capital, cheap land and cheap resources. Cost distortions also contributed to oversized investment and exports. In fact, factor market cost distortion estimates seem to provide a better explanation for movements of the current account over the past ten years than many other factors identified in the literature, such as the exchange rate.

Therefore, factor cost distortion was a fundamental cause behind China's growing external imbalances, including massive trade surpluses, large official capital outflows and extraordinary foreign exchange reserves. These, in turn, contributed to development of the global imbalance problems, as China is now a major surplus country in the world economy.

The growing risks for Chinese economic growth, however, suggest that the current growth pattern may not be able to continue for long. The Chinese government under Wen Jiabao's leadership has spent the past seven years trying to improve the quality of growth and rebalance the economy. But in the end almost all those policy measures failed. During the past seven years, almost all imbalance problems became worse: current account surpluses became larger, the investment share of GDP increased, and consumption weakened further relative to GDP.

The fundamental reason for the policy failure in adjusting economic structure was because the government did not attack its root cause — the incentive structure related to factor market cost distortions. For instance, if capital is extremely cheap, the NDRC cannot succeed in controlling investment by slowing down the approvals for new projects. Similarly, the Ministry of Finance (MOF) is not able to narrow external imbalances significantly by reducing export tax rebates by a couple of percentage points.

A much more effective approach for dealing with the imbalance problem is to implement a comprehensive package of factor market reforms.[6] Policymakers will have to eliminate distortions in the incentive structure and production costs. And this essentially calls for an end to the asymmetric approach to market liberalisation. Steady liberalisation of factor markets and elimination of cost distortions should be the top priority for the next stage reform. Only by so doing, will China be able to rebalance the economy, reduce the risks to economic performance, and place the economy on a more sustainable growth path.

In fact, the Chinese government has already started its process of factor market liberalisation, evidenced by recent freeing of resource prices and accelerating reform of the household registration system. If these reform efforts continue and succeed, then China will soon become a true engine of growth for the region.

REFERENCES

Bai, C.-E. and Qian, Z. (2009a). "Factor Income Share in China: Stories behind Statistics." *Economic Research Journal (Jing Ji Yan Jiu)*, 3.

Bai, C.-E. and Qian, Z. (2009b). "Who Has Eroded Residents' Income? An Analysis of China's National Income Distribution Patterns." *Social Sciences in China (Zhong Guo She Hui Ke Xue)*, 5, pp. 99–115.

Bergsten, C. F., Freeman, C., Lardy, N. and Mitchell, D. J. (2008). *China's Rise: Challenges and Opportunities.* Washington, D.C: Peterson Institute of International Economics.

Bongiorni, S. (2007). *A Year Without "Made in China": One Family's True Life Adventure in the Global Economy.* New Jersey: John Wiley & Sons.

Caprio, G. Jr., Atiyas, I. and Hanson, J. A. (1994). *Financial Reform: Theory and Practice, Cambridge University Press.* New York and Melbourne: Cambridge University Press.

Chang, G. G. (2001). *The Coming Collapse of China.* New York: Random House.

Chen, J., Hou, W. and Jin, S. (2008). "A Review of the Chinese Gini Coefficient from 1978 to 2005." Available at SSRN, http://ssrn.com/abstract=1328998.

Clive, W. R. and Williams, J. (2008). "Estimates of the Equilibrium Exchange Rate of Renminbi: Is There a Consensus and If Not, Why Not?" In M. Goldstein and N. Lardy (Eds.), *Debating China's Exchange Rate Policy.* Washington D.C.: Peterson Institute of International Economics.

Drysdale, P. and Song, L. (Eds.) (2000). *China and WTO: Strategic Issues and Quantitative Assessments.* Routledge.

Fan, G. (1994). "Incremental Changes and Dual-Track Transition: Understanding the Case of China." *Economic Policy*, 9(19, Supplement: Lessons for Reform), pp. 100–122.

Garnaut, R. (1989). Australia and Northeast Asian Ascendancy: Report to the Prime Minister and the Minister for Foreign Affairs and Trade. Australian Government Publishing Services, Canberra.

Goldstein, M. and Lardy, N. R. (2009). *The Future of China's Exchange Rate Policy*. Washington D.C., US: Peterson Institute for International Economics.

Huang, Y. (1998). *Agricultural Reform in China: Getting Institutions Right*. Cambridge: Cambridge University Press.

Huang, Y. (2001). *China's Last Steps Across the River: Enterprise and Banking Reforms*. Canberra: Asia Pacific Press.

Huang, Y. (2010). "Great Ascendancy and Structural Risks: Consequences of Asymmetric Market Liberalization." *Asian Pacific Economic Literature*, forthcoming.

Huang, Y. and Tao, K. (2010). "Causes and Remedies of China's External Imbalances." Working Paper Series No. 2010002, China Center for Economic Research, Peking University.

Ito, T. (2010). "RMB as Number One: When will the Chinese RMB become a Regional Key Currency." Paper presented at the Asian Economic Policy Review Conference, April 10, Tokyo.

Lardy, N. R. (2002). *Integrating China into the World Economy*. Washington D.C.: Brookings Institution.

Li, H. and Zhou, L.-A. (2005). "Political Turnover And Economic Performance: the Incentive Role of Personnel Control in China." *Journal of Public Economics*, 89(9–10), pp. 1743–1762.

Lin, J. Y. (1992). "Rural Reform and Agricultural Growth in China." *American Economic Review*, 82(1), pp. 34–51.

Lin, J. Y. (2009). *Economic Development Transition: Thought, Strategy and Viability*. Cambridge: Cambridge University Press.

Lin, J. Y. (2010). "Dealing with Global Imbalances." Presentation at the Korean Development Institute and International Monetary Fund Conference *Reconstructing the World Economy*, 25 February, Seoul, Korea.

Lin, J. Y., Cai, F. and Li, Z. (1995). *The China Miracle: Development Strategy and Economic Reform*. Hong Kong: The Chinese University of Hong Kong Press.

Maddison, A. (2006). "Asia in the World Economy, 1500–2030." *Asian Pacific Economic Literature*, 20(2), pp. 1–37.

Naughton, B. (1995). *Growing Out of the Plan: Chinese Economic Reform, 1978–1993*, Cambridge University Press.

Pei, M. (2006). *China's Trapped Transition: The Limits of Development Autocracy*. Cambridge: Harvard University Press.

Perkins, D. H. (1986). *China: Asia's Next Economic Giant?* Seattle and London: University of Washington Press.

Sachs, J. D. and Woo, W. T. (2000). "Understanding China's Economic Performance." *Journal of Policy Reform*, 4, 1, pp. 1–50.

Song, G. (1994). "From Unified Purchase and Marketing System to Land Tax (in Chinese)." In Q. Zhou (Ed.), *Rural Change and Chinese Development: 1978–1989 (II)*. Hong Kong: Oxford University Press.

Wang, X. (2010). "An Index of Financial Repression for China." Unpublished note, China Center for Economic Research, Peking University, Beijing.

Wen, J. (2006). "Government Work Report." Delivered at the National People's Congress meeting, 5 March.

Woo, W. T. (2006). "The Structural Nature of Internal and External Imbalances in China." *Journal of Chinese Economic and Business Studies*, 4(1), pp. 1–19.

Woo, W. T. and Huang, Y. (2004). "Some Key Challenges to the Sustainability of Economic Growth in China." In Y.-S. Nam (Ed.), *Rising China and the East Asian Economy* (in Korean). Seoul: Korean Institute for International Economic Policy.

Yao, Y. (2010). "The End of Beijing Consensus." *Foreign Affairs*.

Yu, Y. (2006). "Global Imbalances and China." Finch Lecture, 17 October, Melbourne University, Australia. Published in *Australian Economic Review*, 40(1), pp. 1–33.

Yu, Y. (2009). "China's Policy Responses to Global Economic Crisis and Its Perspective on the Reform of International Monetary System." Paper presented at the Asia Europe Economic Forum Conference, 7–8 July, Kiel Institute of World Economy, Kiel, Germany.

NOTES

1. The only person who correctly predicted 10% annual growth for China during the last quarter of the 20th century was Australia's first Ambassador to China Stephen FitzGerald. Ambassador FitzGerald is political scientist, not an economist. And he made his very brave call in

1976, even before China started economic reform. For some details about the story, see Garnaut, J. (2009). "Braving New Heights in Beijing." *Sydney Morning Herald*, 28 September.

2. Masahiro Kawai, Dean of the Asian Development Bank Institute, formulated this hypothesis at a series of conferences in Tokyo during 2009.
3. These were estimates provided in person by former Ministry of Finance official Zhai Fan in 2001.
4. For detailed methods of estimation, please refer to Huang and Tao (2010).
5. Song Guoqing's article was written in late 1982.
6. The need for more comprehensive approaches, rather than exclusive focus on the currency, was supported by Woo (2006) and Goldstein and Lardy (2009), although they approached the issue from different angles.

5

China's Economic Rise and Regional Trade

Rafael Leal-Arcas*

Queen Mary University of London

ABSTRACT

In the context of a current global economic crisis and an unfinished World Trade Organization (WTO) Doha Round, multilateralism is at its weakest point. The proliferation of bilateral and regional trade agreements seems to be the natural consequence of failed multilaterlism. In this difficult context, this chapter argues that the attitude of China — one of the three global economic superpowers — to multilaterlism is questionable or unclear. China poses a major challenge to the world economy by virtue of being a new global economic superpower.

For a country to be considered a global economic superpower, it must meet three criteria: 1) it must be large enough to significantly affect the world economy; 2) it must be sufficiently dynamic to contribute meaningfully to global growth; and 3) it must be open enough to trade and capital flows to have a major impact on other countries. China meets these criteria, but is a unique global economic superpower in three ways. First, it is still a poor country with a Gross Domestic Product (GDP) per capita of around $6,000 in terms of purchasing power parity. Second, China is not yet a democracy in the Western conception of the term. And third, it is not yet a market economy according to some WTO members. Nevertheless, China's rapidly growing economic, political, and cultural engagement and influence in today's world is both undeniable and remarkable, even if China's rise in global power is not yet at the level of the US during the 20th century or Great Britain during the 19th century.

China's trade expansion started in 1978, when the country initiated reforms and opening-up policies. For the past decade, its position as a strong player in international trade had been remarkable. Structural reforms in China, including trade liberalisation, have resulted in annual real GDP growth rates in excess of 10% over the past 4 years, rising per capita income and poverty reduction. In the process, China has become the world's second largest trader. And yet, it is argued that China should play an even more prominent role in international economic institutions and governance and assume a responsibility commensurate with the benefits it derives from the world trading system. Why? Because with greater power and a greater voice comes greater responsibility.

As opposed to playing a proactive role in the world trading system, China attempts to establish itself as a gravity centre in Asia by concluding many low-quality, politically motivated bilateral free-trade agreements in the region (for example, the China-ASEAN FTA or China in the APEC context). In this sense, the chapter argues that China's trade policy strategy is the creation of a powerful Asian trading bloc, given China's strong position in Asia. In fact, few regional initiatives are undertaken by other countries without first considering what China thinks or how China might react.

If multilateralism continues to weaken, the likelihood of an East Asia Free Trade Area led by China within the next decade is very high as part of China's strategy of promoting regional identity. Should this crystallise, one could envisage a tripolar global trade regime with a new Asian pole to counteract the already existing power centres in the European Union and the US. Moreover, it would most likely mean further deterioration of the current multilateral trading system. Furthermore, China's policy towards regional trade agreements will have a major impact on the international trading system, the debate about regionalism and multilateralism, and the policy of the WTO concerning regional trade agreements.

Keywords: Global economic power; multilateral trade; regionalism; regional trade; WTO; East Asian Free Trade Area; Doha Round; China: accession to WTO; China: status as developing country; China: role in Doha Round; China: attitude to multilateralism.

INTRODUCTION

This chapter argues that China's attitude to multilateral trade is unclear. Moreover, China should assume more responsibility in upholding the standards of global economic governance. In other words, China should hide less behind the status of a developing country and stand up to its own ambition of new leadership. For example, China has often been perceived as going against "traditional" powers (mainly the US), and tends to focus on South-South regionalism.[1] The results of the July 2008 World Trade Organization (WTO) mini-ministerial conference, composed of a trade G-7,[2] are evidence of this. At the mini-ministerial, WTO members' latest attempt to salvage a deal in the Doha round broke down. Import-sensitive China and India were pitted against the US's demands for predictable market access for farm products.[3]

In addition, while China had been criticised as "not prepared to play entirely by the rules",[4] by the 1990s China had fully accepted the identity of statehood and the rights and duties implied by sovereignty.[5] It accepted these pluralist rules at a time when the rules of the game were changing.[6]

The dynamics of this changing order were driven by economic liberalisation and the advance of liberal values and purposes including universal human rights. In 2005, then US Deputy Secretary of State Robert Zoellick, gave a speech entitled "Whither China: From Membership to Responsibility",[7] which focused on the rise of

China's international influence and the management of a Sino-US great power relationship. Zoellick expressed anxiety about China's remarkable economic growth and growing influence as well as uncertainties about how China will use its power. He said "[M]any countries hope China will pursue a peaceful rise, but none will bet their future on it".[8]

The idea of China as an international stakeholder has been reinforced by US foreign practitioners and scholars in many documents and speeches related to US foreign policy. For example, the 2006 US National Security Strategy reaffirmed China's international status as a global player and urged that "[China] must act as a responsible stakeholder that fulfills its obligations and works with the United States and others to advance the international system that has enabled its success".[9] It is therefore argued in this chapter that it is necessary to pave the way for responsible multilateralism[10] for the common goal[11] of establishing peace, security, and prosperity in the 21st century.[12]

The chapter is divided into four parts. After the introduction, the second part deals with the criteria to be a global economic superpower, making the case that China is one of the three global economic superpowers today (the US and the EU being the other two; the EU remains the world's biggest economy[13]). The third part examines China's attitude toward multilateral trade, making the case for China's preference for regionalism, and analyses China's position at the WTO. The last part presents some concluding remarks.

A NEW GLOBAL ECONOMIC SUPERPOWER ON THE BLOCK

The establishment of the People's Republic of China took place in 1949. Since then, not only has China undergone an extraordinary transformation domestically, but it has had a rapid rise as one of the pre-eminent states in regional and global politics, both in terms of hard power and through public diplomacy.[14]

The economic rise of China over the past three decades has been extraordinary. China today is the largest exporter in the world and the largest lender to the US. Accordingly, the global order is shifting, and the structure of power and the parameters of action that have characterised the international system over the past half century are being altered. Recent talk of a G-2 composed of the US and China reflects this shift and indicates that China is now regarded as a near equal power to the US. As part of its growing influence, China is recently actively engaging in economic diplomacy through a wide range of means: from its entry into the WTO in December 2001 to bilateral trade agreements, foreign aid and investment projects in Africa to cooperation on international financial regulation and climate change. This has brought China to the table of most major policy arenas on the international stage.

Compared to other major world economies, Chinese leaders seem to see a triumphant future because Europe and Japan — suffering from the deepest post-war recession — are barely worth considering as rivals, and the US — one of the three global economic superpowers — has passed its peak.[15] Predictions are that by 2027 China will have overtaken the US to become the country with the largest economy in the world.[16] This would spell an end to the US's long reign as the driving force in the global economy.

The definition of a global economic superpower is key to understanding the analysis we are trying to present. According to Fred Bergsten, for a country to be considered a global economic superpower, it must meet three criteria: 1) it must be large enough to significantly affect the world economy;[17] 2) it must be sufficiently dynamic to contribute meaningfully to global economic growth;[18] and 3) it must be open enough to trade and capital flows to have a major impact on other countries.[19] China meets these criteria.[20] These are, undoubtedly, material criteria which leave out the social dimension of a global economic superpower.

As Fred Bergsten has argued, China poses a major challenge to the world economy by virtue of being a new global economic superpower.[21] It is a historically unique global economic superpower in three ways. First, it is still a poor country with a Gross Domestic Product (GDP) per capita of around \$6,000 in terms of purchasing power parity, compared to \$48,000 in the case of the US and \$34,000 in the case of the EU.[22] Second, China is not a democracy in the Western conception of the term. And third, it is not yet a market economy.[23]

This third point, however, is very debatable. Some countries have granted China market-economy status in the anti-dumping field. It follows from Article 15 of the WTO Accession Agreement of China that it is left entirely to the other WTO members on a bilateral basis to give China a market-economy status in anti-dumping cases. For example, countries such as Australia, Argentina, Brazil, and several Asian countries treat China as a market economy in anti-dumping cases, whereas the EU and the US treat China as a non-market economy.[24] China's economy since the late 1970s has changed from a centrally planned system that was largely closed to international trade, to a more market-oriented economy that has a rapidly growing private sector and is a major player in the global economy.[25] Reforms started in the late 1970s with the phasing out of collectivised agriculture and expanded to include the gradual liberalisation of prices, fiscal decentralisation, increased autonomy for state enterprises, the foundation of a diversified banking system, the development of stock markets, the rapid growth of the non-state sector, and the opening to foreign trade and investment.[26] China has generally implemented reforms in a gradualist or piecemeal fashion. In recent years, China has re-invigorated its support for leading state-owned enterprises in sectors it considers important to economic security, explicitly looking to foster globally competitive national champions.[27]

Despite the fact that it is a historically unique global economic superpower, China's rapidly growing economic,[28] political, and cultural[29] engagement and influence[30] in today's world is both undeniable and remarkable,[31] even if China's rise in global power is not yet at the level of the US during the 20th century or Great Britain during the 19th century.[32] China's economy is 70 times bigger than when leader and former General Secretary of the Chinese Communist Party Deng Xiaoping ditched hard-line communist policies in favour of free-market reforms in 1978. After overtaking the UK and France in 2005, China became the third nation to complete a spacewalk, hosted the Olympic Games, and surpassed Japan as the biggest buyer of US Treasuries.[33] Certainly, China's rise has come much sooner than expected.

According to Robert Zoellick and Justin Lin, China and the US must cooperate and become the engine for the G20. "Without a strong G-2, the G-20 will disappoint".[34] In this sense, UK foreign secretary David Miliband has argued that China is the 21st century's indispensable power with a decisive say on the future of the global economy, climate change, and world trade. In Miliband's view, the EU could join the US and China as a third world power only if it manages to speak with a single voice vis-à-vis the rest of the world.[35] The pre-Lisbon-Treaty-ratification situation had still left the EU with a need for a hard-power emphasis, more coordination within the EU-27 Member States, lack of efficiency, and asymmetry. With the ratification of the Lisbon Treaty in December 2009, it is expected that the EU will overcome these deficiencies.

According to Pierre Defraigne, China's rise since 1978 has been made possible by several dysfunctions of global economic governance: 1) the collapse of the Bretton Woods system on 15 August 1971 with the decoupling dollar/gold,[36] floating exchange rates,[37] and the quick liberalisation of capital flows in just a decade had created the right conditions for capital to move to China; 2) the historical decision taken by China to adopt market capitalism under a new brand, i.e., a socialist market economy, epitomised by China's accession to the World Trade Organization (WTO); and 3) the building up of massive structural external imbalances between the US and Asia because of the US's over-consumption which is directly connected with the severe aggravation of income and wealth inequalities in the US. These imbalances forced a massive over-indebtedness among the average and poor American households, which translated into a structural trade deficit for the US and a trade surplus for China.[38]

CHINA'S ATTITUDE TOWARD MULTILATERAL TRADE

China was one of the original contracting parties to the 1947 General Agreement on Tariffs and Trade (GATT). It ceased to be a member in the aftermath of the 1949 Chinese Revolution and establishment of an alternative seat of government by the Nationalist Party in Taiwan. Following more than 15 years of negotiations, China once again became a member of the world trading system, joining the WTO as its 143rd member in December 2001.[39]

China's trade expansion started in 1978, when the country initiated reforms and opening-up policies. For the past decade, its position as a strong player in international trade has been remarkable.[40] Structural reforms in China, including trade liberalisation, have resulted in annual real GDP growth rates in excess of 10% over the past four years, rising per capita income and poverty reduction.[41] Nevertheless, Defraigne argues that, because China's export sector has been severely hit by the 2008 world recession, it must change its growth model in three ways: 1) from export-driven to domestic demand-driven growth; 2) more egalitarian growth; and 3) more sustainable growth.[42]

In the process, China became in 2008 the world's third largest trader,[43] compared to having been the 11th largest trade power in 1998 and the 32nd in 1978.[44] Yet, in the eyes of Bergsten, China has been playing at best a passive role and at worst a disruptive role with respect to the global trading system because China's current account surplus in 2007 was around 11% of its GDP, its annual global surpluses were around $372 billion (by far the largest in the world), and its hoard of foreign currency exceeded $1.8 trillion by mid-2008 and is by far the world's largest. These figures place serious pressures on the global trading system.[45]

Although recently less so, why has China been so passive at the WTO? Is it because it only wants to take the benefits of the world trading system, but no obligations? It is pertinent to remember that, in the early 1990s, Deng Xiaoping brought forward his views on how China should approach international affairs: "Observe calmly; secure our position; cope with affairs calmly; hide our capacities and bide our time; be good at maintaining a low profile; and never claim leadership". However, given China's size in the world economy, it can no longer afford to follow Deng Xiaoping's suggestion of assuming a passive role in world affairs because, even if China is passive, it has a *de facto* impact on world affairs.

China's preference for regionalism

Multilateralism and regionalism/bilateralism are not mutually exclusive. As a matter of fact, several countries in different regions of the world work intensively on regional treaties about integrating regional markets and free trade. The EU is one example. Even though European countries have worked for a European integration in several areas, such as market integration, for more than 50 years, European countries — with the European Community on the sideline with wide influence in the GATT and now the EU as a member of the WTO — have worked to improve the multilateral system.[46]

In the case of Africa, there is the African Economic Community (AEC),[47] and in South America there is the Union of South American Nations (Unión de Naciones Suramericanas — UNASUR),[48] the Andean Community,[49] and Mercosur.[50] Those organisations all work for a deeper integration of regional markets, but the various countries that belong to these regional organisations are making serious efforts on the multilateral level as well. The Doha Round has been quite challenging, making only slow progress since the beginning, but it must be noted that in the Doha Round, several agreements are being negotiated and 153 WTO members, all with different interests, are taking part in these multilateral negotiations. Looking historically at the GATT/WTO, the number of multilateral agreements has increased, even though regional agreements have been concluded by GATT/WTO members.

In general, Chinese leaders and strategists have preferred the predictability and manipulability of bilateral relationships to the inherent messiness and complexity of multilateralism. Evidence of this is the fact that not all the WTO agreements seem to fit China's needs.[51] China attempts to establish itself as a gravity centre in Asia by concluding many bilateral free-trade agreements (FTAs)[52] in the region.[53] In fact, few regional initiatives are undertaken by other countries without first considering what China thinks or how China might react. For example, China's free-trade agreement with the Association of Southeast Asian Nations (ASEAN),[54] the biggest FTA in the world by population coverage, which covers only a small share of China's trade with ASEAN so as to diminish ASEAN's fears of being swamped by China.

Moreover, although limited, some progress has taken place with countries seeking economically meaningful free-trade agreements with China. The exception is New Zealand, with which China has a very good FTA, signed in early 2008, seemingly due to the fact that New Zealand is the first WTO member to approve China's WTO accession and the first to grant it market-economy status. In this sense, this chapter argues that China's trade policy strategy is the creation of a powerful Asian trading bloc, given China's strong position in Asia[55] and how difficult it is to move forward multilaterally.

Towards the creation of an East Asian free trade area: China's commitment to good-neighbour diplomacy

If multilateral trade continues to weaken, and given that there are already many common Asian values in the region, the likelihood of an East Asia Free Trade Area[56] of a like-minded group of countries (namely, China, Japan, South Korea, and Vietnam) led by China acting as the *prima donna* or *prima inter pares*[57] within the next decade is very high as part of China's strategy of promoting regional identity.[58] Should this crystallise, one could envisage a tripolar global trade regime with a new Asian pole to counteract the already existing power centres in the EU and the US. Moreover, it would most likely mean further deterioration of the multilateral trading system. According to Francis Snyder, China's policy towards regional trade agreements will have a major impact on the international trading system, the debate about regionalism and multilateralism, and the policy of the WTO concerning RTAs.[59] From a broader perspective, China's grand strategy is arguably about multipolarity,[60] the acquisition of more power on the world stage, the protection of Chinese national interest, and independence within interdependence.

An example of China's strategy to shape a new regional structure is the economic and political cooperation between China and ASEAN. This has partly been triggered by the fact that the Americans have left the region and it is seen as an opportunity for China's market access.[61] China-ASEAN cooperation has brought a new type of intra-Asian regional cooperation with China, which reflects China's commitment to good-neighbour diplomacy. In November 2001, China and ASEAN began negotiations to set up a free trade area. In 2002, a framework agreement for the planned free-trade area was signed.

The new Asian regionalism stimulated by the China-ASEAN free-trade agreement would dominate the future economic landscape of Asia, although doubts remain as to whether the deal will have real teeth given that there is no rigourous mechanism for settling disputes.[62] This China-ASEAN FTA took effect for China and six ASEAN countries (Brunei, Indonesia, Malaysia, The Philippines, Singapore, and Thailand) in January 2010, thereby eliminating barriers to investment and tariffs to trade on 90% of products, and will expand to the remaining four ASEAN countries (Myanmar, Cambodia, Laos, and Vietnam) by 2015.[63] The idea behind all these efforts is, *inter alia,* water transport along the Upper Lancang/Mekong River covering China, Myanmar, Laos, Thailand, and Vietnam; as well as rail and road links between Yunnan Province of China and Chiang Rai in Thailand.[64]

Another example of China's interest in Asian regionalism is the fact that China signed a bilateral FTA with Singapore in October 2008, investment agreements with The Philippines, harmonised food safety standards with Thailand (to facilitate agricultural trade), and many agreements with the Mekong Delta countries (China, Cambodia, Laos, Myanmar, Thailand, and Vietnam). Politics around the various agreements between China and ASEAN (whether as a bloc or its member states individually) are delicate as ASEAN member states want to avoid China's domination but at the same time build their economies by interacting with China.[65]

The argument of creating a powerful Asian bloc is also true in finance. With the idea of the creation of an East Asian version of the

International Monetary Fund (IMF),[66] China is browbeating trading partners into using the RMB as opposed to US dollars, and floating ideas about creating a new international reserve currency, even though many analysts argue that there is no immediate alternative to the dollar as the vehicle for international trade. China wants to promote the global use of its own currency. If more world trade will be denominated in RMB — which is China's hope — China's contribution to the new IMF-like East Asian reserve fund may mean that a crisis-prone country in the region will borrow partly in RMB.[67] On monetary affairs, it is interesting to note the proposal by Zhou Xiaochuan, governor of China's Central Bank, who has suggested creating a "super-sovereign reserve currency" to replace the dollar over the long run.[68]

China's economic rise is driving East Asian regional integration. Without a doubt, the progress of East Asian regional integration depends very much on the pace of China's economic advancement in the region. Major economic powers in Asia have reacted to China's successful advance: Japan's comprehensive economic partnership initiative with ASEAN in January 2002 is an example of a prompt response to China's FTA initiative with ASEAN mentioned above; in the same manner, India is accelerating its pace of negotiating FTAs with various ASEAN countries. As it stands, these agreements between India and ASEAN countries cover only trade in goods, but they will be extended to trade in services, investment, and other areas of economic cooperation over time.[69] China is trying to make use of its strategic location to extend its influence in economic development for broader market access in Southeast Asia.[70] With all certainty, China's most important trading partner is East Asia and Southeast Asia.

China's position at the WTO

One wonders the extent to which China is serious about multilateralism, given China's minimal involvement in it.[71] However, according to China's own accounting, it has joined more than 130 intergovernmental international organisations and committed to

267 multilateral treaties.[72] China is a strong economic power with increasingly sophisticated production in the coastal regions. Peter Sutherland argues that, since joining the WTO in December 2001, China has enjoyed significant economic growth.[73] The rigourous economic regulation requirements needed to join the WTO have worked as a catalyst for Chinese political and economic reform.[74] For the last 30 years, no other country has benefited more from globalisation than China. Hundreds of millions of Chinese have come out of poverty to become middle class.[75]

Yet, China insists on keeping the status of a developing country[76] despite its size both economically (as of 2010, the second largest economy in the world, compared to the 11th in 1978) and demographically (the most populated country in the world). That said, China's claim of status as a developing country is solely a political decision, not a legal one. There are no definitions of a developing or developed country in the WTO framework. Only least-developed countries are defined with reference to the definition provided within the United Nations framework. Claiming to be a developing country at the WTO is subject to political negotiations among the various WTO members.

Being a developing or least-developed country at the WTO may offer an advantage since, according to the various WTO agreements, it implies obtaining a special and differential treatment granted from other WTO members thanks to the enabling clause. However, even though the various WTO agreements grant special treatment to developing and least-developed countries, such rules might not always be applicable in the WTO dispute settlement system. In a few cases, panels have refused to impose obligations on developed countries if the rule of special treatment is not precise or if it is undefined.[77]

Throughout most of the Doha Round of negotiations, China declared that it should have no liberalisation obligations and even came up with a new category of membership ("recently acceded members")[78] to justify its relatively passive role during multilateral trade negotiations. At the Cancún WTO Ministerial Conference, China made the point that it had already undertaken heavy commitments by way of tariff cuts and so it would be improper to expect newly acceded members to take on further commitments without giving them the benefit of special and differential treatment provisions as had been made clear in the joint proposal on agriculture by the G-20.[79] With such an initiative, China seemingly was giving signals of not being proactive in the world trading system. For China, a major global trading partner, to hide behind such loopholes certainly creates international tension. Moreover, China has risen so much recently that it no longer needs financial aid from the EU through the generalised system of preferences.[80]

All this said, China is not just any developing country. Although technically a developing country, China should not be economically compared with other developing countries such as Guatemala or El Salvador. Rather, it should be compared to the other BRIC countries[81] that are WTO members (i.e., Brazil and India), with whom China is on a par economically,[82] even if this comparison is not perfect either, but it is less imperfect than economically comparing China with Guatemala. That said, it is acknowledged in this chapter that there are areas where China differs significantly from Brazil or India — for instance politically, in terms of legal culture, philosophically, and socially — thereby making some reservations in the comparison.[83] When comparing China with India and Brazil, we see that China plays a rather timid role both in the Doha Round of multilateral negotiations[84] as well as in the WTO's dispute settlement system.

In fact, in the first few years right after China's accession to the WTO,[85] China's inclination was to handle trade disputes through negotiation rather than WTO adjudication.[86] When threatened with WTO litigation during its initial years of WTO membership, China opted to compromise to avoid formal WTO complaints.[87] Up until September 2009, China had only brought six cases before the WTO as complainant,[88] compared to more than 15 cases brought by India and more than 20 by Brazil. Nevertheless, since 2006, China's interactions with the world trading system have shown a marked shift from an initial focus on amending domestic legislation in order to comply with WTO rules and disciplines, to a more confrontational stance.

Moreover, for the Doha negotiations to succeed, greater leadership from China is necessary. In fact, no global solution will be possible without China. Other emerging economies similar in size and economic weight to China, such as Brazil and India, are playing important roles multilaterally. For example, in the agricultural G-20 (not to be confused with the G-20[89] of finance ministers and central bank governors established in 1999), both Brazil and India seem to act as leaders.[90]

Why has China arguably been so passive at the WTO? Presumably, because China is a rather young WTO member; it still needs to improve its skills and competences on WTO matters — although it is well known that Chinese diplomats are very skilled and capable.[91] Culturally, it tends to avoid disputes as going to court is not an honourable thing to do[92] and because China has much influence from Confucius (which means that China has more than a two-thousand-year-old tradition of settling disputes by using mediation instead of using courts as is the case in the western world).[93] In this sense, the understanding of Chinese culture can be an important issue when understanding China's role in both political negotiations of the Doha Round and in the development of international trade law, where China cannot be disregarded.

Legally, China also tends to avoid the WTO dispute settlement system for fear of retaliation,[94] and its bureaucracy still has scope for improvement. This attitude of being less active at the WTO is slowly changing to a more aggressive and proactive role of China in the WTO.[95] One should also acknowledge the fact that, since China entered the WTO in December 2001, in nearly every trade dispute where China was not a complainant or respondent, it intervened as a third party. From this point of view, China is slowly contributing to the development of WTO law.

CONCLUSION

Undoubtedly, the world needs to adjust to China's re-emergence, but China should also provide more globally. As analysed earlier, China has behaved like a small country without taking up much responsibility to maintain international order. China needs to take up a more proactive approach in maintaining international order in global economic governance.

There is widespread expectation for China to assume a multilateral responsibility commensurate with the benefits it derives from the world trading system. Why? Because with greater political power and a greater voice comes greater responsibility. China therefore appears to lack an internationalist view to multilateral trade affairs, being instead more focused on its internal development and concluding essentially regional FTAs.

China should therefore play a more prominent multilateral role, not only at the WTO, but also at the IMF and the World Bank as well as in international economic governance. For example, at the IMF — where China is pushing for a greater say for itself and other developing countries — the voting power of each member is calculated on the basis of its donations. According to the IMF, China's share of votes at the IMF is 3.66% of the total because it only contributes 3.72% of the total funding.[96] The US contributes 17% of the funding, whereas the EU contributes over 31% of the total funding. In this sense, major actors such as the European Commission expect China to donate more money to the IMF and to assume a responsibility commensurate with the benefits it derives from the world trading system.[97]

NOTES

*Senior Lecturer in International Economic Law & European Union Law, and Deputy Director of Graduate Studies, Queen Mary University of London (Centre for Commercial Law Studies), UK. B.A., J.D. (Granada University); M.Phil. (London School of Economics and Political Science); LL.M. (Columbia Law School); JSM (Stanford Law School); M.Res., Ph.D. (European University Institute, Florence). Member of the Madrid Bar. Author of the books *International Trade and Investment Law: Multilateral, Regional and Bilateral Governance* (Edward Elgar Publishing, 2010) and *Theory and Practice of EC External Trade Law and Policy* (Cameron May, 2008). The author can be contacted at: r.leal-arcas@qmul.ac.uk

1. That said, according to the United Nations Conference on Trade and Development, as global indicators continue to reveal the breadth of the 2008 financial crisis, developing countries in general may soften the impact on their economies by increasing cooperation with other nations of the South. See *Bridges Weekly Trade News Digest* (2009). "UN Urges Increased South-South Cooperation in Response to Crisis." 13, 5, 12 February.
2. This trade G-7 should not be confused with the finance G-7 representing the most industrialised nations in the world. The trade G-7 has replaced the so-called "Quadrilateral Trade Ministers' Meeting" and is composed of the Quad plus China, India, and Brazil. Its purpose is to see how key trade and investment matters can be moved forward.
3. For further details, see Leal-Arcas, R. (2008). "Services as Key for the Conclusion of the Doha Round." *Legal Issues of Economic Integration*, 35, 4, pp. 301–321.
4. Foot, R. (2001). "China and the Idea of a Responsible State." In Y. Zhang and G. Austin (Eds.), *Power and Responsibility in Chinese Foreign Policy*. Canberra: Asia Pacific Press, p. 24.
5. Gong, G. (1991). "China's Entry into International Society: Beyond the Standard of 'Civilization'." *Review of International Studies*, 17, pp. 3–16.
6. See, for example, Donnelly, J. (1998). "Human Rights: The New Standard of Civilization?" *International Affairs*, 74, 1, pp. 1–23.
7. Zoellick, R. (2005). "Whither China: From Membership to Responsibility?" Remarks to the National Committee on US-China Relations, New York City, September 21.
8 *Ibid.*, pp. 3–4.
9 The White House (2006). "The National Security Strategy of the United States of America."
10. On Chinese responsibility in international relations, see Zhang, Y. and Austin, G. (2001) (Eds.), *Power and Responsibility in Chinese Foreign Policy*. Canberra: Asia Pacific Press.
11. Bruno Simma proposes other goals, in addition to peace and security: solidarity between states at different levels of development; environmental health; and the protection of human rights. These are explained in more detail in Simma, B. (1997). "From Bilateralism to Community Interest." *Rec. des Cours*. The Hague/Boston/London: Martinus Nijhoff

Publ., pp. 236–243. See also Erika de Wet, E. (2006). "The International Constitutional Order." *Int'l & Comp. L.Q.* 51, pp. 54–57 (describing the emergence of the international community as a process by which international and regional organisations as well as individuals were brought under the reach of international law that had formerly been reserved to states).

12. See remarks by Thomas Christensen before the US-China Economic and Security Review Commission (2006). "China's Role in the World: Is China a Responsible Stakeholder?" 3 August. Available at http://hongkong.usconsulate.gov/uscn_state_2006080301.html#top.
13. Central Intelligence Agency, The World Factbook, "Country Comparison: GDP." Available at https://www.cia.gov/library/publications/the-world-factbook/rankorder/2001rank.html.
14. For an analysis of China's transformation, see Brandt, L. and Rawski, T. (2008) (Eds.), *China's Great Economic Transformation.* New York: Cambridge University Press; B. Eichengreen, Ch. Wyplosz and Y. Park, (2008) (Eds.), *China, Asia, and the New World Economy.* New York: Oxford University Press; "Changing China," *Foreign Affairs,* 87, 1, January/February 2008, pp. 1–66; Oi, J., Rozelle, S. and Zhou, X. (2009) (Eds.), *Growing Pains: Tensions and Opportunity in China's Transformation.* Stanford University: The Walter Shorenstein Asia-Pacific Research Center (presenting an accurate view of China's current reforms in privatisation and markets, governance, questions of health care, environmental degradation, and social inequality).
15. "How China Sees the World." *The Economist,* 21 March 2009, p. 13.
16. Faulconbridge, G. and Stott, M. (2009). "Crisis Speeds BRIC Rise to Power: Goldman's O'Neil." *Reuters,* 9 June. Available at http://www.reuters.com/article/wtUSInvestingNews/idUSTRE5583ZA20090609.
17. In 2008, the International Monetary Fund ranked China as the third wealthiest nation in the world in absolute terms. See International Monetary Fund (2009). "World Economic Outlook Database." October, showing a nominal GDP list of countries. According to the CIA, China's economy is already the second in the world as a country, only behind the US, see https://www.cia.gov/library/publications/the-world-factbook/rankorder/2001rank.html?countryName=China&countryCode=ch&regionCode=eas&rank=3#ch.

18. According to the International Monetary Fund, China has been growing economically in a very impressive and fast manner in the last years. See IMF, "World Economic Outlook, Update," Available at http://www.imf.org/external/pubs/ft/weo/2009/update/01/pdf/0109.pdf; see also Aziz, J. (2006). "Rebalancing China's Economy: What does Growth Theory Tell Us?" *IMF Working Paper*, WP/06/291, December. Moreover, while the world is in crisis, China continues to grow economically at a pace of 6% to 8% annually.
19. See for example China's recent investment in Africa and the Middle East. Predictions are that by 2015, China will take over from the EU and the US regarding Middle East energy markets.
20. See Bergsten, F. (2008). "China's Challenge to the Global Economic Order." In F. Bergsten, Ch. Freeman, N. Lardy and D. Mitchell, *China's Rise. Challenges and Opportunities.* Washington, DC: Peterson Institute for International Economics & Center for Strategic and International Studies. p. 9.
21. *Ibid.*, p. 10.
22. See The World Factbook, "China." Available at https://www.cia.gov/library/publications/the-world-factbook/geos/ch.html#Econ.
23. Under WTO law, there is no definition of market economy. One valid definition, however, is "an economy in which the price mechanism determines what is produced and traded, though too often price signals are distorted by subsidies, industry policy and other types of government intervention". See Goode, W. (2007). *Dictionary of Trade Policy Terms*, 5th ed. Cambridge University Press, p. 274. For an analysis of what features of a legal structure suited to a market economy are missing in the case of China, see Clarke, D. (2007). "China: Creating a Legal System for a Market Economy." The George Washington University Law School Public Law and Legal Theory Working Paper, No. 396.
24. For an overview of anti-dumping and the non-market economy treatment of China by the EU and the US, see Snyder, F. (2001). "The Origins of the Nonmarket Economy: Ideas, Pluralism and Power in EC Anti-Dumping Law about China." *European Law Journal*, 7, 4, pp. 369–434.
25. See Central Intelligence Agency, "The World Factbook: China." Available at https://www.cia.gov/library/publications/the-world-factbook/geos/ch.html.

26. *Ibid.*
27. *Ibid.*
28. Early economic analyses on China's rapid integration in the world economy are, for example, The World Bank (1997). "China Engaged: Integration with the Global Economy." September.
29. See for example the World Expo 2010 in Shanghai.
30. According to a study conducted in late 2007 by the Bertelsmann Foundation of Germany among residents in Brazil, UK, China, France, Germany, India, Japan, Russia, and the US, 50% of people who participated in a public opinion poll viewed China as a world power today, and 57% said it would be a superpower by 2020.
31. A clear example of China's engagement and influence in today's world is the Beijing 2008 Olympic Games.
32. Bergsten, F., Freeman Ch., Lardy N. and Mitchell D. (2009). *China's Rise. Challenges and Opportunities.* Washington, DC: Peterson Institute for International Economics & Center for Strategic and International Studies. p. 209.
33. Piboontanasawat, N. and Hamlin, K. (2009). "China Passes Germany to Become Third-Biggest Economy (Update 3)." *Bloomberg,* 14 January. Available at http://www.bloomberg.com/apps/news?pid=20601087&sid=aShY0wM1pD_Y&refer=home.
34. Zoellick, R. and Lin, J. (2009). "Recovery Rides on the 'G-2'." *The Washington Post,* 6 March. Available at http://www.washingtonpost.com/wp-dyn/content/article/2009/03/05/AR2009030502887_pf.html.
35. Borger, J. (2009). "David Miliband: China Ready to Join U.S. as world power," *The Guardian,* 18 May, Main section, p. 1. Available at http://www.guardian.co.uk/politics/2009/may/17/david-miliband-china-world-power.
36. On 15 August 1971, after the US gold stocks were approaching the symbolic level of $10 billion, compared to $13 billion in 1967 and $25 billion in 1949, the US government decided to take action. In a dramatic Sunday night broadcast, President Nixon announced that the US would no longer convert foreign-held dollars into gold or other reserve assets, "except in amounts and conditions determined to be in the interests of monetary stability and in the best interests of the United States". See address of President Nixon of 15 August 1971. Public

Papers of the Presidents: Richard Nixon 1971, 263. For the actual broadcasting of President Nixon to the US nation, see YouTube, "Nixon Ends Bretton Woods International Monetary System." Available at http://www.youtube.com/watch?v=iRzr1QU6K1o.

37. Floating exchange rate is the "movement of a foreign currency exchange rate in response to changes in the market forces of supply and demand". Currencies strengthen or weaken based on a nation's reserves of hard currency and gold, its international trade balance, its rate of inflation and interest rates, and the general strength of its economy. See Downes, J. and Goodman, J. (1998). *Dictionary of Finance and Investment Terms*, 5th ed., Barron's, p. 215.
38. Defraigne, P. (2009). "Opening Speech of the International Workshop on EU-China Partnership." *EU-China Observer*, Issue 2, pp. 22–26.
39. For further information on China at the WTO, see http://www.wto.org/english/thewto_e/countries_e/China_e.htm.
40. Zhao, R. (2007). "China and India: A Comparison of Trade, Investment and Expansion Strategies." Chatham House, 1 June. p. 2.
41. See Economist Intelligence Unit (2008). "Country Report for China." 4 June.
42. See Defraigne, P. (2009). "Opening Speech of the International Workshop on EU-China Partnership." *EU-China Observer*, Issue 2, pp. 22–26.
43. See generally World Trade Organization (2008). "Trade Policy Review: China."
44. Embassy of the People's Republic of China in Switzerland (1999). "Statistics Show China's 50-Year Economic Development." 3 October.
45. See Bergsten, F. (2008). "China's Challenge to the Global Economic Order." In F. Bergsten, Ch. Freeman, N. Lardy and D. Mitchell, *China's Rise. Challenges and Opportunities.* Washington, DC: Peterson Institute for International Economics & Center for Strategic and International Studies. p. 14.
46. For an overview of the EC in the world trading system, see generally Leal-Arcas, R. (2008). *Theory and Practice of EC External Trade Law and Policy.* London: Cameron May; Leal-Arcas, R. (2008). "50 Years of Trade Policy: Good Enough or as Good as it Gets?" *Irish Journal of European Law*, 15, 1 and 2, pp. 157–182.

47. For more information, see http://www.uneca.org/itca/ariportal/abuja.htm.
48. For more information, see http://www.comunidadandina.org/ingles/sudamerican.htm.
49. The Andean Community is a trade bloc comprising until recently five South American countries: Venezuela, Colombia, Peru, Ecuador and Bolivia. In 2006, Venezuela announced its withdrawal, reducing the Andean Community to 4 member states. The trade bloc was called the Andean Pact until 1996, and came into existence with the signing of the Cartagena Agreement in 1969. Its headquarters are located in Lima, Peru.
50. MERCOSUR stands for Mercado Común del Sur (Common Market of the Southern Cone) and is composed of Brazil, Argentina, Paraguay, and Uruguay. On 9 December 2005, Venezuela was accepted as a new member, but not scheduled to be officialised until later. It was founded in 1991 by the Treaty of Asunción, which was later amended and updated by the 1994 Treaty of Ouro Preto (17 December 1994). Its purpose is to promote free trade and the fluid movement of goods, peoples, and currency.
51. For example, China has not signed the WTO Government Procurement Agreement because it does not suit the large state sector. See Wang, P. (2007). "Coverage of the WTO's Agreement on Government Procurement: Challenges of Integrating China and Other Countries with a Large State Sector into the Global Trading System." *Journal of International Economic Law*, 10, 4, pp. 887–920.
52. See GATT Article XXIV for a definition of a free-trade agreement.
53. On this point, see the views by Fred Bergsten in Bergsten, F. Freeman, Ch. Lardy, N. and Mitchell, D. (2008). *China's Rise. Challenges and Opportunities.* Washington, DC: Peterson Institute for International Economics & Center for Strategic and International Studies.
54. ASEAN is composed of ten members. The six Founding Countries of ASEAN are Malaysia, Indonesia, the Philippines, Singapore, Thailand, and Brunei. The rest of countries are Vietnam, Laos, Cambodia, and Myanmar. The aims and purposes of the Association are to accelerate economic growth, social progress and cultural development, and to promote regional peace and stability.

55. Bergsten, F., Freeman, Ch., Lardy, N. and Mitchell, D. (2008). *China's Rise. Challenges and Opportunities.* Washington, DC: Peterson Institute for International Economics & Center for Strategic and International Studies. p. 16.
56. Urata, S. (2004). "Towards an East Asia Free Trade Area." *Policy Insights,* No. 1, OECD Development Centre, March.
57. On East and South Asian regionalism, see Wang, J. Y. (2006). "China, India, and Regional Economic Integration in Asia." *Singapore Yearbook of International Law,* 10, pp. 269–305; Kawai, M. and Wignaraja, G. (2009). "Asian FTAs: Trends and Challenges." Asian Development Bank Institute Working Paper, No. 144, August.
58. Bergsten, F. (2008). "China's Challenge to the Global Economic Order." In F. Bergsten, Ch. Freeman, N. Lardy and D. Mitchell, *China's Rise. Challenges and Opportunities.* Washington, DC: Peterson Institute for International Economics & Center for Strategic and International Studies. p. 16.
59. See Snyder, F. (2009). "China, Regional Trade Agreements and WTO Law." *Journal of World Trade,* 43, 1, pp. 1–57.
60. On multipolarity in the world trading system, see Narlikar, A. and Wickers, B. (2009) (Eds.), *Leadership and Change in the Multilateral Trading System.* Dordricht: Republic of Letters.
61. On new regionalism in Asia, see Sen, R. (2006). "'New Regionalism' in Asia: A Comparative Analysis of Emerging Regional and Bilateral Trading Agreements involving ASEAN, China and India." *Journal of World Trade,* 40, 4, pp. 553–596.
62. The development of infrastructure also within China has been a key focus for the Chinese government in its economic development initiatives. See KPMG (2009). "Infrastructure in China: Foundation for Growth." Hong Kong, September.
63. Bilaterals.org (2009). "China-ASEAN." April. Available at http://www.bilaterals.org/rubrique.php3?id_rubrique=95.
64. Asian Development Bank (2005). "Greater Mekong Subregion Flagship Initiative: North-South Economic Corridor." 26 June.
65. Bilaterals.org (2009). "China-ASEAN." April. Available at http://www.bilaterals.org/rubrique.php3?id_rubrique=95.

66. The International Monetary Fund's original role was to help nations with short-term cash crunches relating to trade financing and to manage the gold-standard currency valuation system. In recent decades, the IMF has morphed into providing long-term loans to developing countries on the condition that these countries recognise their laws and economies to prioritise servicing debt, for instance, by cutting government budgets, such as education and health spending, liberalising trade and investment policies and providing new intellectual property and investor protections. One after another, countries which followed the IMF policy formula — and who were touted as poster children of success — have collapsed economically and socially, such as the case of Argentina in 2001. See Wallach, L. (2005). *Public Citizen Pocket Trade Lawyer. The Alphabet Soup of Globalization.*
67. Mallaby, S. (2009). "Beijing's Would-Be Houdinis." *The Washington Post*, 26 May. Available at http://www.cfr.org/publication/19489/.
68. For an analysis on the matter, see Bergsten, F. (2009). "We Should Listen to Beijing's Currency Idea." *Financial Times*, Op-ed, 8 April. See also China Briefing (2009). "Central Bank Governor Proposes SDR as Main Reserve Currency." 24 March. Available at http://www.china-briefing.com/news/2009/03/24/central-bank-governorproposes-sdr-as-main-reserve-currency.html.
69. International Centre for Trade and Sustainable Development (2009). "India Boosts Asian Trade Ties." *Bridges Monthly*, 13, 2, June. Available at http://ictsd.net/i/news/bridges/48551/.
70. Liu, F.-K. (2008). "Beijing's Regional Strategy and China-ASEAN Economic Integration." *China Brief*, 8, 10, May 13.
71. Recent FTAs signed by China include those with ASEAN countries, Hong Kong, Macao, Pakistan, as well as the Gulf countries. See "WTO Trade Policy Review, Report by the People's Republic of China." WT/TPR/G/161, 17 March 2006, paras. pp. 77–82.
72. See State Council Information Office White Paper (2005). "China's Peaceful Development Road." 22 December. Available at http://english.people.com.cn.
73. Sutherland, P. (2008). "Transforming Nations." *Foreign Affairs*, 87, 2, March/April, pp. 125–136.
74. For an analysis of the argument that China's economic growth will rely on its successful integration into the global economy, see Yueh, L.

(2005). "China's Economic Growth with WTO Accession: Is it Sustainable?" Asia Programme Working Paper, No. 1, Royal Institute of International Affairs, May.

75. "How China Sees the World." *The Economist*, 21 March 2009, p. 13.
76. In fact, China continues to use its self-proclaimed status as the "world's largest developing nation." On this note, see Mitchell, D. (2007). "China and the Developing World." *The China Balance Sheet in 2007 and Beyond*, Washington, DC, May.
77. See anti-dumping cases about the Anti-Dumping Agreement, Article 15, first sentence; *US — Steel Plate*, WT/DS206/R, para. 7.110; and *EC — Tube or Pipe Fittings*, WT/DS219, para. 7.68. None of those sections was appealed to the WTO Appellate Body.
78. See Government of India, Ministry of Commerce & Industry (2003). "India, China Re-emphasise Solidarity on WTO Issues at Cancun." 11 September. Available at http://commerce.nic.in/pressrelease/pressrelease_detail.asp?id=221. In addition to China, the other countries under the category of "newly acceded members" were: Albania, Armenia, Bulgaria, Croatia, Ecuador, Former Yugoslav Republic of Macedonia, Jordan, Kyrgyzstan, Moldova, Mongolia, Oman, Panama, Saudi Arabia, and Chinese Taipei.
79. The Group of 20, or G-20, is a group of developing countries focused on tearing down industrialized countries' barriers to agricultural trade. In March 2006, the group included 21 countries: Argentina, Bolivia, Brazil, Chile, China, Cuba, Egypt, Guatemala, India, Indonesia, Mexico, Nigeria, Pakistan, Paraguay, the Philippines, South Africa, Thailand, Tanzania, Uruguay, Venezuela, and Zimbabwe.
80. The idea of granting developing countries preferential tariff rates in the markets of industrialised countries was originally presented by Raul Prebisch, the first Secretary-General of UNCTAD, at the first UNCTAD conference in 1964. The Generalised System of Preferences was adopted at UNCTAD II in New Delhi in 1968. Under the standard GSP, preferential access to the EU market is provided to 176 developing countries and territories in the form of reduced tariffs on around 6,400 goods when entering the EU market, with no expectation of reciprocal treatment.
81. BRIC is a term used in economics to refer to the combination of Brazil, Russia, India, and China. General thinking is that the term was first prominently used in a thesis of the Goldman Sachs investment bank.

Goldman Sachs argues that the economic potential of Brazil, Russia, India, and China is such that they may become among the four most dominant economies by the year 2050. This will certainly affect the four European Union (EU) member states which are members of the G-7. The thesis was proposed by Jim O'Neill, chief global economist at Goldman Sachs. These countries encompass over 25% of the world's land coverage and 40% of the world's population. The BRIC countries have taken steps to increase their political cooperation, mainly as a way of influencing the United States position on major trade accords, or, through the implicit threat of political cooperation, as a way of extracting political concessions from the United States, such as the proposed nuclear cooperation with India. For further detail on the BRICs, see Goldman Sachs (2007). *BRICS and Beyond*. The Goldman Sachs Group. For a thorough analysis of the trade relations between the EU and the BRICs unilaterally, bilaterally, and multilaterally, see Leal-Arcas, R. (2009). "The European Union and New Leading Powers: Towards Partnership in Strategic Trade Policy Areas." *Fordham International Law Journal*, 32, 2, pp. 345–416.

82. We are referring here to Brazil and India, the public lobbyists on behalf of the emerging markets, which are much more multilaterally pro-active than China. For a comparison between China and India in the WTO, see Qin, J. Y. (2008). "China, India, and the Law of the World Trade Organization." *Asian Journal of Comparative Law*, 3, 1.
83. One way to compare developing countries of the WTO is by looking at the various WTO Agreements and comment on whether those agreements are sufficiently suited to take into account the degree of development in the specific countries. For example, in the draft proposal for a "new" plurilateral Government Procurement Agreement — to which China is not yet a party, but in which it has observer status — individual examinations of the needs of the developing country would need to be made. See the revision of the Agreement on Government Procurement, GPA/W/297 of 11 December 2006, Article IV.
84. When asked by the US to issue a joint statement in support of the DDA in 2006, China refused. See BNA WTO Reporter (2006). "China Balked at Joint Statement of Support for WTO Talks, US Official Says." 19 April.

85. For an analysis on China's reasons to join the world trading system in 2001 in the face of the reputedly onerous accession commitments it was required to fulfill, see He, L.-L. and Sappideen, R. (2009). "Reflections on China's WTO Accession Commitments and Their Observance." *Journal of World Trade*, 43, 4, pp. 847–871.
86. Quite the opposite to China's approach, it is interesting to note that Robert Hudec encouraged the judicialisation of trade disputes. See Hudec, R. E. (1992). "The Judicialisation of GATT Dispute Settlement." In M. M. Hart and D. P. Steger (Eds.), *In Whose Interest? Due Process and Transparency In International Trade*; see also Jackson, J. H. *et al.* (2008). *Legal Problems of International Economic Relations* 12, 5th ed.; Trubek, D. M. (2008). "Transcending the Ostensible: Some Reflections on Bob Hudec as Friend and Scholar." *Minn. J. Int'l L.* 1, 3–4; Schneider, A. K. (2006). "Not Quite a World Without Trials: Why International Dispute Resolution is Increasingly Judicialised." *J. Disp. Resol.* 119, 119–124 (arguing that certain international disputes are increasingly judicialised).
87. See, for example, BNA WTO Reporter (2004). "EC Threatens WTO Suit Against China Unless it Lifts Coking-Coal Restrictions." 25 May.
88. United States — Definitive Safeguard Measures on Imports of Certain Steel Products, WT/DS252 (30 May 2008); United States — Preliminary Anti-Dumping and Countervailing Duty Determinations on Coated Free Sheet Paper from China, WT/DS368 (18 Sept. 2007); United States — Definitive Anti-Dumping and Countervailing Duties on Certain Products from China, WT/DS379; United States — Certain Measures Affecting Imports of Poultry from China, WT/DS392; European Communities — Definitive Anti-Dumping Measures on Certain Iron or Steel Fasteners from China, WT/DS397; United States — Measures Affecting Imports of Certain Passenger Vehicle and Light Truck Tyres from China, WT/DS399.
89. This so-called G-20 is composed of the finance ministers and central bank governors of 19 countries: Argentina, Australia, Brazil, Canada, China, France, Germany, India, Indonesia, Italy, Japan, Mexico, Russia, Saudi Arabia, South Africa, South Korea, Turkey, the United Kingdom, and the United States. The European Union is also a member, represented by its rotating presidency and the European Central Bank. To ensure that global economic *fora* and institutions work together, the Managing Director of the International Monetary Fund (IMF) and the President of

the World Bank, plus the chairs of the International Monetary and Financial Committee and Development Committee of the IMF and World Bank, also participate in G-20 meetings on an ex-officio basis. For further information, see http://www.g20.org/about_what_is_g20.aspx. "The G-20 thus brings together important industrial and emerging-market countries from all regions of the world. Together, member countries represent around 90% of global gross national product, 80% of world trade [including intra-EU trade] as well as two-thirds of the world's population. The G-20's economic weight and broad membership gives it a high degree of legitimacy and influence over the management of the global economy and financial system." *Ibid.*

90. This new phenomenon of India and Brazil playing hardball at the WTO is clearly explained by Fareed Zakaria in Zakaria, F. (2008). *The Post-American World.* Allen Lane. p. 37.
91. See Runnalls, D., Ye R., von Moltke K., and Yan W. (2002) (Eds.), "Trade and Sustainability: Challenges and Opportunities for China as a WTO Member." International Institute for Sustainable Development.
92. On this point, see Gao, H. (2005). "Aggressive Legalism: The East Asian Experience and Lessons for China." In H. Gao and D. Lewis, (Eds.), *China's Participation in the WTO.* London; Cameron May. pp. 315–351.
93. See, for example, Zakaria, F. (2008). *The Post-American World.* Allen Lane. pp. 109–114, explaining the correlation between the Chinese legal system and Confucianism. Also, Farah, P. (2008). "L'influenza della concezione confuciana sulla costruzione del sistema giuridico e politico cinese." In G. Bombelli and B. Montanari (Eds.), *Identità europea e politiche migratorie.* Vita e pensiero. pp. 193–226.
94. Information gathered from Zhang Xiaotong, economic and commercial Attaché at the Chinese Mission to the European Communities, on 4 April 2009 in Bruges, Belgium.
95. See Gao, H. (2007). "China's Participation in the WTO: A Lawyer's Perspective." *Singapore Yearbook of International Law,* pp. 1–34. p. 34.
96. For a list of IMF members' voting power, see International Monetary Fund, "IMF Members' Quotas and Voting Power, and IMF Board of Governors." Available at http://www.imf.org/external/np/sec/memdir/members.htm#3.
97. European Commission, "Global Europe. EU-China Trade and Investment: Competition and Partnership." p. 14.

6

The Role of China in Asia-Pacific Trade Framework in the Context of APEC

Emile Kok-Kheng Yeoh*, Im-Soo Yoo† and *Lionel* Wei-*Li Liong**

**University of Malaya, †Ewha Womans University*

ABSTRACT

For the past three decades, China has opened and greatly strengthened her diplomatic relations and expanded its trading network. With a real gross domestic product growth at an average annual rate of 10% since its opening up, China's economic reforms have transformed China into a major trading power. This is evident in the growth of China's exports from $14 billion in 1979 to $1,429 billion in 2008. China has accumulated the world's largest foreign exchange reserves, totalling nearly $2.447 trillion as of March 2010. The rapid rise of China as a major economic power within a short span of three decades has been described as one of the greatest economic success stories in modern times. With the rise of China as a colossal trading power, it is important and timely to study the role of China in shaping the regional trade pattern between China,

East Asian countries and ASEAN countries. Focusing on trade relations between China, Malaysia and countries in the East Asian region, this chapter examines the role of China in the Asia-Pacific trade framework in the context of APEC as well as analyses the possible regional implications of ACFTA as part of a paradigm shift in China's trade policy with particular reference to Sino-Malaysian economic relations. The examination of the various FTAs and collaborations between China, other East Asian countries and Southeast Asian countries in regional trade in this chapter suggests that with proper coordination and cooperation, intra-regional trade among the aforesaid countries would benefit one another on a mutual, rather than subjugatory, basis.

Keywords: APEC; China; ASEAN-China Free Trade Agreement (ACFTA)/China-ASEAN Free Trade Agreement (CAFTA); Foreign Direct Investment; World Trade Organization.

INTRODUCTION

Free trade system is one of the dynamic factors for economic development as it could bring the best welfare among trade partners, increasing productivity as well as consumer wellbeing. Thus, on the world level more negotiations for free trade have been agreed upon. Moreover, almost all advanced countries have already been more open on the free trade idea and in-bound investment capital flows though the developing countries have often argued for more protections for their own domestic trade and industry.

Nevertheless, free trade negotiation between advanced and developing countries involves a long process. It was due to certain conflicting interests, with some success stories and some failures. In 1995, the World Trade Organisation (WTO) was successfully formed, and it has been trying to build up world-wide negotiation for free trade in the world. The world has since seen more negotiations at the world trade level. After the launching of the WTO, the Doha Development Agenda (DDA) was started in 1997 but the negotiation has continued with talks for seven years but still failed to bring about any conclusions and arrangements. Many parties believe that a successful agenda could not be reached in a few years' time but will take much more time and effort.

A reason why the WTO/DDA could not reach a consensus is the increasing influence from developing countries, for example China, India and Brazil who want to drive the negotiations to their benefits. These countries now have more power to influence the negotiation in their own interests. These emerging economic powers are requesting for more agricultural and industrial product markets to be opened for their interests but in terms of raw materials, the Third World has wanted more protections against attempted liberalisation from the advanced-countries-to-be.[1] This problem cannot be solved in just one day.

On the world trade level, the WTO/DDA programme is not successful due to many reasons. Hence in the due process, many countries in the region have integrated on their own account. Perhaps, the second best way for them is the regional and multilateral cooperation in terms of free trade (FTA) and monetary cooperation. In Southeast Asia, ASEAN cross-border trade within the region has accounted for 60% of the world trade and Malaysia, Singapore, Thailand and Indonesia are playing an important role in East Asia, while Japan, South Korea and China are countries which do not have any regional FTA among themselves. They are underway in finalising an agreement with one another but they have yet a single three-country FTA. This is due to historical problems and differences in interests. But these three countries in the Northeast Asian region have started to agree with an ASEAN+3 FTA, although currently each of them has separate agreements with the ASEAN countries. Therefore this has motivated them to foster one family with the ASEAN community.

On another separate perspective, China is also focusing on making the ASEAN-China/China-ASEAN Free Trade Agreement (ACFTA/CAFTA)[2] a success but there were some unsettled issues, not least among the ASEAN countries themselves. Therefore China has also been interested to form bilateral agreements with separate ASEAN countries like Malaysia, in a counteraction against Japan and South Korea.

The phenomenal rise of China since the 1980s has seen the country emerge as a major global economic power in recent years. For the past three decades, China has opened and strengthened diplomatic relations and expanded her trading network. With a real gross domestic product growth at an average annual rate of 10%,[3] China's economic reforms have transformed China into a major trading power. This is evident in the growth of China's exports from US$14 billion[4] in 1979 to US$1,429 billion in 2008 (Morrison, 2009: 8). Thanks to her trade surpluses, China has accumulated the world's largest foreign exchange reserves, totalling nearly US$1.95 trillion, as reported in 2008 (Setser and Pandey, 2009: 1).

For close to half a century, the United States of America (US) has enjoyed a position of superpower among all nations, in part because of her strong intellectual, economic and military power. However, the People's Republic of China has experienced tremendous growth in the past decade. If China continues to grow at the same rate, a "major reallocation of power among the world leaders" is expected to occur in the next 20 years with China rivalling the US for the world leadership position.[5] As a growing trade power, China has gradually replaced the US as the most important export market for Southeast Asian countries. At present, China has trade deficits as large as tens of billions of US dollars with neighbouring countries and regions.[6] Japan, the hitherto dominant player in the Asian region, is ceding this status to China.

Due to the rise of China, the Asia-Pacific region has drawn growing attention in recent years as a region that is integrating successfully into the global economy. With the rise of China as a colossal trading power, it is important and timely to study the role of China in shaping regional trade pattern between China, the East Asian countries and the ASEAN countries. Focusing on trade relations between China, Malaysia and countries in the East Asian region, this chapter examines the role of China in the Asia-Pacific trade framework in the context of the Asia-Pacific Economic Cooperation (APEC) forum.

In addition, this chapter also analyses the possible regional implications of ACFTA/CAFTA as part of a paradigm shift in

China's trade policy with particular reference to Sino-Malaysian economic relations. In this context, past trade and investment patterns between China and Malaysia are examined. The growing level of pre-ACFTA Sino-Malaysian trade in some way suggests that ACFTA has the potential to yield substantial economic benefits for the trading partners concerned in the years to come.

In the analysis of bilateral and multilateral trade relations, various FTAs[7] and collaborations between China, other East Asian countries and Southeast Asian countries in regional trade are examined in this chapter. It is suggested that with proper coordination and cooperation, intra-regional trade among the aforesaid countries would benefit one another. However, to further assert herself as a global power, China needs to solve her domestic problems and change her political strategy in the near future. In addition, China should actively participate in various agreements and bring new ideas to the table making win-win policies for all.

REGIONAL ECONOMIC INTEGRATION

Major regional economic integrations have developed in the Americas, Europe and the Asia-Pacific region in the last century.

In the case of the European Union (EU), regional economic integration has developed for more than 50 years since the Cold War. In the early 1940s, the Benelux (Belgium, Netherland and Luxembourg) union was formed for cultural, economic and geographic integration.[8] In the early 1950s these three countries were joined by France, West Germany and Italy to form the European Coal and Steel Community which was the first European continent community.[9] The Benelux countries created the community to coordinate economic activities among them to promote sustainable growth within the community. In addition, the countries also established the Benelux Court of Justice in Brussels "to promote uniformity in the application of common rules of law".[10]

The US has been successful in her economic integration with Canada and Mexico. The North American Free Trade Agreement (NAFTA) was launched by the US, Canada and Mexico.[11] The agreement created "a trilateral trade bloc" in North America.[12] This agreement removed most barriers related to trade and investment among the countries.[13] However, this trilateral trade bloc is still at an infant stage compared with the EU's economic integration. In a way, NAFTA can be seen as a channel for the US to fulfil her own dream. George Bush Sr, during his tenure as the US president, introduced the Enterprise of the Americas Initiative (EAI), "a hemispheric program that he projected would establish a free-trade zone stretching from Anchorage to Tierra del Fuego, expand investment and provide a measure of debt relief to the countries in Latin America and the Caribbean".[14] Among the member countries of NAFTA, the US is a much bigger nation and possesses much more power than her counterparts. Thus, the US has taken the leadership of the continent and this leadership position has provided the catalyst for the US's economic success.

Turning to the Asia-Pacific region, APEC, which was created in 1989,[15] has not seen much result. Compared to the NAFTA and the EU, APEC covers a huge geographic region and major economic disparities exist among its member nations. Thus, the member countries of APEC are characterised more by heterogeneity rather than homogeneity, whether in terms of level of economic development and resource endowment or in terms of cultural heritage.

Since the launching of the "Open and Reform" policy, China has strengthened herself and is now ranked first in terms of exports, overtaking Germany recently, in the global community. China has transformed herself into an industrial nation and it is now the right time for China to provide the impetus for integrating the countries in the Asian region. In this respect, China has started forming FTAs with many Asian nations and is in the process of playing an even more important role in the Association of Southeast Asian Nations (ASEAN) and ASEAN Free Trade Area (AFTA).

On the other hand, Japan who has long been the major player in the Asian region is losing her power to China. China has taken several steps in recent years to gain influence. Apart from exerting her influence over the region through the ASEAN+3, she has taken up an active role in the East Asian region. Japan has always supported the US in several trade-related issues. The US wants to engage in further economic integration with the ASEAN and Pacific regions and assume leadership position. However, in the last decade, we have seen that the WTO has failed to achieve its goals. No solutions were found for various regional trade problems and the US has also shown little interest to resolve the WTO issues. At the same time, Japan has also started to engage several other countries for her benefit. ASEAN+3 (ASEAN, China, Japan, South Korea) and ASEAN+3+3 (ASEAN, China, Japan, South Korea, India, New Zealand, Australia) countries are now in the process of building an East Asian Community.

The three consecutive years from 2009 to 2011 provide the best chance for the US to exert her influence over trade-related matters in her own interest. In the recent 2009 APEC conference in Singapore,[16] the US has made progress in relation to playing a more important role in ASEAN. After the 2010 APEC conference held in Japan, an allied nation of the US, the 2011 APEC conference will be held in the US.[17] The US, with support from Singapore and Japan, will attempt to prepare a better model for regional economic integration based on her own leadership. The Obama Administration has already started working on improving trade relations with the Asia-Pacific region. The US is trying to gain support from the Asia-Pacific region so that she can increase her exports. In the 2009 Singapore APEC conference, different countries received different agendas from the US, mostly related to deregulation and financial support. The 2010 APEC conference in Japan provides the US an opportunity to collect information and feedbacks from the countries so that she can formulate a new model for the Asia-Pacific region. Finally, the US is expected to make concrete policy recommendations during the 2010 APEC conference so that tangible results could be obtained in the near future. If an FTA can be formed between the Asia-Pacific countries and the US, the US would benefit by having greater access to the Asia-Pacific market.

APEC AND WHAT HAS IT ACHIEVED SO FAR?

APEC is designated to be the main forum for "facilitating economic growth, cooperation, trade and investment in the Asia-Pacific region".[18] Since the birth of APEC in 1989, it has grown to encompass 21 members from four continents. It represents the "most economically dynamic region in the world".[19] Created "to enhance economic growth and prosperity in the region" and "to strengthen the Asia-Pacific community", the forum accounts for approximately 40.5% of the world's population, 54.1% of world GDP and 43.7% of world trade.[20]

The 21 APEC member economies of APEC include Australia, Brunei, Canada, Indonesia, Japan, Republic of Korea, Malaysia, New Zealand, the Philippines, Singapore, Thailand and the US who joined in 1989, Taiwan (Chinese Taipei), Hong Kong and People's Republic of China who joined in 1991, Mexico and Papua New Guinea who joined in 1993, Chile who joined in 1994, and Peru, Russia and Vietnam who joined in 1998.

APEC is a unique organisation which has been revolving around dialogues with no binding obligation.[21] APEC member countries have already held several meetings with no fruitful results. Since its establishment in 1989, many have claimed that APEC is merely "a loose discussion forum", and in fact, many claim that APEC will remain as such (Liao *et al.*, 2006: 1). Therefore APEC still faces a momentous task to make things happen at the regional level rather than merely "talking" about the issues.

Nevertheless, the diversity of member countries and the coverage of an extensive geographical area make APEC a relevant avenue for regional collaborations. Since the 1995 Osaka meeting, APEC has expanded international interaction and increased its national level activities. It has widened both its membership and scope. (*ibid.*: 3) APEC greatly differs from other regional organisations due to the "high diversity of its members". The member nations of APEC do not share "cultural ties", "common history" or any "big historical trauma" (*ibid.*: 2).

Asian countries so far have not been as inclusive as their Western counterparts. Comparing with the European Union, Asian countries neither have enough widening policy nor deepening efforts for regional collaboration. Unlike Western countries, Asian countries do not have many trade agreements which can help to integrate the region. They have also hardly taken any initiatives to deepen integration.

At the beginning of 2010, China and Southeast Asia established the largest FTA in the world, "liberalising billions of dollars in goods and investments" which covers "a market of 1.7 billion consumers".[22] In eight years' time, it is expected that ACFTA will "rival the European Union and the North American Free Trade Area in terms of value and surpass those markets in terms of population" while expanding "Asia's trade reach" and "boost intra-regional trade" against the backdrop of China having become ASEAN's "third largest trading partner" after overtaking the US and widely believed to leapfrog Japan and the EU within a few years of the inception of ACFTA.[23]

Trade between ASEAN countries and China has "exploded in the past decade", increasing from US$39.5 billion in 2000 to US$192.5 billion in 2009.[24] Therefore, China has the advantage in terms of trade negotiation, monetary cooperation and investment in the region. In addition, the average tariff rate that China charges on ASEAN goods would be cut to 0.1% (from 9.8%) and the average tariffs imposed on Chinese goods by ASEAN countries will fall to 0.6% (from 12.8%).[25]

China's influence on the region and in the globe has increased significantly in the last 20 years. With growing trade deals and several bilateral agreements, China will likely obtain more trade and investment deals in the Asian region in the near future. The growth of China's influence in the region has sparked fear and anxiety from the US and Japan.

The ongoing WTO negotiations have brought no significant outcomes and this explains why the US would be interested in signing bilateral agreements with countries in the Asia-Pacific region. The 2009 APEC meeting was successfully held in Singapore and subsequent meetings for 2010 and 2011 will be held in Japan and the US. The US will utilise the opportunities provided by the APEC meetings held in these consecutive years to advance her position in the region in a bid to rival the rise of China. The three advanced nations are allies of the US and fully support the US's proposal for a Free Trade Area of the Asia-Pacific (FTAAP).

Despite the fact that APEC is not a binding organisation, its significance in the region will gradually grow and APEC is expected to emerge as a powerful organisation in the near future. With more than 2.7 billion consumers and nine member countries in the G20,[26] APEC will liberalise various sectors in its member countries, provide an impetus for the growth of the member countries and spur trade across the Asia-Pacific region.

In November 1994, the APEC Economic Leaders Declaration[27] was adopted in Bogor, Indonesia, with the goal of freeing and opening trade and investment in the Asia-Pacific region (see especially Clause 6 of the declaration), no later than 2010 in the case of the industrialised economies and 2020 in the case of the developing economies.

Prominent Asian scholar Dr Hadi Soesastro pointed out in a Shorenstein seminar that the Bogor Declaration outlined seven major principles regarding the goal of trade and investment liberalisation (see Soesastro *et al.*, 1995), and he also noted that, immediately after the APEC meeting, "the Malaysian and Thai governments expressed some reservations and clarifications of their positions on the Bogor Declaration" in separate statements. There were three points in common in these statements (*ibid.*):

1. The goal is "not to create an exclusive Asia-Pacific free-trade area in the sense of the European Union or NAFTA".
2. The "target dates of 2010 and 2020 are not binding commitments".
3. The "elimination of trade and investment barriers in the region will proceed gradually".

As pointed out, there is a widespread agreement among the APEC leaders that the timetable is nonbinding. Although the "nonbinding" nature of the timetable "raises questions about the value of the agreement", it was pointed out that the "political commitment" by the APEC leaders is an important "confidence-building step" that will encourage "trade liberalisation across the region" (*ibid.*).

To achieve the Bogor Goals, APEC carries out work in three main areas, namely trade and investment liberalisation, business facilitation, and economic and technical cooperation.[28] With average trade barrier in the region reduced from 16.9% when APEC was established in 1989 to 5.5% within a span of 15 years (which will gradually diminish to zero), APEC has taken several reform efforts in the area of business facilitation: the costs of business transactions across the region being reduced by 6% during 2002–06 and an additional 5% reduction in business transaction costs between 2007 and 2010 was hoped for.[29]

Since the inception of APEC, many countries have initiated several cooperative programmes for human resource development (education and training, especially for improving management and technical skills), the development of APEC study centres, cooperation in science and technology (including technology transfer), measures aimed at promoting small- and medium-scale enterprises (SMEs) and steps to improve economic infrastructure, such as energy, transportation, information, telecommunications and tourism, with the aim of contributing to sustainable development.[30]

Financial crises have actually strengthened cooperation within the region. Asian countries have recently gone through two major financial crises: the first one in 1997–98 and the second one in 2008–09. In the aftermath of the Asian financial crisis many ASEAN countries suffered liquidity problems. Countries like Thailand, the Philippines and South Korea were supported by the International Monetary Fund (IMF) through bailout programmes. These countries have repaid the debts and their economies have recovered. Several other countries like Malaysia, took their own steps to overcome the difficulties. Asian countries have learnt from the financial crisis that they need to cooperate with one another in terms of trade, investment and finance for the sustainable growth of their economies.[31]

The 1997–98 Asian financial crisis has led to strong cooperation among the Asian countries, and in recent years the "institutionalisation of the ASEAN Plus Three (APT) process has started to take shape" (Stubbs, 2002: 440). Government leaders and officials from ASEAN and the three Northeast Asian states (China, Japan, and South Korea) are "consulting on an increasing range of issues" (*ibid.*). The emergence of ASEAN+3 "raises questions about relations between it and other regional groupings such as the Asia-

Pacific Economic Cooperation (APEC) forum and ASEAN itself", and due to the differences among the East Asian countries, a number of obstacles to the development of ASEAN+3 had arisen (*ibid.*). The Asian economic crisis has enhanced the importance of ASEAN+3. Indeed, the regional grouping now has "the potential to become the dominant regional institution in East Asia". At present, ASEAN+3 "continues to hold annual conferences and meetings", while it is also trying "to form a better monetary cooperation in order to avoid any future financial crisis" (*ibid.*: 454).

To "address the short-term currency liquidity problem", the finance ministers and central bank governors of the ASEAN countries, China, Japan and the Republic of Korea (ASEAN+3), as well as the Hong Kong Monetary Authority have signed the Chiang Mai Initiative Multilateralisation (CMIM) which was reached on all main aspects of creating a US$120 billion regional reserve pool to "provide emergency liquidity for countries and regions in financial crisis", with the objective of addressing problems related to balance of payment and short-term liquidity in the region.[32] China and Japan will contribute US$38.4 billion each, the Republic of Korea will contribute US$19.2 billion and the 10 ASEAN nations will provide a combined US$24 billion to the liquidity pool (Rajan, 2009: 18). In addition, under the Chiang Mai Initiative (CMI), "a full series of bilateral swap and repurchase agreements between the ASEAN+3 countries" will be made, and under such an arrangement, member countries can swap their local currency for major international currencies (de Brouwer, 2005: 25).

The 2008–09 global financial crisis, which was triggered by the US subprime mortgage crisis, has significantly affected the EU and Asian countries. Having experienced the 1997–98 crisis, most Asian countries have restructured their financial and banking industry. Their previous experience and cooperation with one another has helped them to recover at a faster rate than their Western counterparts.

The Asian countries like Japan, China and South Korea are better placed than their G20 counterparts. The G7 countries alone are unlikely to be able to solve the financial crisis without the cooperation from the Asian countries. The fact that emerging economic powers are now playing a very important role in the world economy can be seen from the choice of Brazil and South Korea as the venues for the next G20 meetings.

The Asia-Pacific region compared to the EU and America differs in a very important aspect. Countries in the Asia-Pacific region have always lacked a strong leadership. APEC, which was formed 20 years ago, is an attempt to promote economic partnership within the region under one leadership. As such, it is hoped that APEC would provide a better platform for all participating countries to engage in well-coordinated economic integration under one leadership.

GROWING ECONOMIC INTEGRATION AND COOPERATION OF CHINA IN THE ASIAN REGION

At the beginning of this year, 2010, China and ASEAN officially launched the ACFTA.[33] China-ASEAN trade is targeted to hit US$200 billion, by 2010 up from US$113 billion in 2005. This will make ACFTA the third largest free trade zone in trade volume after the EU and NAFTA.[34] China sees the free trade agreement as a way of securing raw materials, while countries in ASEAN see opportunities in China's huge market.[35] China and ASEAN signed an initial FTA in November 2002 and some tariffs have been reduced since 2005, while from 2010, tariffs on 90% of goods traded with China will be eliminated for Malaysia, Indonesia, Brunei, the Philippines, Singapore and Thailand and by 2015 for Laos, Vietnam, Cambodia and Burma.[36] Companies from ASEAN which are interested in entering China's service market (business services, tourism, etc.) are given preferential access and vice versa.

For Malaysia, ACFTA is seen as having the potential to accelerate the development of economic relations between her and China and the economic growth of the two countries, and trade tariff barriers between the two countries will be eliminated following the full establishment of the FTA.[37] The FTA will "bring business and trade between the two countries to a new height" and also "benefit the banking industry which serves as a bridge of economic promotion and trade development". The Bank of China (Malaysia) is said to be "committed to promoting trade activities actively between China and Malaysia by rendering value-added services" and presently more than 100 corporations from China have established operations in Malaysia".[38]

However, some Indonesian and Philippine manufacturers are against ACFTA, claiming that ASEAN member countries will only become the supply chain for China's booming economy which will be further propelled by gradual trade liberalisation under ACFTA. Industry players in Indonesia have formally requested for the postponement of the treaty implementation for fear of the entry of cheap Chinese products undermining their manufacturing businesses. The Indonesian industries submitted a list of 228 items including iron and steel, textiles, machinery, electronics, chemicals and furniture covered by the FTA.[39]

It is submitted that ASEAN countries and China should seek to promote proper coordination and cooperation in economic integration. Looking at US-China trade relations, it is observed that a failure to do so would bring about highly disruptive effects. Recently, the US government took the decision to approve extra tariffs of 35%, 25% and 20% over the next three years, in addition to the regular 4% levy on tires imported from China, and since then China has imposed import tariffs or restrictions on imports of US nylon, industrial acid, chicken and other products, besides having initiated an investigation into whether US automakers are selling below cost ("dumping") cars in China, with the US retaliating by looking into allegations of dumping in other products and imposing tariffs on imports of Chinese steel pipes, and this growing tension has "exacerbated protectionist fears on both sides of the Pacific" and is "one reason global trade talks once against collapsed in Geneva last year".[40]

Against this background, China and ASEAN should learn from the China-US experience and avoid trade war or other conflicts. Proper coordination and cooperation is needed for the benefit of both China and ASEAN.

ROLE OF CHINA IN THE ASIA-PACIFIC REGION

Japan and the US are losing their power in the Asian region and China's influence is increasing in the region. As such, Japan and the US are trying to strengthen their diplomatic relations with other Asian countries. In addition, the US is also trying to increase their export activities in the region. In recent years, the US is becoming very aggressive in approaching Asian countries for establishing economic relations. Politically, the US wants to limit China's influence in the Asian region.

With her growing economy, China has increased her economic activities with other Southeast Asian countries. For example, she is supporting the ruling regime of Burma to build a sea harbour in the Indian Ocean. On the other hand, the US's allies like Japan, the Philippines, Thailand and Singapore provide support for the presence of the US marine in the region. Most trading activities in Asian countries pass through the Strait of Malacca. The security of this waterway, particularly in the context of maritime terrorism, is therefore a great concern for many countries. Furthermore, China has also gradually expanded her activities in the waters of the Taiwan Strait and South China Sea, much of which she claims to be under her sovereignty. In recent years, China is spending more money on naval activities than she did before.

The rise of the Chinese economy has not only brought development for the country but also created some problems. China is trying to acquire raw materials and other natural resources, but this also creates problems for the global society. The Western nations and Japan realise that the integration of China into the Asian region will increase the superiority of China and decrease their powers in the global arena. This leads to the US and Japan attempting to expand their regional FTAs from the Asian region to the Asia-Pacific region. In addition, there are plans to include countries which do not come under these regions. Countries like India, Mongolia, Pakistan, Laos, Bangladesh, Colombia, and Ecuador are now seeking membership in some of these FTAs.

China, India and ASEAN are growing at a very fast rate and are playing major roles in the global economy. The rapid growth of these emerging economic powers and the ASEAN+3 economies has stimulated world economic recovery after the global financial crisis. During the Cold War era, Japan dominated the region. She exported manufactured goods and in return received raw materials and agricultural products. Several ASEAN countries have criticised the Western countries as they have not shared similar level of foreign direct investment (FDI) and technological transfer. While Japan was fully supported by the US during the era, Asian countries have now sought for Japanese assistance for capital and technology through forging closer ties. However, at present, the Japanese export market is falling due to the rise of South Korea and China. China has dominated the region and now initiating several investment and monetary cooperation with other Asian countries. It is widely believed that China will succeed in creating a proper platform for investment and monetary cooperation in the region. When this is achieved, countries in the region will be the first to benefit.

In the last few years, China has replaced Japan as the dominant player in the Asian market. She is expected to overtake Japan and become the second largest economy after the US sometime in 2010. The WTO has failed to meet the expectation of both developed and developing countries, but it has surely made the US the most powerful developed country in the world. Recently, however, the emergence of new and potential economic powers like Brazil, Russia, India and China (BRIC), and particularly the growing influence of China, is causing much anxiety among many advanced nations.

However, China's financial market is underdeveloped in comparison with those of the Western countries. This is probably due to her socialist capital market system. Recently, the Chinese government has announced her commitment to stimulate the economy, by building Shanghai into an international financial centre and maintaining economic growth which would stabilise the capital market.[41] Shanghai is likely to become the financial centre of the future for China as well as for the Asia-Pacific region. The global financial crisis of 2008–09 has momentarily halted the global expansion of financial markets. To become the global leader in the financial market, China in the next phase needs several major reforms aiming at improving market infrastructure and functionality, improving market regulation and supervision, and strengthening her legal framework. She also needs to increase the level of competitiveness among financial institutions, improve her market mechanism and corporate governance.

China has often been accused of "manipulating the exchange rate". It is true that the Chinese government needs to purchase dollars in large quantities to keep the yuan exchange rate "within certain target levels". Even though the yuan appreciated significantly after the July 2005 reforms against the US dollar, many people believe that it "remains highly undervalued against the dollar" (Morrison, 2009: 20). In addition, it is believed that the Chinese government's policy could "undermine long-term economic stability" as it causes "overproduction in various sectors", increases the quantity of non-performing loans and causes inflation, for the reason that China's currency policy has rendered the economy "overly dependent on exports and fixed investment for growth" and, furthermore, "promotes easy credit" (*ibid.*: 20–21).

China has grown so fast that she has realised that she might become a global power much faster than she thought, and has been treated as a *de facto* global power by the US, at least with regard to economic matters, with the two countries for all intents and purposes forming a "G2".[42] China is already a major trading country, and there is little doubt that it will be a strong financial market player in the near future. This is the best time for China to change her policy to rise and become a strong financial power in accordance with her position as a G2 country.

Since the last decade, China has accumulated trade surplus on a yearly basis. The country's exports have consistently exceeded her imports. Accumulating foreign reserve through trading, China currently possesses a foreign exchange reserve of over US$2 trillion.

In terms of trade, China has gradually replaced the US as the main export market for Southeast Asian countries and now has trade deficits of tens of billions of US dollars with neighbouring countries and regions, and this explains why "the process of RMB regionalisation has started with the ASEAN members adjoining the PRC".[43] The RMB has been used in "cross-border trade settlement". In this respect, China has "signed bilateral currency swap deals with several countries and regions around the world since the beginning of 2009" (Nie, 2009). However, several steps must be taken before the regionalisation of the RMB takes place: firstly, the implementation of RMB settlements must be carried out "within surrounding countries" first before moving to "broader regionalisation", and to achieve this, the Chinese government has declared that "Guangdong, the Yangtze River Delta Area, Hong Kong, Macao, Guangxi Zhuang Autonomous Region and Yunnan Province would begin quoting prices and settling accounts in RMB in trade with ASEAN" from the end of 2008 (*ibid.*). In addition, the People's Bank of China has "signed a currency swap agreement valued at RMB650 billion with monetary authorities in Hong Kong, the Republic of Korea, Malaysia, Indonesia, Belarus and Argentina".[44]

This is the beginning of the rise of the RMB as the leading international currency. With a huge foreign exchange reserve, China is well positioned to advance in the financial world. With faith in the US dollar waning, China can begin to strengthen its financial infrastructure and gradually open up her financial market and elevate the RMB to the status of a leading international currency. This is important for China if she wants to exert her influence in the region.

SINO-MALAYSIAN EXPERIENCE

With the changing global trade patterns and proliferation of preferential trading agreements (PTAs), a small open economy like Malaysia is set to see changes in her international trade partners. In the past, the US, Japan and the EU have been the major trading partners of Malaysia. However, with rapid economic growth, the emerging and transforming economic entities in East Asia, China in particular, are going to become more integrated, through trade and capital flows, with other East Asian countries, including Malaysia. As

China is anticipated to sustain relatively high growth rates in the foreseeable future, Malaysia is positioning herself to take advantage of the growth opportunities. This could explain Malaysia's enthusiasm in getting actively involved in negotiations with the other ASEAN members to sign the ACFTA agreement with China not only to promote an increase in intra-regional trade but also to enhance market integration. Malaysia sees the FTA in terms of substantial potential gains through competition and scale effects, which could be used strategically to serve the growth objective. However, positive outcomes are only possible with careful policy design including detailed consideration of the implications of the agreement, identification of the readiness of the industries for liberalisation and market access opportunities in partner countries, and ensuring effective enforcement mechanisms (Yeoh and Ooi, 2007b: 5).

Basically in response to certain ASEAN members' doubt regarding the real benefits of ACFTA for them, China proposed a fast-track trade liberalisation of agricultural products to "let ASEAN pick the peaches and taste the sweetness first" (Ravenhill and Jiang, 2007: 18). This was the "Early Harvest Programme" (EHP) negotiated on a bilateral basis between China and the individual ASEAN members. Member countries can exempt certain products from the programme's coverage under the Exclusion List. Conversely, there is a Request List for the inclusion of certain products not covered by the programme but mutually agreed by China and the concerned ASEAN member. Commenced in January 2004, EHP enables the reduction of tariff for certain products before ACFTA is fully implemented. These products include 562 items at 8/9 digit level in Chapters 1–8 in the Harmonised System of tariffs (ASEAN Secretariat, 2002).

According to the Malaysian Ministry of International Trade and Industry (MITI), Malaysia has placed 590 products under EHP in which 503 are categorised as unprocessed agricultural products and 87 as processed and manufactured products. Malaysian exporters have benefited from the EHP[45] since its inception in 2004 with total exports amounting to US$135 million. Malaysia has placed 87.3% of (or 10591) products in the normal track and 6.5% (or 418) in the sensitive track. Products in the sensitive list are swine, milk and cream, wood products, cement, automotive, iron, steel and others. For Malaysia, 0.6% of the products, comprising alcoholic beverages, arms and weapons, tobacco refuse, and used tires, are excluded from tariff liberalisation under ACFTA. In 2005, a total of 3780 Preferential Certificates of Origin were issued by Malaysia for EHP exports to China amounting to US$540.3 million. Malaysian products which have benefited under EHP and TIG (Trade in Goods) agreements included chemical products, palm oil, stearic acid, rubber products, and detergent and soaps. On the other hand, Malaysia imported goods worth US$3.7 million from China under the EHP and TIG agreements in 2005 (MITI, 2006a: 189–190).

Investment profile

Historically, Malaysia relies heavily on foreign direct investment (FDI) for her economic expansion and industrial upgrading. Table 1 shows that China was the 8th largest foreign investor in Malaysia from 2001 to 2005. The amount of investment stood just below the Republic of Korea and surpassed investments from Taiwan and the Netherlands. According to MITI (2006b), Malaysia was the 6th

Table 1. Approved FDI Projects in Malaysia — Top 10 Sources, 2001–05 (RM million)

Country	2001	2002	2003	2004	2005	Total
US	3412	2668	2182	1059	5155	14476
Germany	2603	5055	170	4724	388	12940
Japan	3366	587	1295	1011	3672	9931
Singapore	2228	1019	1225	1515	2920	8907
United Kingdom	123	168	3870	151	99	4411
United Arab Emirates	–	0.9	3952	–	–	3952.9
Republic of Korea	1703	369	447	325	674	3518
Mainland China	2923	55	247	187	40	3452
Taiwan	1140	252	622	415	431	2860
Netherlands	69	607	316	99	1674	2765

Source: Yeoh and Ooi (2007b: 6), Table 2. Data of 2001 and 2002 are from IDE-JETRO and SERI (2004: 10), Table 5. Data of 2003 to 2005 are from MITI

largest source of imports and the 15th largest export destination of China in 2005 (Devadason, 2007:138) and Sino-Malaysian trade reached US$16.5 billion for the first six months of 2006 and expected to reach US$50 billion by 2010.[46] The statistics published by the Malaysian Industrial Development Authority (MIDA) show that the approved projects from China totalled 10 as compared to the total of 705 approved projects from foreign investors in 2001, with the investments amounting to RM2923 million,[47] or 15.46% of total foreign investment in Malaysia. The number of projects approved was 9 with a total amount of RM55 million in 2002; it accounted for only 0.47% of the total foreign investment in Malaysia. Investment from China regained its strength as it grew by more than four-fold to RM247 million; this accounted for 1.58% of the total foreign investment in Malaysia in 2003. Investments from China in 2004 and 2005 were RM187 million and RM40 million respectively, with a share of 1.42% and 0.22% of the total foreign investment in Malaysia. However, mainland China has since dropped out from the top 10 FDI sources (Table 2).

Table 2. Approved FDI Projects in Malaysia — Top Sources, 2005–09 (RM million)

Country	2005	2006	2007	2008	2009*
US	5155.0	2476.6	3020.0	8669.0	288.5
Australia	155.9	2560.1	1685.1	13105.8	307.0
Netherlands	1674.0	3284.2	1690.4	1795.7	457.9
Hong Kong	105.4	84.5	59.8	83.6	116.3
Indonesia	52.5	214.9	41.2	22.1	2.2
Japan	3671.7	4411.6	6522.7	5594.9	6466.1
Germany	387.7	232.3	3756.8	4438.3	198.0
Republic of Korea	673.6	437.8	1118.8	197.6	431.8
Singapore	2919.9	1884.7	2952.2	2004.3	1613.9
Taiwan	430.7	405.5	408.7	911.6	610.4
United Kingdom	99.2	642.0	385.3	850.5	166.9
Others	2557.3	3593.8	11785.1	8425.5	1501.5
Total	17882.9	20227.9	33425.9	48098.8	12160.4

* January–August

Source: Malaysian Ministry of Finance, *Economic Report 2009/2010*

Table 2 shows the FDI inflows to Malaysia for the period of 2005–09. The top five sources of foreign investment were Japan (RM26667 million), the US (RM19609 million), Australia (RM17814 million), Singapore (RM11375 million), and Germany (RM9013 million). FDI to Malaysia increased from 2005 to 2008 with a total of 521 projects involving foreign investment in 2008. Total foreign investment in approved projects increased by 43.90% from RM33425.9 million in 2007 to RM48098.8 million in 2008. This reflected the fact that Malaysia remained an attractive investment destination in this region during the period. However, total FDI inflow to Malaysia dropped sharply to RM12160.4 million. The decrease is likely to be caused by the global financial crisis. The electrical and electronics (E&E) industry received the highest amount of FDI with a total of RM11.3 billion or 63% of the total foreign investment approved in 2005. This was followed by investments in scientific and measuring equipment with a total of RM1.4 billion, chemicals and chemical products worth RM596.1 million, plastic products worth RM594.8 million.[48]

Table 3 shows the source of FDI from ASEAN members and China to Malaysia. Singapore accounted for the highest amount of investments with RM17362 million from 2001 to 2009. Investments

Table 3. Sources of FDI to Malaysia — Comparison of China with ASEAN Countries, 2001–09 (RM million)

Country	2001	2002	2003	2004	2005	2006	2007	2008	2009*
Singapore	2228	1019	1225	1515	2920	1885	2952	2004	1614
China	2923	55	247	187	40	–	–	–	–
Indonesia	76	12	48	87	52	215	41	22	2
Thailand	68	9	264	37	142	–	–	–	–
Philippines	–	1	34	215	–	–	–	–	–
Vietnam	–	3	–	–	–	–	–	–	–
Burma	–	2	–	–	–	–	–	–	–

* January–August

Source: Yeoh and Ooi (2007b: 7), Table 3. Data of 2001 and 2002 are from IDE-JETRO and SERI (2004: 10), Table 6. Data of 2003 to 2005 are from MITI. Data of 2006 to 2009 are from Malaysian Ministry of Finance, *Economic Report 2009/2010*

from Singapore have recorded an increasing trend from 2002 to 2005 and from 2006 to 2007. The increasing investments were mainly due to major expansion projects in the E&E industry. From 2007 to 2009, investments from Singapore decreased. In 2007, investments from Singapore amounted to RM2922 million, the highest during the period of 2001–09. Singapore was the second largest source of foreign investments in 2009.

Compared to ASEAN countries, FDI from China to Malaysia is second only to Singapore and well ahead of the second largest ASEAN source of FDI, viz. Indonesia. A total of 214 projects from China have been approved from 2001 to 2005. Investments from China are involved in the following industries: E&E, chemical and chemical products, wood and wood products, non-metallic mineral products, machinery manufacturing, food manufacturing, and plastic products manufacturing.

In the case of ASEAN, China's FDI in the grouping amounted to only about 1% (US$226 million) of the total FDI in ASEAN in 2004. For the period of 1995–2004, China's cumulative FDI in ASEAN, just exceeding US$1 billion, amounted to only less than the 0.5% of ASEAN's total inbound FDI for the period (Table 4). FDI inflow from China has been constantly increasing from 2002 to 2008. However, FDI inflow from China still amounted to only around 2% of ASEAN's total inbound FDI from 2006 to 2008. On the other hand, Singapore topped the recipient list of China's outward FDI in ASEAN. ASEAN's cumulative investment in China surpassed US$4000 million by the end of 2007, accounting for more than 4% of China's total inbound investment. Singapore alone accounted for more than 70% of China-bound FDI flows from ASEAN (Table 5).

FTA and FDI

In the 1980s and early 1990s, ASEAN economies grew rapidly, at an average pace of 7% annually. Rapid input factor accumulation, especially capital from FDI, was essential to this growth. Since 1997, FDI into ASEAN countries has declined as a proportion of global FDI and FDI directed to developing countries. Furthermore, the Japan

Table 4. Foreign Direct Investment in ASEAN Countries (US$ million)

	1997	2002	2003	2004	2005	2006	2007	2008
Within ASEAN	*5235.7*	*3634.4*	*2301.8*	*2432.7*	*4217.7*	*7602.3*	*9408.6*	*11070.8*
Rest of the World	*28694.7*	*10070.3*	*16145.2*	*19371.1*	*34738.3*	*45767.9*	*59106.0*	*49355.2*
EU	8326.5	5087.5	6674.7	6357.7	10015.6	10672.2	18383.5	12445.3
US	4950.1	357.6	1395.3	5051.9	3945.8	3406.4	6345.6	3392.5
Japan	5229.5	3366.2	2317.7	2538.2	6655.0	10222.8	8382.0	7653.6
Taiwan	914.0	270.7	826.9	1186.6	−6.8	785.3	872.3	1463.1
South Korea	721.8	92.4	632.0	896.5	507.0	1253.8	3124.7	1279.1
Hong Kong	1884.8	204.5	100.1	344.9	586.4	1278.8	1622.4	619.5
Mainland China	62.1	−80.9	188.7	225.9	537.7	1016.2	1226.9	1497.3
Others	6605.9	772.4	4009.8	2769.5	12497.6	17132.4	19148.6	21004.8
Total	33930.5	13704.7	18447.0	21803.9	38956.0	53370.2	68514.6	60426.0

Source: HKTDC, 2006; ASEAN Statistical Yearbook 2008

Table 5. Actual Foreign Investment by ASEAN Countries in China (US$ million)

	1997	1998	2003	2004	2005	2006	2007
Singapore	2606.4	3404.0	2058.4	2008.1	2204.3	2260.5	3184.6
Malaysia	381.8	340.5	251.0	385.0	361.4	393.5	397.3
Philippines	155.6	179.3	220.0	233.2	188.9	134.3	195.3
Thailand	194.0	205.4	173.5	178.7	95.9	144.8	89.5
Indonesia	80.0	69.0	150.1	104.5	86.8	100.7	134.4
Brunei	0.1	1.8	52.6	96.1	160.4	294.2	376.9
Cambodia	5.5	2.9	12.5	20.7	2.8	2.1	6.3
Burma	2.7	5.1	3.5	8.8	3.7	7.4	3.3
Laos	0.4	1.1	0.4	4.3	–	–	3.0
Vietnam	1.5	14.1	3.3	1.1	1.3	13.7	0.7
Total	3428.0	4223.2	2925.4	3040.5	3105.5	3351.2	4391.3

Source: HKTDC, 2006; China Trade and External Economic Statistical Yearbook, 2007 and 2008

External Trade Organisation found that ASEAN bore the brunt of the decline of Japan's FDI to East Asia in recent years. Japanese investments in Indonesia, Malaysia, the Philippines and Thailand declined by more than half between 1997 and 1999. The decline has been attributed to the competition with China for FDI (Saywell, 2001), the lack of liberalisation and the Asian financial crisis. Hence, the formation of ACFTA, it was hoped, would promote investments in the region and to recoup some of the shares of FDI to China. Besides, China and ASEAN could become a whole piece of platform for FDI with the formation of an FTA. When the tariff rates are reduced to zero, the region will have the potential of becoming an attractive FDI destination (Yeoh and Ooi, 2007a: 3).

On the part of China, it is obvious that she now sees FTAs as a crucial means to enhance economic development through expanding market size and establishing market coordination mechanisms to improve the investment environment and attract more investments from outside the region. This is in line with Beijing's need to guarantee the supply of energy and raw material from ASEAN and to help diversifying export markets. (Ravenhill and Jiang, 2007: 19).

The formation of ACFTA has the potential to further increase Malaysia's investment opportunity in China with both sides having entered into negotiations in order to progressively liberalise the investment regime. China's large market, abundant human resource and low production cost in combination may provide great opportunities for Malaysian firms to invest there. MIDA's statistics on Malaysian investment in China suggested opportunities in the China market, e.g. one of the Malaysian firms, Hytex Integrated Berhad has invested some US$25 million to set up a new garment factory in China. Another, Karyon Industries Berhad, with a joint-venture with a China firm, will produce lead-free metal stabilisation in China.[49] With rising labour costs and shortage of workers in the domestic market, Malaysia is no longer a cost-competitive location for labour-intensive operations, and this leads to the option for labour-intensive manufacturers to relocate to cost-competitive countries like China and Vietnam. For instance, certain Malaysian firms have shifted the labour-intensive operations such as shoemaking and garment industries to China, seeking lower labour costs, lesser capital outlays, and higher profit margin. In short, the formation of ACFTA has the potential of generating opportunities for Malaysian firms to invest in low-cost and labour-intensive sectors within the FTA (Yeoh and Ooi, 2007a: 11).

Trade relations and market access opportunities

Bilateral trade between Malaysia and China has increased significantly since 1994 and China was Malaysia's fourth largest trading partner in 2005, having replaced Taiwan since 2001. Trade flows between Malaysia and China have increased significantly from US$4.264 billion to US$46.386 billion for the 1998–2007 period, reflecting the mutual efforts of the governments and the intrinsic increasing domestic needs for the rapid economic development of both countries (Table 6). Malaysian exports to China increased more than 10-fold from US$1.596 billion to US$17.689 billion for the 1998–2007 period (see more details in terms of product group and commodity composition in Table 7 and Table 8). Bilateral trade between China and Malaysia is even higher if trade flows between Malaysia and Hong Kong are included. In 2005, the total value of trade between Malaysia and Hong Kong was RM42 billion, with exports amounting to

RM31.21 billion and imports totalling RM10.79 billion. Between 1998 and 2007, imports from China rose by more than 10-fold from US$2.668 billion to US$28.697 billion. Malaysia recorded trade surplus with China for the 1994–96 period; this was followed by a trade deficit of RM1.02 billion in 1997. Malaysia recorded trade surplus for the 1998–99 period, followed by a trade deficit of RM0.81 billion in the year 2000. Trade deficit was also recorded from 2002 to 2005 (Yeoh and Ooi, 2007a: 18). However, ideally with the establishment of an FTA, the abolition of trade barriers will lead to trade expansion through trade creation or diversion. In the future, with China increasing her share in Malaysia's total trade, there is a likelihood that Malaysia will gain from the trade integration of China and ASEAN.

As noted earlier, an Early Harvest Programme (EHP) was introduced in the early 2000s to eliminate tariffs on an agreed list of products prior to the actual implementation of the ACFTA as a gesture of the earnestness of the countries involved. The EHP was implemented on 1 January 2004 and the elimination of tariffs was scheduled to complete by 1 January 2006 for the six original members of ASEAN (ASEAN-6) and 2010 for Cambodia, Laos, Burma and

Table 6. Trade between China and Malaysia, 1998–2007 (US$ billion)

Year	China's export to Malaysia	China's import from Malaysia	Total China-Malaysia trade	Total China-ASEAN trade
1998	1.596	2.668	4.264	23.5
1999	1.674	3.606	5.28	27
2000	2.565	5.48	8.045	39.5
2001	3.22	6.205	9.425	41.6
2002	4.975	9.296	14.271	54.8
2003	6.141	13.987	20.13	78.3
2004	8.087	18.174	26.26	105.8
2005	10.607	20.096	30.703	130.4
2006	13.537	23.572	37.109	160.838
2007	17.689	28.697	46.386	202.533

Source: Data for 1998–2005 from Li (2006: 128), Table 9.1 (data source: *Yearbook of China's Foreign Trade and External Economic Cooperation*, 1998–2005, China Foreign Economic Relations and Trade Publishing House). Data for 2006–2008 are from *China Trade and External Economic Statistical Yearbook*, 2007 and 2008

Table 7. Malaysian Exports to China by Product Group (RM billion)

Description	Year 1994	Year 2004
TOTAL EXPORTS	5.06	32.14
E&E products	0.17	12.70
Palm oil	1.91	5.29
Chemicals & chemical products	0.07	3.92
Crude petroleum	0.13	1.57

Source: Kwek and Tham (2007:125), Table 6.2. Data from MATRADE

Table 8. Commodity Composition of Exports to China from Malaysia (%)

Year	Agriculture-intensive	Mineral-intensive	Labour-intensive	Capital-intensive
1990	78.7	7.5	1.4	12.5
1995	66.3	6.2	4.3	23.2
2000	21.5	9.5	2.4	66.7
2003	14.4	7.7	1.3	76.7

Source: Li (2006:129), Table 9.2. Computed with data from UN Comtrade database

Vietnam (CLMV). Covered under the EHP are agricultural and primary products in the HS Chapters 1 to 8 (Table 9) of the Customs Duties Order (unless specifically excluded by a member country) and specific products in Chapters 9, 15, 18, 27, 34, 38, 40 and 70. Malaysia has offered 590 products under the EHP, which include 503 unprocessed agricultural products and 87 specific products including coffee, cocoa and cocoa products, animal and vegetable fats/oils, mineral fuel, soap and stearic acid, articles of rubber and glass envelopes for cathode-ray tube (Table 10). China has offered 581 products under the EHP. Take the year 2004 as an example: Malaysian exporters could be seen to have benefited by exporting these products to China. A total of 2046 Form E (Preferential Certificates of Origin under ACFTA) were issued for exports to China. Total amount of exports under EHP was RM514.1 million. Meanwhile, no imports from China were recorded under the EHP in 2004, pointing to the unequal nature of the agreement as noted earlier. Malaysia's exports under the EHP had further increased to RM540.3 million in 2005 (MITI, 2006a: 189–190). The Agreement on Trade in Goods (TIG) came into force on 20 July 2005. Malaysia's exports under the agreement are encouraging with a total of 1381 Form E being issued by Malaysia for exports to the China market. The value of exports under this agreement totaled RM756.5 million. In terms of imports from China, a total value of RM3.7 million was recorded in 2005 (*ibid.*).

Table 9. Early Harvest Programme Tariff reduction commenced from 1 January 2004, 0% tariff rates by 2006. It covers more than 500 products, mostly agricultural products listed in the first 8 chapters of HS Code

Chapter	Description
01	Live animals
02	Meat and edible meat offal
03	Fish
04	Dairy produce
05	Other animal products
06	Live trees
07	Edible vegetables
08	Edible fruits and nuts

Table 10. Malaysia's Main Exports under ACFTA, 2005

Product Category	RM million	Share of Malaysia's total export under ACFTA (%)
TOTAL	1296.8	100
Chemical products	613.1	47.3
Palm oil	196.7	15.2
Stearic acid	134.5	10.4
Rubber products	105.3	8.1
Detergent and soaps	95.9	7.4
Cocoa products	74.9	5.8
Fish and crustaceans	19.1	1.5
Mangosteen, watermelon and papaya	18.9	1.5
Cathode-ray tubes for television	13.2	1.0

Source: Yeoh and Ooi (2007b: 22–23), Table 13. Data from MITI

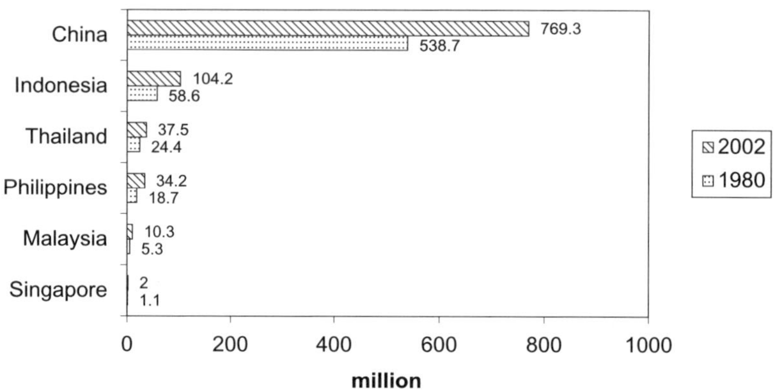

Figure 1. Total Labour Force of ASEAN-5 and China
Source: Mukhriz and Nor' Aznin, 2005: 18, Table 7

On the other hand, it should be noted that the formation of ACFTA could also create challenges for Malaysia, one of which is the fact that the labour force in China is undeniably huge compared to ASEAN-5, hence giving China a definite advantage in the labour-intensive sectors, although annual growth rate of labour force in China was the lowest among these economies (Figure 1). Monthly wages of unskilled production workers for some companies in the eastern seaboard cities of China could be 20–70% lower, as compared to Malaysia. Some companies in Malaysia, such as Motorola, Sony Electronics, Acer Technology and Philips Semiconductor have relocated some of their operations to China to take advantage of the lower labour costs (UNDP, 2006: 73). Furthermore, the formation of ACFTA and the removal of trade barriers will enable the competitive exporter with cheaper products to access the region's markets easily. Hence, Malaysian manufacturers will face greater competition in the domestic market as well as in the third-country markets of ASEAN involving many lines of textile and clothing, plus consumer electronics, footwear, toys and plastic products. In particular, garment producers in Malaysia have faced negative impacts from home-market penetration and third-market displacement by China in recent years (Yeoh and Ooi, 2007b: 30). According to Yeoh (2001), Malaysia's Associated Chinese Chamber of Commerce and Industry reported that out of over 4,000 small and medium enterprises involved in the garments and textiles sector, some 3,000 had closed down. In addition, China has developed competitiveness in a wide range of other manufactures, including machinery and electrical appliances, optical instruments, clocks and watches, metal products and several chemicals. In fact, these manufactured goods accounted for about 70% of all ASEAN imports from China (Wattanapruttipaisan, 2003). There are worries in Malaysia that the shift in the composition of China's exports to higher value-added products and the rising domestic production of components would eventually make China a more favourable location than Malaysia particularly in outsourcing activities as according to the A.T. Kearney Offshore Location Attractiveness Index, Malaysia ranked third for business process outsourcing after India and China (*Third Industrial Master Plan, 2006–2020*, MITI; Devadason, 2007: 139). Due to the reallocation of the production base towards China, in mid-2003, electrical and electronic firms in Malaysia, the state of Penang in particular, employed 17% fewer workers than in 2000 (Woo, 2004, cited in Devadason, 2007: 139). For further illustration, Malaysia's "revealed comparative advantage" (RCA) with respect to China was computed in Table 11 to identify niches for exporting to China, while Table 12 shows her opportunity for importing from China.[50]

Regarding trade overlap between Malaysia and China, Li (2006: 131) found the Sino-Malaysian intra-industry trade (IIT) having steadily increased during 1998–2001, reaching around 50%, although IIT had been relatively low (less than 30%) till the mid-1990s (Figure 2) (Li, 2006: 131), concurring with the finding of Wong (2004). Similarly, Devadason (2007) has found that the extent of Sino-Malaysian IIT has experienced steady increase between 1980 and 2005, reaching almost 50% of total trade by 2001, exceeding Malaysia's IIT with the US and Japan (Devadason, 2007: 144). Li also found that the Sino-Malaysian IIT (Grubel-Lloyd index) is below that of Singapore, above that of the Philippines and Indonesia, rather parallel to that of Thailand after 2002.

Table 11. RCA for Malaysia, 2004

Code	Product	RCA
15	Animal, vegetable fats and oils, cleavage products, etc.	12.91
80	Tin and articles thereof	6.83
44	Wood and articles of wood, wood charcoal	2.82
85	Electrical, electronic equipment	2.45
40	Rubber and articles thereof	2.44

Source: Yeoh and Ooi (2007a: 23), Table 17. Computed with data from ITC database, UNTACD

Table 12. RCA for China, 2004

Code	Product	RCA
46	Manufactures of plaiting material, basket work	9.31
66	Umbrellas, walking-sticks, seat-sticks, whips, etc.	8.27
67	Bird-skin, feathers, artificial flowers, human hair	6.63
42	Articles of leather, animal gut, harness, travel goods	4.84
43	Fur skins and artificial fur, manufactures thereof	4.41
95	Toys, games, sports requisites	4.18
63	Other made textile articles, sets, worn clothing etc.	4.10
64	Footwear, gaiters and the like, parts thereof	3.75
61	Articles of apparel, accessories, knit or crochet	3.33
62	Articles of apparel, accessories, not knit or crochet	3.33
58	Special woven or tufted fabric, lace, tapestry etc.	2.88
81	Other base metals, cements, articles thereof	2.74
96	Miscellaneous manufactured articles	2.62
60	Knitted or crocheted fabric	2.31
94	furniture, lighting, signs, prefabricated buildings	2.3
54	Manmade filaments	2.14
52	Cotton	2.06

Source: Yeoh and Ooi (2007a: 24), Table 18. Computed with data from ITC database, UNTACD

Reduction in over-dependence on developed countries

Besides expanding trade between Malaysia and her partner countries, ACFTA could also reduce her exports dependence on developed countries. Although trade between Malaysia and the other member countries of ACFTA would increase greatly, Malaysia's exports are heavily dependent on developed countries such as the US, the EU and

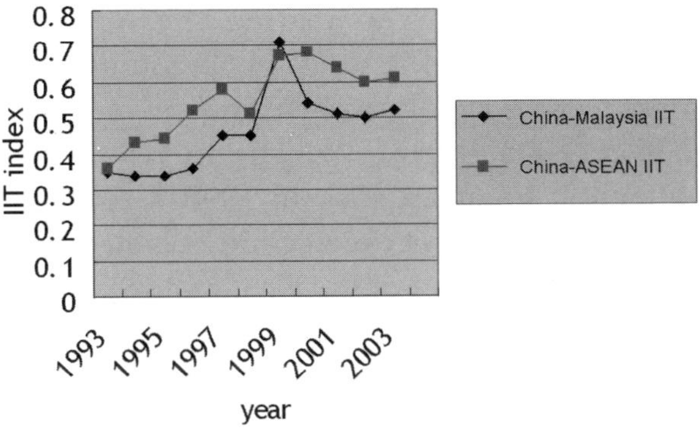

Figure 2. China-Malaysia and China-ASEAN Intra-industry Trade (IIT)
Source: Li (2006: 131), Figure 9.1 (data from *http://www.aseansec.org*)

Table 13. Percentage Share of Malaysia's Exports to US, EU and Japan

	Year				
Country	1970	1980	1990	2000	2005
US	13	16.4	16.9	20.5	19.7
EU	19.2	16.9	14.9	13.7	11.7
Japan	18.2	22.8	15.8	13.1	9.4

Source: UNDP (2006: 31), Table 2.4

Japan (Table 13). The total share of exports of these countries accounted for 56.1% of Malaysia's exports in 1980. The share of exports decreased to 47.6% in 1990, 47.3% in 2000 and 40.8% in 2005. (Yeoh and Ooi, 2007a: 25) Sluggish economic growth is the key factor for the decline in exports demand in these major markets. Japan was a major exports market for Malaysia in the 1980s and 1990s. However, exports to Japan dropped significantly to 13.1% in 2000. In 2005, Malaysia's exports to Japan accounted for only 9.4%. This was due to Japan's low economic performance that decreased her market demand. That may be the biggest problem of over-dependence on a single export market.

In terms of trade intensity, Kwek and Tham (2007) has found that Malaysia's trade ties with China have grown faster than her trade ties with the rest of the world, with the trade intensity index of

Malaysia's trade with China (comparing the relative intensity of Malaysia's trade with China relative to her trade with the rest of the world) having increased significantly from 1.60 in 1995 in 2000 and further to 6.04 in 2003 (Figure 3). The increase was particularly remarkable after the financial crisis in 1998. Growth in exports to China and ASEAN could offset the decline of Malaysia's share in her key market with the formation of the FTA. Malaysia's exports market has been widening with China's accession to the WTO and the agreement to establish an FTA with ASEAN. These could gradually reduce Malaysia's over-dependence on the developed countries. Considering these factors, it leaves greater room for the future development and expansion in trade between Malaysia and the other members of ACFTA. In the context of global economic slowdown, and years of recession of the regional economic power, Japan, ACFTA by enhancing trade flows of the member countries will be especially beneficial. On the part of China, from the geopolitical perspective, she is of course happy to see that with the implementation of ACFTA, ASEAN's traditional economic dependence on the US, Europe and Japan would be gradually shifted to herself, although both she and ASEAN are still facing a risk in the over-concentration in electronics whose final market is over-dependent on the US (Ravenhill and Jiang, 2007: 21).

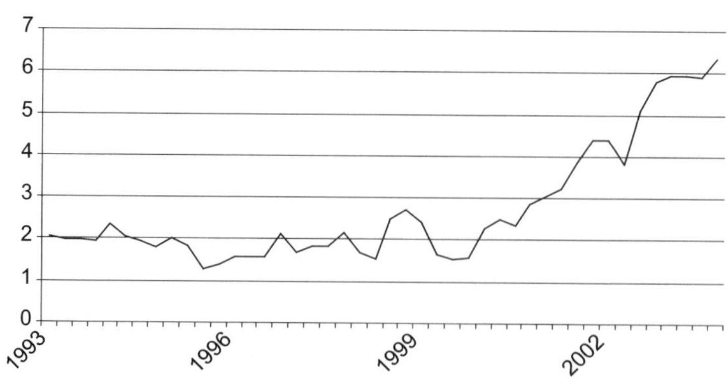

Figure 3. Quarterly Trade Intensity Index of Malaysia's Trade with China (1993:Q1–2003:Q4)

Source: Kwek and Tham (2007: 127), Figure 6.1

Table 14. Malaysia and China: Pre-AFCTA Import Duties on Selected Products (%)

	Malaysia	China
Product sector	Import duty	Import duty
Wood Products	5	17–27
Rubber Products	30–40	29.9–30
Furniture and Parts	Nil	20.7
Food and Beverage	0–25	22–45
Chemicals and Chemical Products	0–20	20–27
Jewellery and Parts	10	40–52
Boiler, Machinery and Mechanical Appliances	0–30	17–40
Electrical Machinery and Equipment, Electronics Parts and Accessories	0–30	17–47
Animal or Vegetables Fats and Oils and their fractions including edible preparations	0–10	22–47
Parts and Accessories for vehicles other than railway or tramway	25–30	23–33

Source: Kwek and Tham (2007: 134), Table 6.6. Data from MITI

Competition to enter the China market

Malaysia has, in general, lower tariffs than China (Table 14);[51] for instance in 2004, Malaysia's average tariff was 9.2% while China's was 17% ACFTA's tariff reduction is poised to increase Malaysian firms' access to the China market with potential customs duty savings arising from the margin of difference between the Most-Favoured Nation (MFN) tariff rate and the lower preferential ASEAN-China tariff rate (Kwek and Tham, 2007: 134).

However, Malaysia will encounter a certain amount of other barriers to enter the China market. There is competition in the substitutes between Malaysia and the other ASEAN members in the China market due to the similarity of their economic structures and commodity exports to the China market.

THE FUTURE: WHAT ROLE CAN CHINA PLAY?

In 2009, APEC celebrated its 20th year of successful establishment. Since its inception 20 years ago, APEC has positioned itself as the premier forum for facilitating economic growth, cooperation, trade and investment in the Asia-Pacific region.[52] Being "the most economically dynamic part of the world",[53] APEC member economies "generated nearly 70% of global economic growth"[54] and the APEC region "consistently outperformed the rest of the world, even during the Asian financial crisis" (APEC Secretariat, 2005: 4). At present, the rapid economic growth of China, Russia and Vietnam still draws much attention from various parts of the world.

APEC's success could be mainly attributed to the "designs and functions of APEC in the region for the economic activities" as the "active participation of private sectors" provides the public sectors in APEC member nations "cutting-edge advices on entrepreneurial developments and high-technology", while through such cooperation between the public and private sectors, problems related to business growth are often effectively solved, and in this respect, APEC members have demonstrated the ability to forge strong public-private sector partnerships within the nations (Chang, 2008: 2). Furthermore, APEC should explore the possibility of expanding its membership. The rise of BRICs is one of the most important economic trends in the 21st century. APEC should "embrace this economic momentum mainly growing from within the region" and "be more aggressive in bringing these other two neighbours, India and Brazil, or their neighbouring countries, into the APEC community" (*ibid.*: 3). Although, since its inception, APEC has become more "dynamic and heterogeneous" through the "enlargement of its membership", providing an "unprecedented opportunity for regional integration" for many member countries, APEC is still primarily an Asian body, and as such, the "Asian nature of APEC" would actually be a "sustaining force", while the "sense of ownership" is also equally important as evident in Japan's participation in the Kyoto Protocol (Liao *et al.*, 2006: 3).

There are many indications which point towards APEC expanding its "scope of competence" while remaining relevant and effective in the future — as interaction between member countries increase, a "sense of common destiny" is likely to be strengthened, and it is this "sense of common destiny" which could even evolve into a "common vision of Asia-Pacific" with consequences far beyond the original objectives of APEC (*ibid.*). As such, APEC is entering a new and complex phase with the expected "development of action plans for liberalisation by each member economy" and their "subsequent continuing review" (Woods, 1995). Thus, it would seem that the strategy for APEC in the future is to act as swiftly as possible to "negotiate and implement a Trans-Pacific Partnership as the first and major step toward a Free Trade Area of the Asia-Pacific" and thereby achieve the "Bogor goals" (Bergsten, 2009).

Looking back at APEC's history, the level of success of the organisation has been primarily judged on the degree of trade liberalisation among its member states, and in this respect, Japan has "taken a very active leadership role within Asia" to "promote a new Asian economic architecture", and "proposed the ASEAN+6 variant" and "initiated the East Asian Summits", giving hope that "a successful realisation of the Trans-Pacific Partnership" would further encourage "trade liberalisation" and "restore the vitality of APEC" (*ibid.*). Since its formation, APEC has grown from 12 founding members to 21. At present, APEC economies account for "more than 40% of the world's population and world trade", and "more than half of global production", while the fact that the most senior-level personnel of member countries continue to attend APEC meetings is evidence of its importance and success.[55]

Due to the current economic uncertainty surrounding the world, it is well nigh impossible to predict the future of APEC with any precision. Even though the 21 countries within APEC have increased regional economic cooperation and coordination considerably, huge economic and developmental disparities continue to exist between APEC member states. In fact, developed countries within APEC are gaining more from the strengthening APEC regional ties than their developing counterparts. In order to narrow the growing discrepancy between the member countries, it would be of utmost importance to ensure that free trade exists among all APEC countries. Within the APEC organisation, the US, Japan and China are the most powerful nations. No one has ever imagined or predicted that China can attain the present level of economic development within such a short span of time. In fact, China has achieved such economic and technological clout that she will soon be replacing Japan to become the second largest economy in the world.[56] It is very possible that China will lead the Asian region, and even the world, in the future. China has attained such a high level of development primarily by exporting her products to the rest of the world. In addition, China has also started making huge investments in the industries of neighbouring countries within the Asian region, benefiting her neighbouring countries in the process while gaining popularity and power. With China's increasing trade within the region, Japan and the US have lost some of their market shares to China. In order to retain her market share, China has taken the initiative to sign several FTAs with other Asian countries. Although similar FTAs are signed by Japan and South Korea within the region, China remains in the leadership position.

In terms of bilateral and multilateral trade agreements, China has focused her attention on establishing the China-ASEAN FTA. The creation of ACFTA has further strengthened China's leadership in the region. It appears that China would not favour including Russia and the US in the FTA. On the other hand, China supported the inclusion of Japan and South Korea. A possible explanation for this is that China does not view Japan and South Korea as too much of a threat in terms of trade in the region. Japan supported explicitly the US's proposition to add more new members to the FTA. China does not seem to worry about this as Japan is gradually losing her power in the region.

The US is very much interested in widening FTA arrangements to include countries in the Asia-Pacific region. She is looking forward to include more countries from the region to join Brunei, Singapore and New Zealand which are already member countries of the FTAAP. The 2009 APEC conference in Singapore, the 2010 conference in Japan and the 2011 conference in the US provide great opportunities for the US to exert her influence in forging stronger ties with other APEC member countries.

The interest of the US in the Asian region is further sparked by the uncertainty shrouding the WTO. The WTO has 153 members (representing more than 95% of total world trade) and 30 observers, all seeking membership.[57] To "enhance equitable participation of the poorer countries", the WTO is currently working on a trade negotiation called the Doha Development Agenda which however has been "dogged by disagreement between exporters of agricultural bulk commodities and countries with large numbers of subsistence farmers" on the "precise terms of a 'special safeguard measure' to protect farmers from surges in imports".[58] With such uncertainties surrounding the Doha Round, the US has become more interested in enhancing her trade relations within the Asia-Pacific region.

It is observed that while China wants the concept of free trade to be restricted to a few countries within the region, the US wants a much wider free trade zone. A probable explanation for China's preference of a more restricted FTA is that China can more easily lead the region and benefit from a restricted FTA because China's strength and influence mainly lie in the Asian region. An FTA which covers both the Asia and Pacific regions will increase the power and influence of the US and Japan in the region. China does not favour a wider FTA for fear of losing influence and advantage in trade in the region.

The US's proposition for a wider free trade zone is based on three major concepts which are summarised in the "goals of the G20 Framework for strong, sustainable and balanced growth": balanced growth, inclusive growth and sustainable growth.[59] In order to achieve these three types of growth, the US suggests that she can contribute significantly at a micro-level in the area of education, technology, SMEs, worker training, microfinance, opportunities for women, etc. The US has marketed herself as a country which can offer the best assistance for fellow nations to achieve long-term economic and trade growth in the abovementioned fields.

The US and China share a complicated relationship in terms of FTA arrangements. China is well aware of the risk of losing her leadership position and power in the region if she accepts the US's proposal of a larger free trade zone. On the other hand, the US also realises that the road towards successful economic integration in the region will be riddled with difficulties without China's cooperation.

It is often advocated that if China can cooperate with the US in developing a wider free trade zone in the Asia-Pacific region, China can gain more political stability and leadership in the region. Apart from that, the US would also be willing to actively work together with China to deal with the nuclear proliferation problem. This will contribute towards overall peace in the region and the world. On the other hand, disputes between China and the US will only bring problems to the global society rather than solve them.

In Asia, Japan is facing the aging problem domestically and is losing power in the continent. The US is trying to build a new model for supporting her allies in Asia. If the US succeeds in exerting further influence in the Asian region, China's leadership position would be shaken. After the recent global financial crisis, it is argued that China has caught up with the US. However, it is submitted that it would be difficult for China to compete with the US unless China further strengthens her economy.

China needs to act strategically on specific domestic and global issues. To strengthen herself as a major power, China needs to resolve her domestic problems and enhance social and economic development. In addition, China should try to make the yuan a key currency in the global market and play a more global role than she is playing right now. Thus, to strengthen her position as a leader in world trade, more specifically in the Asia-Pacific region, China will not only need to develop her economic and trade cooperation with countries in the region, but will also need development on all fronts.

REFERENCES

APEC Secretariat (2005). "APEC at a Glance." http://www.apec.org/apec/enewsletter/jan_vol7/publication.primarycontentparagraph.0002.LinkURL.Download.ver5.1.9.

ASEAN Secretariat (2002). "Framework Agreement on Comprehensive Economic Co-Operation between ASEAN and the People's Republic of China." http://www.aseansec.org/13196html.

ASEAN Secretariat (2008). *ASEAN Statistical Yearbook 2008*. Jakarta: ASEAN Secretariat.

ASEAN Secretariat (2009). *ASEAN Statistical Yearbook 2009.* Jakarta: ASEAN Secretariat.

Balassa, B. (1961). *The Theory of Economic Integration.* London: George Allen and Unwin.

Bergsten, C. F. (2009), "The Future of APEC and Its Core Agenda." Keynote speech delivered to the APEC 2010 Symposium, Tokyo, Japan, 9 December http://www.piie.com/publications/papers/paper.cfm?ResearchID=1447.

Chang, H. (2008). "APEC: A View from Asian Business 'The Future of APEC.'" *Journal of Commerce and Industry*, 1. http://www.cacci.org.tw/Journal/2008%20Vol%201/HarveyChang.pdf.

China Trade and External Economic Statistical Yearbook 2007. Beijing: China Statistics Press.

China Trade and External Economic Statistical Yearbook 2008. Beijing: China Statistics Press.

Nie, S. (2009). "Shanghai's New Impetus towards China's Wall Street." http://www.sinoptic.ch/shanghaiflash/texts/pdf/2009/200904_Shanghai.Flash.pdf.

de Brouwer, G. (2002). "The IMF and East Asia: A Changing Regional Financial Architecture." *Pacific Economic Papers*, No. 324, February. http://dspace-prod1.anu.edu.au/bitstream/1885/40645/2/pep-324.pdf.

Devadason, E. (2007). "Malaysia-China Trade Patterns in Manufactures: How Big Is Production Sharing?" In E. K.-K. Yeoh and E. Devadason (Eds.), *Emerging Trading Nation in an Integrating World: Global Impacts and Domestic Challenges of China's Economic Reform.* Kuala Lumpur: Institute of China Studies, University of Malaya, pp. 138–152.

Hong Kong Trade Development Council (HKTDC) (2006). "China-ASEAN Free Trade Area and Implications for Hong Kong as a Trade Hub." Economic Forum, 29 June. http://www.tdctrade.com/econforum/tdc/tdc060602.htm.

Institute of Developing Economies-Japan External Trade Organisation (IDE-JETRO) and Socio-Economic & Environmental Research Institute (SERI) (2004). "Trade, Investment and Economic Cooperation between China and Southeast Asia: The Case of Malaysia." Report of IDE-JETRO and SERI joint research project, November 2003–February 2004.

"Is Globalization Inevitable?", Free Media Productions, 2009. http://www.freemediaproductions.info/Editorials/author/maverick/.

Kiyota, K., Sazanami, Y. and Wong, Y. C. (2005). "Intra-regional Trade in Asia: Dynamics of Production Sharing." http://www.univ-lehavre.fr/actu/itlcsge/kiyota_2.pdf.

Kwek, K.-T. and Tham, S.-Y. (2007). "Trade between Malaysia and China: Opportunities and Challenges for Growth." In E. K.-K. Yeoh and E. Devadason (Eds.), *Emerging Trading Nation in an Integrating World: Global Impacts and Domestic Challenges of China's Economic Reform.* Kuala Lumpur: Institute of China Studies, University of Malaya, pp. 123–137.

Li, Y. (2006). "An Analysis of Recent Sino-Malaysian Trade Relations." In E. K.-K. Yeoh (Ed.), *China and Malaysia in a Globalizing World: Bilateral Relations, Regional Imperatives and Domestic Challenges.* Kuala Lumpur: Institute of China Studies, University of Malaya, pp. 127–136.

Liao, A., Liner, C. and Müller, S. (2006). "A Bright Future for APEC." Position paper for roundtable discussion "Whither Regionalism in Asia and the Pacific?" in "Governance and Regional Integration" course, Graduate Institute of International Studies, Geneva. http://hei.unige.ch/sections/sp/courses/0506/dupont/roundtable/Bright%20future%20for%20APEC.pdf.

Malaysia External Trade Development Corporation (MATRADE) (2004). *Malaysia's Trade Performance, 1994–2003.* Kuala Lumpur.

Malaysia External Trade Development Corporation (MATRADE) (2005). *Malaysia's Trade Performance, 2004.* Kuala Lumpur.

Malaysian Ministry of Finance (2010). *Economic Report 2009/2010.* Kuala Lumpur: Percetakan Nasional Malaysia Berhad.

Malaysian Ministry of International Trade and Industry (MITI) (2004). *Malaysia – International Trade and Industry Report 2003.*

Malaysian Ministry of International Trade and Industry (MITI) (2006a). *Malaysia – International Trade and Industry Report 2005.*

Malaysian Ministry of International Trade and Industry (MITI) (2006b). *Third Industrial Master Plan, 2006–2020: Malaysia — Towards Global Competitiveness.* Kuala Lumpur: Percetakan Nasional Malaysia Berhad.

Morrison, W. M. (2006). "China's Economic Conditions." CRS Issue Brief for Congress, No. RL33534, Congressional Research Service.

Mukhriz, I. A. A. and Abu Bakar N. A. (2005). "The Export Competition between China and ASEAN-5 Countries in the U.S. and Japan: A Survey on Manufacturing Sectors." Paper presented at the conference "WTO, China, and the Asian Economies, III: Economic Integration and Economic Development," 25–26 June, Xi'an Jiaotong University, Xi'an, China.

PricewaterhouseCoopers (2009). "Greater China IPO Watch 2008." PWC China/Hong Kong Capital Market Services Group. http://www.pwccn.com/home/webmedia/633795312509403786/gc_ipo_survey_rpt_jun2009.pdf.

Rajan, R. S. (2009). "Crises, Private Capital Flows and Financial Instability in Emerging Asia." UNESCAP Working Paper, WP/09/06, UNESCAP Macroeconomic Policy and Development Division. http://www.unescap.org/pdd/publications/workingpaper/wp_09_06.pdf.

Ravenhill, J. and Jiang, Y. (2007). "China's Move to Preferential Trading: An Extension of Chinese Network Power?" Paper presented at the International Conference "Made in China vs. Made by Chinese: Global Identities of Chinese Business", Collingwood College, Durham University, Durham, United Kingdom, 19–20 March.

Saywell, T. (2001). "Powering Asia's Growth." *Far Eastern Economic Review*, 164, 30, 40–43.

Setser, B. W. and Pandey, A. (2009). "China's $1.5 Trillion Bet: Understanding China's External Portfolio." CGS Working Paper, Council on Foreign Relations Press.

Soesastro, H., Noland, M. and Emmerson, D. K. (1995). "The Jakarta-Bogor APEC Summit: A Vision for 2020." Shorenstein Reports on Contemporary East Asia, Number 3, January. http://ieas.berkeley.edu/shorenstein/1995.01.html.

Stubbs, R. (2002). "ASEAN Plus Three: Emerging East Asian Regionalism?" *Asian Survey*, 42, 3, pp. 440–455.

The People's Bank of China (2009). "Strengthen Regional Financial Cooperation and Actively Conduct Currency Swap" 31 March. http://www.pbc.gov.cn/english//detail.asp?col=6400&ID=1299.

The Development GAP (1992). "The Enterprise for the Americas Initiative: Description and Up-date." October. http://www.developmentgap.org/americas/EAI_Description_and_Update.pdf.

United Nations Conference on Trade and Development (UNTACD) (2006). "International Trade Statistics: General Trade Data 2000–2004." International Trade Center (ITC). http://www.intracen.org/tradestat/welcome.html.

United Nations Development Programme (UNDP) (2006). *Malaysia: International Trade, Growth, Poverty and Human Resource Development.*

Wattanapruttipaisan, T. (2003). "ASEAN-China Free Trade Area: Advantages, Challenges, and Implications for the Newer ASEAN Member Countries." *ASEAN Economic Bulletin,* April.

Wong, K.-Y. (2004). "China's WTO Accession and its Trade with the Southeast Asian Economies." Paper presented at the Conference "WTO, China and the Asian Economies: Free Trade Areas and New Economic Relations", Beijing, China, 18–19 June.

Woo, W. T. (2004) "The Economic Impact of China's Emergence as a Major Trading Nation." Mimeo, University of California at Davis.

Woods, J. M. L. (1995). "Achieving the 2020 Vision – The Future of APEC and Its Impact on World and Regional Trade." Paper presented at the 22nd International Trade Law Conference, 27–28 October, Canberra. http://www.apec.org.au/docs/future.htm.

Yeoh, E. K.-K. and Ooi, S.-M. (2007a). "China, Malaysia and ACFTA: FDI, Trade and Comparative Advantage." ICS Working Paper Series 2007–4, Institute of China Studies, University of Malaya, March.

Yeoh, E. K.-K. and Ooi, S.-M. (2007b). "China-ASEAN Free Trade Area: Implications for Sino-Malaysian Economic Relations." Copenhagen Discussion Paper Series, No. 17, Asia Research Centre, Copenhagen Business School, April.

Yeoh, M. (2001). "China's WTO Accession – Likely Impact on Malaysian Companies." Paper presented to Malaysia's National Economic Action Council's Consultative Group on Globalization, 5 December. http://www.asli.com.my/China.htm.

NOTES

*Dr. Emile Kok-Kheng **Yeoh** 楊國慶, Director and Associate Professor, Institute of China Studies, University of Malaya, Malaysia. Email: emileyeo@correo.nu, emileyeo@gmail.com. Dr. Im-Soo **Yoo** 유임수/劉壬洙, Emeritus Professor of Economics, Ewha Womans University, Seoul, Republic of Korea; President,

Asia-Europe Perspective Forum; former President, Korean Association for Contemporary European Studies, Korean-German Association of Social Science and Korean-German Association of Economics and Management. Email: isyoo@ewha.ac.kr, isyoo42@gmail.com. Lionel Wei-Li **Liong** 梁偉立, Project Research Officer, Institute of China Studies, University of Malaya, Malaysia. Email: iliew84@yahoo.com.

1. See "The Doha Round…and Round…and Round…" *The Economist Print Edition*, 31 July 2008. http://www.economist.com/finance/displaystory.cfm?story_id=11848592.
2. China calls the proposed FTA the China-ASEAN Free Trade Area (CAFTA); ASEAN calls it ASEAN-China Free Trade Area (ACFTA). To avoid confusion with another CAFTA (Central American Free Trade Agreement), the acronym "ACFTA" is used in this chapter.
3. http://www.chinability.com/GDP.htm.
4. "Billion" = thousand million.
5. "Is Globalization Inevitable?" Free Media Productions, 2009. http://www.freemediaproductions.info/Editorials/author/maverick/.
6. Gu, X. (2009). "China Tries RMB Regionalization Measure." *China Today*, 19 June http://www.chinatoday.com.cn/ctenglish/se/txt/2009-06/19/content_203295.htm.
7. However, Ravenhill and Jiang (2007: 1) preferred the term "preferential trading agreements" (PTAs) to "regional agreements" (RAs) or "free trade agreements" (FTAs) for the fact that their membership is often not "regional" in any conventional geographic sense of the word and "relatively few of the large number of preferential arrangements negotiated in the last decade come close to conventional criteria for 'free' trade".
8. For more details about Benelux, reference can be made to http://www.benelux.be/en/home_intro.asp (Benelux Economic Union), http://www.benelux-parl.org/ (Benelux Parliament), http://www.courbeneluxhof.info/ (Benelux Court of Justice) and http://www.boip.int/en/homepage.php (Benelux Office for Intellectual Property).
9. http://europa.eu/legislation_summaries/institutional_affairs/treaties/treaties_ecsc_en.htm.
10. http://www.pict-pcti.org/courts/beneluxCJ.html.
11. Details about NAFTA can be found at http://www.sice.oas.org/Trade/NAFTA/naftatce.asp.

12. http://www.international.gc.ca/trade-agreements-accords-commerciaux/agr-acc/nafta-alena/index.aspx.
13. http://www.fas.usda.gov/itp/Policy/nafta/nafta.asp.
14. The Development Gap. (1992). "The Enterprise for the Americas Initiative: Description and Up-date." October. http://www.developmentgap.org/americas/EAI_Description_and_Update.pdf.
15. http://www.apec.org/apec/about_apec/achievements_and_benefits.html.
16. Details about the 2009 APEC Conference can be found at http://www.apec.org/apec/leaders__declarations/2009.html.
17. http://www.apec.org.
18. *Ibid.*
19. http://www.apec2007.org.
20. http://www.apec.org/apec/about_apec.html.
21. http://www.apec.org/apec/about_apec.html.
22. Coates, S. (2009). "ASEAN-China Open World's Largest Free Trade Area." *Industry Week*, 30 December. http://www.industryweek.com/articles/asean-china_open_worlds_largest_free_trade_area_20729.aspx.
23. "Asian Opening." *Lanka Business Online*, 30 December 2009. http://www.lankabusinessonline.com/fullstory.php?nid=182100356.
24. "ASEAN, China Open World's Biggest Free Trade Area." *Borneo Post Online*, 31 December 2009. http://www.theborneopost.com/?p=2142.
25. http://www.thefreelibrary.com/ASEAN-China+open+free+trade+area-a01612103457.
26. http://www.america.gov/st/business-english/2009/November/20091104135511dmslahrellek0.9469721.html.
27. This summary of the Bogor Declaration can be found at http://www.apec.org/apec/leaders__declarations/1994.html.
28. These three pillars of the Osaka Action Agenda is discussed in detail in the Joint Statement of the 7th APEC Ministerial Meeting, 1995.
29. http://www.apec.org/apec/about_apec/achievements_and_benefits.html.
30. http://www.asianlii.org/apec/other/agrmt/2aeldocr429/.
31. http://en.wikipedia.org/wiki/1997_Asian_Financial_Crisis.
32. "ASEAN+3, HK Sign Chiang Mai Initiative to Address Currency Liquidity." *China Daily*, 28 December 2009. http://www.chinadaily.

com.cn/bizchina/2009-12/28/content_9238573.htm/ http://news.xinhuanet.com/english/2009-12/28/content_12717353.htm.

33. "Launch of China-ASEAN FTA Significant Event in Asia: Singapore Scholar." Xinhuanet, 29 December 2009. http://news.xinhuanet.com/english/2009-12/29/content_12723814.htm.
34. Gooch, L. (2009). "Asia Free-Trade Zone Raises Hopes, and Some Fears about China." *The New York Times*, 31 December. http://www.nytimes.com/2010/01/01/business/global/01trade.html.
35. *New York Times*, 31 December 2009.
36. http://www.smidec.gov.my/node/957.
37. "China-ASEAN FTA to Speed Up China-Malaysia's Economic Growth." *Global Times*, 26 December 2009. http://business.globaltimes.cn/china-economy/2009-12/494529.html.
38. "Launch of China-ASEAN FTA Significant Event in Asia: Singapore Scholar." Xinhuanet, 29 December 2009. http://news.xinhuanet.com/english/2009-12/29/content_12723814.htm.
39. http://www.textileasia-businesspress.com/.
40. Miller, J. W. (2010). "WTO to Probe US-China Tire Rift." *The Wall Street Journal*, 13 January. http://online.wsj.com/article/SB126323846798625041.html.
41. "Foreword." In PricewaterhouseCoopers (2008).
42. "First BRIC Summit Concludes." *Deutsche Welle*, 16 June 2009. http://www.dw-world.de/dw/article/0,4335954,00.html.
43. Gu, X. (2009). "China Tries RMB Regionalization Measure." *China Today*, 19 June. http://www.chinatoday.com.cn/ctenglish/se/txt/2009-06/19/content_203295.htm.
44. The People's Bank of China (2009). "Strengthen Regional Financial Cooperation and Actively Conduct Currency Swap." 31 March. http://www.pbc.gov.cn/english//detail.asp?col=6400&ID=1299.
45. Malaysia has no exclusion of any products for China and the other ASEAN member states under the EHP.
46. *The Star* (Malaysian daily), 2006, cited in Devadason (2007: 138).
47. "RM" = (Malaysian) ringgit. RM1 is equivalent to about US$0.295.
48. MIDA, http://www.mida.gov.my.
49. MIDA, http://www.mida.gov.my.

50. Identified by the product groups, where China's RCA is greater than two, while Malaysia's RCA is less than 1 (*ibid.*: 24).
51. MATRADE (http://www.matrade.gov.my) gave an average tariff rate of 20.4% for agricultural goods, 11.5% for chemical products, 14.6% for machinery and parts, 6.9% for metal products, 27.2% for textiles and 12.9% for wood and related products (Kwek and Tham, 2007: 134).
52. http://www.apec.org/apec/about_apec.html.
53. http://www.apec.org/apec/about_apec/achievements_and_benefits.html.
54. http://www2.ed.gov/about/inits/ed/internationaled/apec.html.
55. "APEC Marks 20 Years, Looks to Future of Regional Trade." VOA News, 10 November 2009. http://www1.voanews.com/english/news/a-13-2009-11-10-voa14-69822382.html.
56. "China Economy Shows Strong Growth in 2009." BBC, 21 January 2010. http://news.bbc.co.uk/2/hi/8471613.stm.
57. "WTO." *International Business Times* (n.d.). http://www.ibtimes.com/topics/detail/266/wto/.
58. http://en.wikipedia.org/wiki/World_Trade_Organization.
59. These three major concepts are thoroughly discussed at http://www.apec.org/apec/news__media/media_releases/20091115_leadersstatement.html.

Part III

Monetary Integration and the Reform of the Reminbi

7

Towards an Effective (More or Less) Monetary Union in Asia

Lok Sang Ho*

Lingnan University

ABSTRACT

This chapter proposes a common anchor for currencies in Asia. The common anchor is based on a basket of major currencies, including the US dollar, the Euro, the Japanese Yen, the British pound, the Canadian dollar, and the Australian dollar. It is proposed that the basket be GDP-weighted. Because GDP figures are subject to revision, data from 2 years ago will be used to update each year's weights. It is demonstrated that pegging with this currency basket effectively stabilises a country's effective exchange rate, and that with a common anchor, de facto currency integration is achieved. Each currency, on transition, can appreciate or depreciate to achieve an effective exchange rate consistent with its economic fundamentals and then keep pegging to the common anchor at such a level until economic fundamentals so change as to warrant a repegging against the common anchor.

Keywords: GDP-weighted currency basket; basket link/peg; monetary union; trade creation; currency integration, de facto; john Williamson; A Rose.

INTRODUCTION

Since the Asian Financial Crisis of 1997–98, the understanding has dawned that Asian countries need to work together to prevent another crisis. Notwithstanding rapid growth and apparent economic success, the countries in Asia have learnt that they are in fact quite vulnerable.

This vulnerability is at least in part related to the fact that many Asian currencies are more or less tied to the US dollar. According to Kawai (2008), who used regression methods to demonstrate his results, "emerging East Asian economies operated de jure or de facto dollar pegs prior to the crisis". This observation has to do with the fact that America was a major market for the exports of all of these trade-oriented economies, and with the fact that the US dollar was the predominant currency for international settlement. Indeed, all the major commodities are quoted and traded in US dollars, and the US dollar is also the predominant currency for denominating bonds. Because of the special status of the US dollar and trade orientation, most trade-oriented Asian countries have tried to maintain stability of their currencies against the US dollar. For years this arrangement appeared to have worked quite well for the East Asian economies, but it turns out that the benefits were not sustainable.

The stability of the exchange rate against the US dollar and general US dollar weakness since 1985 boosted trade and investment in the region. As can be shown in Figure 1, the relative exchange rate of the US dollar against a standard basket of currencies (defined as a GDP-weighted average of the exchange rates of the US dollar, the constituent currencies of the Euro as in 1999, the Japanese Yen, the British pound, the Canadian dollar, the Australian dollar), dropped from around 130 to around 90 from 1985 through 1995. The various Asian currencies that had tied to the US dollar enjoyed a period of strong export competitiveness, inflow of capital, and prosperity, but also inflation. To be fair, inflation was not very high, though certainly uncomfortable by today's standards, ranging from 5.8% to 7.9% in 1996 among the three economies most affected by the crisis, namely

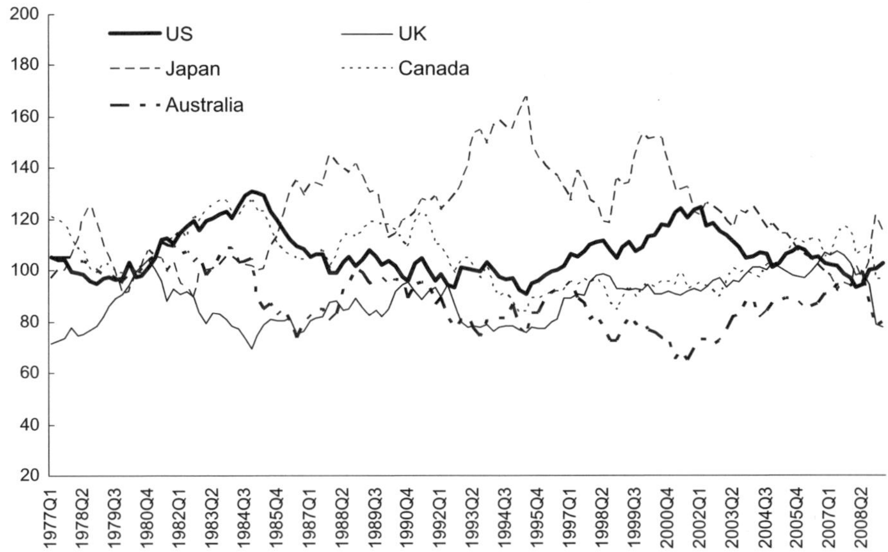

Figure 1. Relative Effective Exchange Rates Index (1980 = 100) 1977–2009Q1

Note: The thick line had been declining from 1985 through 1995, but then began to rise appreciably ahead of the Asian Financial Crisis in 1997 and kept rising through the end of 2002 before staging another decline

Source: Ho (2010b)

Thailand, South Korea, and Indonesia. Judging from the fact that 3 month interest rates averaged over 13% for these countries in 1996, inflation expectations were even higher (Tables 1 and 2).

Mirroring the inflow of capital (Table 3) is increasing indebtedness and an asset price bubble. With increasing indebtedness and an asset price bubble and high interest rates, plus currency appreciation that started in 1995 with a strengthening US dollar, any rumor would easily trigger a capital flight; any sign that neighbouring countries were in trouble would generate panic. Table 3[1] shows that Thailand in particular was having capital inflows at around 10% of the GDP throughout the 1990s before the crisis struck.

For some time Japan has been advocating more regional integration in East Asia. Japanese Prime Minister Yukio Hatoyama, soon after he took office in September 2009, specifically suggested the

Table 1. Key Variables in 1996: The Asian Tigers Before the Crisis

	Investment as a proportion of GDP[a] (%)	Gross savings rate (%)	Trade as a proportion of GDP[b] (%)	Share of world GDP (%)	Real GDP growth (%)	Consumer inflation (%)
Hong Kong	31.3	30.6	122.9	0.6	4.9	6.0
Indonesia	32.1	31.2	20.4	0.8	8.0	7.9
Malaysia	42.2	42.6	78.9	0.4	8.6	3.5
Philippines	23.2	15.6	31.2	0.3	5.7	8.4
Singapore	36.5	50.1		0.3	6.9	1.4
South Korea	36.8	35.2	28.9	1.8	7.1	4.9
Taiwan	21.2	25.1	40.1	1.0	5.7	3.1
Thailand	42.2	35.9	34.9	0.7	5.5	5.8

Notes: [a]GFCF plus inventories (GFCF only in the cases of Hong Kong and Singapore)
[b]Average value of exports plus imports as a proportion of GDP (including re-exports in the case of Hong Kong, given its status as an entrepôt)
Sources: Goldman Sachs, "International Economics Analyst", February/March 1998 p xii; IMF, "World Economic Outlook", May 1998 tables 5 and A2; BIS, "68th Annual Report", 1998 table II1.2; IMF, "World Economic Outlook: Interim Assessment", December 1997 table A1; ROC Council for Economic Planning and Development, Taiwan Statistical Data Book 1998, June 1998 tables 3.1, 3.14a, 3.9 and 11.4; Government Information Services Department, "Hong Kong 1997", appendix 6

idea of an East Asian Community. Liu Hongcai, vice-minister of the International Department of the Communist Party of China Central Committee, welcomed this as a long term goal (*China Daily*, November 3, 2009). Monetary integration, if not monetary union, will be an important step in the direction.

A TRUE MONETARY UNION IS DESIRABLE BUT INFEASIBLE

Monetary unions are certainly favourable to trade. Rose (1999) and Glick and Rose (2002) contended that the effects of monetary unions on trade were huge. "German managers can expect unprecedented competition from firms as far-flung as Portugal and Finland. Of course the elimination of the monetary barrier is also an opportunity. Unencumbered by exchange rate worries, French producers

Table 2. Exchange and Interest Rates During the Asian Crisis

	3-month interest rates			Change in dollar exchange rate	Change in real exchange rate	Move in stock market
	Average in 1996 (%)	Peak level[a] (%)	Date of 1997 peak	Jun.1997 to Sep.1998[b] (%)	Jun. 1997 to Sep. 1998[c] (%)	during 1997 (%)
Hong Kong	5.5	25.0	October	0.0	16.1	−18.7
Indonesia	13.8	27.7	October	−77.7	−56.3	−37.0
Malaysia	7.3	8.8	November	−39.8	−27.2	−52.2
Philippines	11.7	85.0	October	−38.3	−26.0	−40.3
Singapore	3.0	10.3	December	−17.6	−2.7	−31.7
Korea	13.3	25.0	October	−33.8	−19.8	−42.6
Taiwan	5.5	9.8	October	−19.4	−12.4	9.3
Thailand	13.0	26.0	December	−36.7	−19.1	−55.2

Notes: [a]Based on 3-month interbank interest rates
[b]Change from 2 July 1997 to 21 September 1998
[c]Change in the bi-laterally trade-weighted real exchange rate index
Sources: BIS, "68th Annual Report", 1998 table VII.10; IMF, "World Economic Outlook", October 1998 table 2.13; IFC, "Emerging Stock Markets Factbook", 1998 various tables; FT, various editions

can look to expand their sales to Ireland and Austria dramatically at much lower cost than before. The increase in competitive pressures may start slowly but could eventually be as or more important than the 1992 elimination of all tariffs and non-tariff barriers inside the European Community. No manager doing business inside the vast market that is euroland can afford to ignore EMU" (Rose, 1999). While the magnitude of the trade creation effect is still subject to debate, there is now general agreement that monetary unions will boost trade noticeably.

Monetary unions are also less susceptible to speculative currency attacks than individual currencies. With a much bigger economic mass, the entire region will stand to benefit from the expectation that the exchange rate with other regions will be more stable. Such expectations may lead to lower interest rates and thus lower borrowing costs. The elimination of the need to convert one currency

Table 3. Asian Economies' Capital Flows as a Proportion of GDP (%)[a]

	1991	1992	1993	1994	1995	1996
Indonesia: Net Private Capital Inflows	4.6	2.5	3.1	3.9	6.2	6.3
of which: foreign direct investment	1.2	1.2	1.2	1.4	2.3	2.8
portfolio investment	0.0	0.0	1.1	0.6	0.7	0.8
Taiwan: Net Private Capital Inflows[b]	−1.2	−3.2	−2.1	−0.6	−3.6	−3.2
of which: foreign direct investment	−0.3	−0.5	−0.7	−0.5	−0.4	−0.7
portfolio investment		0.2	0.5	0.4	0.2	−0.4
Korea: Net Private Capital Inflows	2.2	2.4	1.6	3.1	3.9	4.9
of which: foreign direct investment	−0.1	−0.2	−0.2	−0.3	−0.4	−0.4
portfolio investment	1.1	1.9	3.2	1.8	1.9	2.3
Malaysia: Net Private Capital Inflows	11.2	15.1	17.4	1.5	8.8	9.6
of which: foreign direct investment	8.3	8.9	7.8	5.7	4.8	5.1
portfolio investment	n/a	n/a	n/a	n/a	n/a	n/a
Philippines: Net Private Capital Inflows	1.6	2	2.6	5	4.6	9.8
of which: foreign direct investment	1.2	1.3	1.6	2	1.8	1.6
portfolio investment	0.3	0.1	−0.1	0.4	0.3	−0.2
Singapore: Net Private Capital Inflows	1.7	−2.7	9.4	2.5	1.3	−10.1
of which: foreign direct investment	8.8	2.1	5.5	4.8	4.9	4.3
portfolio investment	−2.1	3.3	0.5	1.1	0.9	−16.2
Thailand: Net Private Capital Inflows	10.7	8.7	8.4	8.6	12.7	9.3
of which: foreign direct investment	1.5	1.4	1.1	0.7	0.7	0.9
portfolio investment	0.0	0.5	3.2	0.9	1.9	0.6

Notes: [a]As well as foreign direct investment (FDI) and portfolio investment, official financing and private sector borrowing contribute to a country's capital inflows

[b]A negative sign indicates an outflow of capital from the country

Source: IMF, "World Economic Outlook: Interim Assessment", December 1997 Table 1

into another in the region reduces transaction costs and risks, and can be expected to promote trade and investment.

The ASEAN plus three countries (China, Korea, and Japan) have established the Chiang Mai Initiative (CMI) after the Asian Financial Crisis, to provide surveillance over financial and currency market developments and facilitate currency swaps that may be deemed necessary. The countries in the region have, however, stopped short of proposing anything like a monetary union, which is deemed unrealistic given the cultural, economic, social, and political diversity of the countries. For most of the countries giving up monetary independence is too heavy a price to pay, and in practice it is difficult to think of a central banker who can command the trust from everyone. Yet this has not prevented the proposal of the currencies pegging to a common anchor. One such proposal was made by Ogawa and Kawasaki (2006).

A BENCHMARK CURRENCY BASKET AS A COMMON ANCHOR

Ogawa and Kawasaki (2006) used the Dynamic Ordinary Least Squares to estimate the cointegrating vector for ASEAN plus three currencies with the currency basket consisting of the US dollar and the euro. They found that the Japanese Yen should be included as an endogenous variable in the long-term relationship as well as other East Asian currencies while the Japanese Yen worked exogenously as well as the euro and the US dollar in the system composed of the East Asian currencies, suggesting that including the Yen in the currency basket makes a lot of sense. They tried to estimate the weights endogenously.

Estimating weights endogenously has the advantage that no prior judgment or assumption was necessary, and that such weights are determined empirically and so "apolitical". The disadvantage is that the weights have to be determined after the fact, and will depend on the econometric model used. Ho (2010b) argued for using GDP weights along the lines of a gravity model: in the final analysis a bigger country tends to import more, either directly or indirectly. In a world with production fragmentation, traditional trade weights are notoriously misleading, especially for such countries as China which export a lot of goods using intermediate goods imported from elsewhere.

Apart from using GDP weights, which will be explained in greater detail in a moment, the proposed basket includes in addition to the US dollar, the euro, and the Yen, also the British pound, the Canadian dollar, and the Australian dollar. The Canadian dollar and the Australian dollar are often regarded as commodity-related currencies, given that Canada and Australia are key commodity exporting countries. The British pound has a long history as an international currency, and Britain has always been an important trader in the world. Ho (2000) had proposed the "World Currency Unit" as a basket of GDPs of the United States, the Euro zone, Japan, the UK, Canada, and Australia. Ho (2010a) demonstrated that this is equivalent to a basket of currencies each indexed against inflation. Ho (2010b) also demonstrated that the unindexed basket of currencies can serve as a benchmark against which the effective exchange rate of any currency can be measured, using the following formula:

$$\mathrm{RER}(iw) = \frac{e_i'}{e_w'} \tag{1}$$

where e_i' is the "*normalised* exchange rate of currency i against the US dollar" while e_w is the "exchange value of the basket of *normalised* currencies against the US dollar". Here "normalisation" means scaling up or down a currency's exchange rate by dividing with its exchange value against the US dollar in the base year. Normalisation will ensure that the exchange rate of any currency i against the US dollar is 1:1 in the base year.

One can make a case to include the Chinese RMB in the currency basket, but since the RMB is presently not yet a fully convertible currency, and because there are still price controls in China, it is believed that including the RMB in the basket should wait until the time when China lifts all price controls and allows full convertibility of the currency. As it turns out, experiments that include the RMB in the basket do not show an obvious improvement in the statistical results.

The benchmark basket of currencies is GDP weighted, using the following formula:

$$\sum_i \frac{\mathrm{GDP}_{i(T-2)} \cdot e_{i(T-2)}}{\Sigma \mathrm{GDP}_{j(T-2)} \cdot e_{j(T-2)}} \cdot \frac{e_{it}}{e_{i0}} \tag{2}$$

Here, $\frac{e_{it}}{e_{i0}}$, otherwise written as e_i', as in (1), is the normalised exchange rate of currency i against the US dollar. 0 is the base year.

Table 4. Explaining Exports with the Relative Exchange Rate

	Cointegrating vector			VECM result	
Country	Ln EX	Ln of exchange rate index	LnGDP	ECM(−1)	R^2
Thailand	1	0.6477 (2.9916)**	−1.9537 (−7.7566)***	−0.1484 (−2.5353)**	0.2955
Korea	1	1.2474 (6.0682)***	−2.1530 (−1.3829)	−0.1139 (−1.6120)	0.5342
China#	1	4.3086 (17.7025)***	−7.6317 (−42.7569)***	−0.0971 (−2.8612)**	0.5094
Hong Kong	1	2.9430 (8.1059)***	−2.8210 (−16.223)***	−0.1159 (−5.6299)***	0.3362

Notes: ** and *** indicate Significance at 5% and 1% respectively
#A dummy variable for the Asian financial crisis was added in VECM model. This "dummy" variable is a non-binary variable computed as the difference between the 12-month forward exchange rate against the US dollar and the spot exchange rate of the HK dollar, normalised to stay between 0 and 1. The presumption is that when the discount was the highest market sentiments were highest for the HK dollar to depreciate. This is assumed to be exactly the time when the currency crisis was at its height. RE: Relative Exchange Rate Index, 2000 = 100, CPI-based; LnEX: Log of total exports of goods and services of Hong Kong/China, current price; LnGDP: Log of OECD GDP Volume Index, 2000 = 100

As can be seen in the formula, we use the GDP of 2 years ago as the weights for the currency basket.

Ho (2010b) has demonstrated that the effective real exchange rate computed using this benchmark basket actually performs remarkably well compared to those published by other international agencies in explaining real exports for the US, the UK, the Euro zone, and Japan. Table 4 shows that the effective exchange rate index also explains total exports very well in a long term cointegrating relationship, for Thailand, Korea, for China, and Hong Kong. Ln GDP is the logarithm of the GDP volume index for OECD countries. In this table, however, we use nominal values and the nominal effective exchange rate, in part because trade volume figures or deflator figures are not readily available, and in part because we want to demonstrate that the unindexed currency basket as defined in equation (2) is a good target to peg against, since pegging a currency against this benchmark currency basket is tantamount to stabilising the effective exchange rate, which counts so much in determining a country's total exports.

The proposal of pegging against a currency basket as opposed to pegging against a single currency has sometimes invited skepticism. There is little doubt that pegging against a single currency is easier than pegging against a currency basket. But as Ho (1990) and Williamson (1996) argued, Hong Kong may simply start to trade US dollars for Hong Kong dollars at a price that would vary depending on the value of the US dollar in the foreign exchange markets vis-à-vis the other currencies in the basket, instead of at a fixed rate. Ho proposed to use the US dollar as the instrumental currency to bring about the intended peg, just as Williamson did. Ho argued that there is advantage in having a transparent currency basket, because then arbitrageurs will actually help bring about the intended peg promptly, as they know that any deviation would trigger the monetary authorities to close the gaps eventually by buying and selling US dollars.

The experience in Hong Kong made it very clear that pegging against the US dollar may cause overheating sometimes and economic stagnation at other times. In 1985, with Hong Kong dollar appreciating along with a very strong US dollar, Hong Kong's exports were very weak, and the economy was on the verge of a recession. In the 1987–91 period, the US dollar was weak, and the Hong Kong economy boomed, with the unemployment rate falling below 2% from 1987–91 and inflation rate at double digit levels from 1989–92. Pegging against a currency basket helps avoid overheating the economy as well as chances of recessions due to an excessively strong currency undermining competitiveness of exports.

To the extent that countries in the region all peg their currencies to a common anchor, the bilateral exchange rates between any pair of countries will be quite stable. This should be favourable to trade and investment and regional integration. Presently, the Centre for Public Policy Studies at Lingnan University is providing daily quotations of the benchmark currency basket at http://www.ln.

edu.hk/cpps/wcu/wcu.php. For example, on April 26, 2010, the benchmark basket with base year 2005 was worth US$1.052770. The currency as a whole has appreciated 5.28% against the US dollar since 2005.

TRANSITION AND PEGGING AT THE RIGHT LEVEL

It is important to set the exchange rate at a "realistic" level, one that is consistent with the macroeconomic fundamentals of the country. This is the level such that, combined with the domestic interest rate, it is possible to achieve full employment and fiscal budget balance (Ho, 2006). Given the interest rate and inflation expectations, asset price levels, and market sentiments, currency appreciation would undercut aggregate demand by reducing foreign demand, while currency depreciation would stimulate aggregate demand by increasing foreign demand. In principle, if private demand is too weak for full employment, it is possible to increase public sector demand by expansionary fiscal policy. The balanced budget requirement at full employment makes sure that the full employment equilibrium is sustainable.

Suppose at time *t*, the exchange rate against the US dollar is e_{it}. Suppose full employment requires that the exchange rate be at $\alpha_i e_w$. Suppose $\alpha_i e_w > e_{it}$. Then there will be a need for a one-time depreciation of the currency against the US dollar. Alternatively, the depreciation can be introduced in phases. Once the level $\alpha_i e_w$ has been reached, the currency may rise or fall against the US dollar, but should remain pegged to the US dollar, until there is a change in economic fundamentals that may then warrant a currency appreciation or depreciation.

The main case for pegging against the currency basket is that this way the effective exchange rate of the currency will not drift up or down simply because the anchor currency drifts up or down.

But in the regional context, having a common anchor currency basket implies intra-region exchange rate stability. Given the theory and the evidence following the launch of the euro, we can expect increasing trade and investment in the region, as well as stronger ability to withstand speculative attacks.

CONCLUSIONS

Back in 1996, Williamson observed that "there is [a] problem that is common to a number of the East Asian countries, which is the instability of the effective exchange rates of the East Asian currencies... 6 of the 8 currencies are more unstable in nominal effective terms than in terms of the dollar, and in most cases the instability of the real effective rate is (somewhat) greater still. One way of curing this problem would be for each of the East Asian countries to peg its currency unilaterally to a trade-weighted basket. But, since the trading patterns of the East Asian countries differ, the currency baskets would differ between countries".

This chapter has dealt with this problem by adopting a GDP weighted currency basket rather than a trade-weighted basket. Given the extent of vertical trade among many APEC countries, trade weighted currency baskets are actually potentially misleading. To the extent that many of the exports from APEC countries are intermediate goods, pegging against a GDP weighted basket may actually work better because GDP is often the final "magnet" for imports, however indirect magnetic force may be.

It has been demonstrated that the GDP-weighted benchmark currency basket provides a convenient common anchor for currencies in the region to peg against and helps stabilise effective exchange rates. Pegging against a common currency basket can be done independently and at a level consistent with any country's economic fundamentals. Once the currencies are pegged to a common basket, intra-regional currency exchange rates will become stable, achieving to a large degree de facto currency integration.

This chapter does not advocate pegging to the inflation indexed basket which preserves purchasing power. Given that the currencies of other countries are not indexed against inflation, pegging against the inflation-indexed currency basket would hurt a country's competitiveness over the long run.

REFERENCES

Baldwin, R., DiNino, V., Fontagné, L., De Santis, R. A. and Taglioni, D. (2008). "Study on the Impact of the Euro on Trade and Foreign Direct Investment." Economic Papers 321, European Commission Directorate-General for Economic and Financial Affairs.

Berger, H. and Nitsch, V. (2008). "Zooming Out: The Trade Effect of the Euro in Historical Perspective." *Journal of International Money and Finance,* 27, 8, pp. 1244–1260.

China Daily, "Asian EU a 'Long Term' Goal." November 3, 2009.

Flam, H. and Nordström, H. (2006). "Euro Effects on the Intensive and Extensive Margins of Trade." CESIfo Working Paper No. 1881, December.

Glick, R. and Rose, A. K. (2002). "Does a Currency Union Affect Trade? The Time-Series Evidence." *European Economic Review,* 46, 6, pp. 1125–1151.

Ho, L. S. (1990). "A Proposal for an Adaptive Linked Exchange Rate System." *Hong Kong Economic Papers,* 20, pp. 89–96.

Ho, L. S. (2003). "Bringing about Realistic Exchange Rates: A Post Asian Financial Crisis Perspective." in L. S. Ho and C.-W. Yuen (Eds.), *Exchange Rate Regimes and Macroeconomic Stability.* Kluwer Academic Publishers.

Ho, L. S. (2006). "The Role of Fiscal and Monetary Policy." *Pacific Economic Review,* 11, 1, pp. 121–127.

Ho, L. S. (2010a). "The World Currency Unit: Has the Time Come for Its Use?" mimeo.

Ho, L. S (2010b). "Globalization, Exports, and Effective Exchange Rate Indices." Mimeo.

Kawai, M. (2008). "Toward a Regional Exchange Rate Regime in East Asia," *Pacific Economic Review,* 13, 1, pp. 83–103.

Muûls, M. and Pisu, M. (2007). "Imports and Exports at the Level of the Firm: Evidence from Belgium." Research Series 200705-03, National Bank of Belgium.

Nitsch, V. and Pisu, M. (2008). "Scalpel, Please! Dissecting the Euro's Effect on Trade." ETH Zurich and National Bank of Belgium.

Ogawa, E. and Kawasaki, K. (2006). "Adopting a Common Currency Basket Arrangement into the 'ASEAN plus three.'" RIETI Discussion Paper Series 06-E-028, June.

Rose, A. K. (2000). "One Money, One Market: The Effect of Common Currencies on Trade." *Economic Policy*, 30, April, pp. 7–45.

UK Parliament (1999). "The Asian Financial Crisis." Research Paper, 99/14.

Williamson, J. (1996). "The Case for a Common Basket Peg for East Asian Currencies." Paper presented to a conference on "Exchange Rate Policies in Emerging Asian Countries: Domestic and International Aspects", Association for the Monetary Union of Europe and the Korea Institute of Finance, November 15–16.

NOTES

* I thank Gary Wong and Owen Rui for research assistance.

1 Tables 1–3 are directly sourced from UK Parliament Research Paper 99/14.

8

On the Reform of RMB Exchange Rate: A Middle Ground Solution

Bin Zhang*

Chinese Academy of Social Sciences

Xiuping Hua

University of Sheffield

ABSTRACT

Just one year after the global financial crisis, the RMB exchange rate is under pressure to appreciate once again. For one thing, the domestic structural problems in the Chinese economy which are related to RMB exchange rate have not yet been solved; for another, expectation for RMB appreciation and speculative inflows of capital returns to China. The reform of the RMB exchange rate regime seems both necessary and inevitable. In this chapter we try to achieve three goals: (1) to provide a systematic evaluation of the current *de facto* dollar peg regime; (2) to evaluate the benefits and shortcomings of four different reform schemes on RMB exchange regime which are popular in debate on this issue; (3) to propose a middle ground solution to the reform of RMB exchange rate regime, which is capable of giving considerations to both macroeconomic stability and rebalancing of resource allocation between tradable and nontradable sectors. The middle ground solution includes: a one time 10% RMB appreciation against the US dollar accompanied by annual ±3% band against the US dollar. Now is a very good time for implementing the middle ground solution to the RMB exchange rate reform.

Keywords: RMB exchange rate reform; one-off appreciation; trade imbalances.

INTRODUCTION

China had started a gradual exchange rate reform since July 2005. But this process has stagnated since July 2008. To reduce uncertainty and help exporters weather a slump in demand triggered by the global financial crisis, China has effectively pegged the RMB at about 6.83 yuan to the dollar since then. At present, namely just one year after the global financial crisis, there is considerable debate at home and much international criticism of the current *de facto* dollar peg regime of RMB exchange rate. The RMB exchange rate faces pressure to appreciate once again. For one thing, the domestic structural problems in Chinese economy have not yet been solved; for another, expectation for RMB appreciation and speculative inflows of capital returns to China. The reform of the RMB exchange rate regime seems both necessary and inevitable.

This paper aims to achieve three goals: (1) to provide a systematic evaluation of the current *de facto* dollar peg system of RMB exchange rate; (2) to evaluate the benefits and shortcomings of four different reform schemes on RMB exchange regime which are popular in debate of this issue, namely (i) gradual appreciation within a narrow fluctuation band; (ii) pegging to a basket of currencies; (iii) real exchange rate appreciation through market oriented factor price reforms and accompanied by moderate inflation, while keeping existing nominal exchange rate fixed; (iv) coordinated basket peg system in East Asia or other exchange rate cooperation plans in East Asia; (3) to propose a middle ground solution to the reform of RMB exchange rate regime, which is capable of giving considerations to both macroeconomic stability and rebalancing of resource allocation between tradable and nontradable sectors. The rest of the paper is organized as follows. The next three sections examine issues concerned with these three goals, respectively, while the last section summarises and concludes.

AN EVALUATION OF THE CURRENT *DE FACTO* US DOLLAR PEG REGIME

Exchange rate is one of the most important prices in an open economy. Either realised adjustments or unfulfilled expectations in the exchange rate will affect imports and exports, consumer product prices and asset prices. An appropriate exchange rate formation mechanism is very important to maintain short-term macroeconomic stability. At the same time, the exchange rate is one of the key factors which determine relative prices of trade goods to non-trade goods. Rapidly changing productivity rates in a fast growing economy like China always require quick adjustments of relative prices of traded and non-traded goods to ensure a reasonable economic structure and avoid the risks of economic imbalances. From the perspectives of maintaining macroeconomic stability in the short run and sustainable economic growth in the long term, this section focuses on evaluating the benefits and shortcomings of current RMB exchange rate formation mechanism.

The evaluation from the macroeconomic stability perspective

Shortcomings

(1) Expectations for RMB appreciation, speculative capital inflows and shocks on aggregate demand

Continued mismatch between supply and demand in the foreign exchange market has led to expectations that the RMB would appreciate. Since 2002, due to many factors such as joining the WTO, a large-scale increase of foreign direct investment, a new wave of heavy industrialisation, and so on, China's trade goods sectors has expanded rapidly, which has greatly enhanced China's import substitution capabilities and accelerated exports. As a result, China's trade surplus has burgeoned dramatically. Pressure for the RMB appreciation in the international community had been triggered since 2003 and much talking had been swirling around the world on the RMB appreciation. Under pressure, China had started a gradual exchange rate reform since July 2005, but this process has stagnated since July 2008. To reduce uncertainty and help exporters weather a slump in demand triggered by the global financial crisis, China has pegged the yuan at about 6.83 per dollar since then. In the high time of global financial crisis, expectation on RMB appreciation was suspended.

The RMB appreciation expectations returned after the financial crisis and the pressure for RMB revaluation will continue to grow in the future. During the financial crisis, the expectations on the RMB appreciation had once disappeared. However, a weakening US dollar and China's impressive economic recovery in 2009 has renewed pressure on the RMB to appreciate. At present, this pressure has intensified with the improving situation of China's international balances (Table 1). On the one hand, growth in China's exports and imports in December 2009 exceeded expectations, and China's exports are now larger than those of any other country.[1] On the other hand, the financial crisis has put great pressure on global economic growth and employment. For instance, over the last two years 7 million jobs have been lost in the United States, including 85,000 in December 2009. In such a circumstance, China's managed exchange rate regime has caused many concerns among trading partners. In their view, the policy of keeping the exchange rate down is equivalent to an export subsidy and tariff, namely, to protectionism. If China keeps on refusing to revaluate the RMB, undoubtedly it will invite complaints from many countries that it is benefiting at their expense.[2]

The RMB appreciation is expected to affect aggregate demand through two channels. The first is to cause pressure on the money supply, which will lead to monetary expansion in case of insufficient sterilised intervention, and hence to stimulate the rises in asset prices and aggregate demand. The trade surplus, FDI surplus, and speculative capital inflows associated with RMB appreciation expectations, increase the imbalance between supply and demand in foreign exchange market. In order to maintain exchange rate stability, monetary authorities have to buy all the excess supply of foreign exchange in the market, which would increase the foreign currency assets of the monetary authorities as well as the corresponding domestic monetary supply. Since 2003, the growth in foreign currency assets has dominated the growth of base money. The growth rate of foreign exchange assets even exceeded the growth rate of broad money, which put much pressures on the monetary authorities to clamp down monetary growth. If the sterilised intervention measures cannot keep up, the money growth will be out of control. After the breaking out of the financial crisis, the growth rate of foreign currency assets has once fallen below that of broad money. However, in the future the growth rate of broad money will fall to normal levels and the short-term capital will re-enter China, and the money supply will soon be under severe pressure again.

Second, even if the monetary authorities has maintained a stable growth rate of broad money supply by successful sterilisation interventions, expectation for RMB appreciation itself will stimulate rises in asset prices and aggregate demand. Expectation on

Table 1. China's Monthly Short-Term International Capital Flows in 2009 (billion yuan)

Month	1	2	3	4	5	6	7	8	9	10	11	12
Increase in foreign currency reserves	−325	−14	417	551	806	421	430	362	618	557	605	104
Trade surplus	391	48	186	131	134	83	106	157	129	240	191	184
FDI	75	58	84	59	64	90	54	75	79	71	70	121
The valuation effect	−395	−107	195	36	252	50	19	93	102	94	62	−256
Short-term international capital inflows	−396	−13	−48	325	356	198	251	37	308	152	282	55

Source: Zhang Ming (2010) China's short-term capital flows in 2009, RCIF Working Papers, No. 2010004

RMB appreciation hits the capital market just like a major new technological revolution, altering expectations on relative return on assets. We may consider a situation that there are two main choices for residents in their portfolio. One is bank deposits with fixed interest rate; the other is risky assets with floating rate of return. Once RMB appreciation is expected, expected returns on those risky assets of non-traded goods sectors, such as real estate, will increase and risky asset price goes up. In this process, even if the broad money supply which is mainly composed of various deposits has not changed, the value of collateral will increase due to rising asset prices, which reduce the actual cost of loans to enterprises and residents, and hence stimulate aggregate demand. It is the so-called financial accelerator effect in Bernanke *et al.* (2000).

(2) US dollar exchange rate fluctuations, import price fluctuations, shocks on aggregate supply and demand

In the dollar peg exchange rate system, substantial fluctuations in the US dollar exchange rate will result in substantial fluctuations in the prices of imported goods. In the literature, one outstanding advantage of the pegged exchange rate regime is that it helps to maintain domestic price stability. But the validity of this argument is questioned in China. During the periods of volatile American economy and US dollar exchange rate, the dollar is not a good nominal anchor and the economies of those countries which chose a dollar peg may suffer from volatile fluctuations too. Figure 1 indicates that the prices of imported goods fluctuate with the nominal dollar exchange rate. It can be found in this figure that when the dollar's trade-weighted exchange rate fall around 10% between the end of 2007 and the middle 2008, the imported prices of Chinese imported goods increase 15%. It can be concluded in such a case, both trade conditions and price stabilities are facing severe shocks in China.

Fluctuations in prices of imported goods may affect the domestic aggregate supply and demand, and is one of the major explanatory factors of the domestic price fluctuations. Fluctuations in the prices of imported goods will change the relative prices of domestic products,

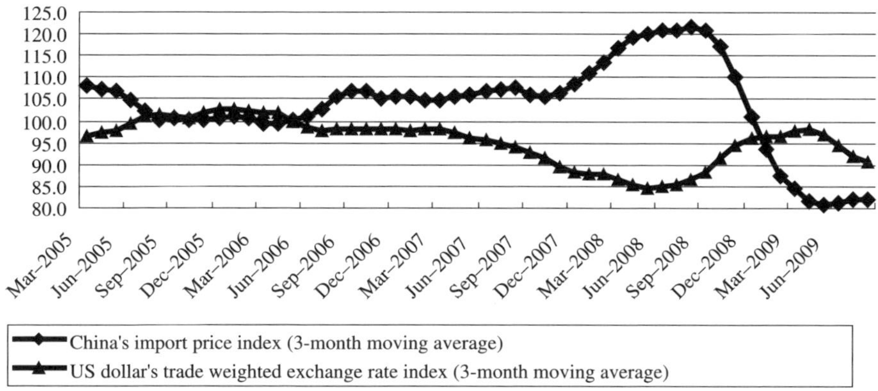

Figure 1. China's Import Prices and the US Dollar Trade-Weighted Exchange Rate (3-month moving average)

Source: CEIC

bring the adjustment to the supply side in a structural sense and change the levels of outputs and prices. Since both ratios of imports and exports to GDP and industrial added value to GDP are very high in China, the price fluctuations of imported goods have prominent effects on domestic prices. Figure 2 shows that the trends in China's domestic Producer Price Index (PPI) and the price index of imported goods are quite consistent. A more detailed research in Gao (2009) indicate that the correlation coefficients between prices of global commodity and China's domestic price index such as PPI and CPI are at quite high values.

Benefits

Pegging to the US dollar is thought to help maintain short-term trade and employment stability. But it may be just a misunderstanding. The competitiveness of export prices is determined by the exported trade-weighted exchange rate, and the costs of imported goods are determined by imported trade-weighted exchange rate. Either to keep competitiveness of exports or relatively stable costs of imports, the policy target shall not be to maintain the stability of exchange rate of RMB against the dollar.

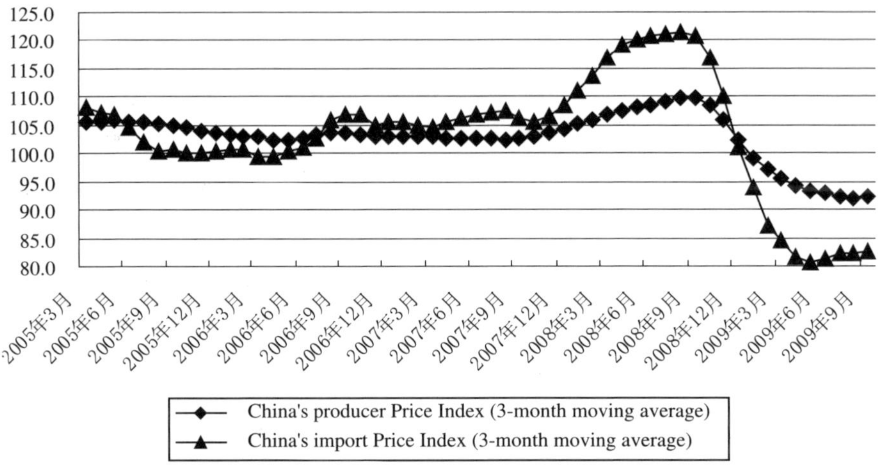

Figure 2. China's Import Prices and Domestic Producer Price Index (3-month moving average)

Source: CEIC

In fact, just as mentioned before, when the exchange rate of the US dollar against other major trading partners fluctuated severely, China's import and export, prices, aggregate supply and demand will face severe shocks.

As the Chinese enterprises generally use the US dollar as the invoicing and settlement currency, pegging to the US dollar is thought to help domestic enterprises to avoid exchange rate risks, but it is not accurate. By pegging RMB to US dollar, exchange rate risks that enterprises are faced have not disappeared, but have just became invisible. For example, an enterprise who exports to Europe employs the US dollar as the invoicing and settlement currency. Its European customers face the risks of exchange rate fluctuations between the dollar and the euro, and to hedge it, they sign a forward contract in the foreign exchange market. However, customers themselves may not bear all the hedging expenses, but would rather decrease the bid prices in the dollar. Hence the hedging costs actually do not disappear but seems invisible to Chinese enterprise, and who will cover such cost is ultimately determined by the bargaining power of Chinese and foreign parties.

Evaluation from the perspective of sustainable economic growth

Shortcomings

In the current dollar peg system, the RMB exchange rate cannot play the role of an effective price instrument to allocate domestic resources between traded goods and non-traded goods, and hence intensifies distortions in economic structure. There are obvious difference between economic fundamentals of the US and China, and the real effective exchange rate of RMB which is dominated by the US dollar effective exchange rate is difficult to adjust to meet the demands of domestic economic restructuring. Cheap RMB helps to maintain the competitiveness of traded goods and improve the employment in the trade sectors. But cheap RMB will hurt the competitiveness and job opportunities of domestic nontradable sectors. It is exactly what has happened in present China. Industry output which mainly comes from production of trade goods occupies a very high proportion of GDP, which is among the highest in the world. The output of service sectors, on the other hand, occupy a very low share of GDP which is not only far below than those of developed countries, but also lower than those of developing countries with similar levels of national incomes (Table 2). Much of industrial outputs cannot be consumed in the domestic markets and have to be exported to international markets. The service sector is also underdeveloped and many demands for better service in medical care, education, environmental improvement and transportations cannot be satisfied.[3]

Distorted development of traded goods sector relative to the non-traded goods sector have negative effects on distribution of income, employment, environment, natural resources, etc. Generally, service sector is much more labour-intensive than the industries. The relative underdevelopment of service sectors is associated with less job opportunities and lower share of labour compensation in national income. The newly added jobs in export industries, in particular those highly capital intensive industries like iron and chemical industry, due to cheap currency is far from able to make up the job losses in service sectors. Excessive influx of resources into more

Table 2. Comparison of the Industrial Structure Across Different Countries

	China	Low-income countries	Low-and middle-income countries	Average level in the world
Proportion of agriculture to GDP	15	25	12	4
Proportion of industrial to GDP	53	25	40	28
Proportion of service sector to GDP	40	50	48	68
Share of employment in service sector	33		33	

Source: World Development Indicators 2009 and China Statistical Yearbook 2009

environmental demanding industrial sectors make a large quantity of energy and environmental resources exported. Pan *et al.* (2008) have done some calculations based on input-output table and found that in 2002 China exports consumed around 240 million tons of standard coal, which accounted for 16% of primary energy consumption. It resulted in a net increase in domestic emissions of 150 million tons. Namely, when China accumulates trade surplus, it has also accumulated a large number of "ecological deficit".

Cheap currency helps expand the relative advantages of traded goods sector over those of foreign counterparts as well as domestic non-traded goods sectors, and hence protect their size. However, it does no good to technical innovations and industrial upgrading in such sectors. The process of currency appreciation hence will be a natural selection process of more innovative enterprises, since enterprises with more innovations in technology and managements will get much more development opportunities than those with less innovations. Recalling the experiences of Japan in the 1980s, it was exactly under tremendous pressure of currency appreciations that many Japanese enterprises with well-known brands chose to accelerate technological innovation and industrial upgrading, and hence laid a firm foundation for competitiveness in technology and management in the world.

Distorted exchange rate hampered other reforms in China as well, in particular reform of the capital account, as well as the increasing use of RMB internationally. Since the RMB is cheap, it is difficult to initiate the reform of capital account under the consistent unilateral expectations of RMB appreciation. Domestic enterprises would slow down their overseas investment and foreign investors would try to enter China. In such a circumstance the main task of capital account management is to guard against the negative impacts of speculative capital inflows, and further reform on China's capital account and financial liberalisation process will thus be delayed as well.

Benefits

At the early stage, the dollar peg mechanism helped to expand the size of industrial sectors and accumulated foreign reserves at an adequate level, which benefited technical developments and stable growth in investment. But such benefits have severely diminished at present. At the early stages of economic development, scale of economy plays an important role in putting forward industrial developments. At the same, a large quantity of investment goods is needed to be imported, and hence there is huge demand for foreign reserves. Competitive local currency helps to attract domestic resources to traded goods sector, to expand the scale of the industrial sectors, to improve quickly accumulations in technology and human capital, to contribute to accumulation of foreign exchange reserves, and hence to ensure steady growth of imports of investment goods and domestic investment. But after 30 years of fast developments, at present the overall scale of industrial sector is not that it is too small, but it is too large; the scale of foreign reserves far exceeds the needs for tackling the international balance of payments dilemmas.

THE EVALUATION OF DIFFERENT POLICY OPTIONS FOR RMB EXCHANGE RATE REFORM

This part turns to evaluation of benefits and shortcomings of four different policy options for reforming RMB exchange rate mechanism. They include (1) gradual appreciation of RMB within a narrow fluctuation band; (2) pegging to a basket of currencies; (3) real exchange rate appreciation through market oriented factor price reforms and accompanied by moderate inflation, while keeping existing nominal exchange rate fixed; (4) coordinated basket peg system in East Asia or other exchange rate cooperation plans in East Asia.

Policy option one: A gradual appreciation of RMB within a narrow fluctuation band

It is a policy choice which was actually the RMB exchange rate formation mechanism just before the outbreak of the financial crisis, namely the RMB exchange rate reform that occurred during the period from mid-2005 to mid-2008. It is somewhat similar to the BBC (Basket, Band and Crawl) regime. The last round of RMB exchange rate formation mechanism had exactly taken into account a basket of currencies, a fluctuation range, as well as a crawling trend. The main difference is that the C (crawling) in the BBC system is often adjusted according to differences in price levels at home and abroad, while China's exchange rate adjustment factors for the crawling trend had not been clearly explained and besides, a clear appreciation trend had showed in the operation. Based on the targets of the RMB exchange rate reform set by monetary authorities, the appreciation trend may be understood as moving closer to a reasonable and equilibrium exchange rate.

Benefits

(i) To achieve a gradual appreciation of the RMB, a slight improvement of the economic structure, and a slight alleviation of many structural problems impeding China's economic growth.

(ii) To introduce fluctuations of the RMB against the US dollar, to increase enterprises' and residents' awareness of hedging exchange rate risks, and to promote the developments of relevant financial products and market for hedging exchange rate risks.
(iii) During the period of rising commodity prices, exchange rate may be employed to alleviate imported inflation pressure.
(iv) To alleviate pressures in the international community partially.
(v) To increase the international community's demand for the RMB, and to increase the usage of yuan in neighbouring countries and regions.

Shortcomings

(1) To trigger consistent expectations on the RMB appreciation and a larger scale of speculative capital inflows, which may result in serious domestic asset price bubbles, as well as a certain degree of economic overheating and inflation risks. Hence it poses a great challenge to short-term monetary policy management and macroeconomic stability.
(2) To increase the uncertainty on profit forecasts of export sectors, to incur modest increase in the export prices in the international market and moderate decrease in import prices, and to bring short-term negative impact on those tradable sectors.

Policy option two: Pegging to a basket of currencies

Pegging to different currency baskets would bring different results. For instance, pegging to a basket of currencies based on import weights helps to maintain the stability of import costs and domestic prices, while pegging to a basket of currencies based on export weights helps to maintain the competitiveness of export. Here we considers the most commonly used way, namely to determine the weights of a currency by considering its import and export volume in China's total foreign trade volume.

Benefits

(1) In the context of the dollar depreciation, it helps to alleviate the dollar-driven depreciation of the RMB trade-weighted exchange rate. In comparison to the US dollar peg regime, it helps relieve the pressures coming from both speculative capital inflows and the international community. But it needs to be pointed out all these benefits are based on the context of the dollar depreciation. If the dollar appreciates, such benefits disappear.
(2) To maintain competitiveness of exports, and stabilise costs of imports and alleviate pressures of imported inflation.
(3) To introduce fluctuations of the RMB against the US dollar, to increase enterprises' and residents' awareness of hedging exchange rate risks, and to promote the developments of relevant financial products and market for hedging exchange rate risks.
(4) To increase the international community's demand for the RMB, and to increase the usage of yuan in the neighbouring countries and regions.

Shortcomings

(1) It is just another form of fixed exchange rate system. In such a regime, the exchange rate does not make automatic adjustment to the changes in domestic foreign exchange market. Given rapid changes in economic fundamentals behind China's foreign exchange market, the level of exchange rate cannot be sustained in the long run and will be associated with pressures from international community and speculative capital inflows in the short run.
(2) Exchange rate cannot be used as an instrument to rebalance the economy.

Policy option three: Substitute factor price reforms and a moderate inflation for exchange rate reform

The main content of this proposal is to adopt a serious of domestic reforms to substitute for exchange rate reform. Reforms include land policy reforms (such as restricting preferential policies enjoyed by industrial enterprises, and making changes in the current government monopoly model of land supply), energy price reforms (such as a more market-oriented price formation mechanism of electricity, water, oil), strengthening protection measures of workers' rights and interests (such as implementing the "Labour Law" more seriously), and other factor price reforms. All these reforms will improve on resource allocation and reduce trade imbalances. Therefore they may be taken as an alternative to exchange rate reform. Considering that reforms in factor prices will be associated with inflation, this proposal advocates tolerance of moderate inflation.

The above-mentioned reforms in the areas of production factors are very important for optimising resource allocation and reduce the imbalances in the domestic economy. However, they are not enough to replace the exchange rate reform. Conducting reforms on both fields of factor prices and exchange rate at the same time are most useful for changing current price distortions and imbalances in resource allocation.

Exchange rate reform is able to solve two problems. First, it is able to overcome one-way RMB appreciation expectations and hence reduces their macroeconomic shocks; second, it is capable of correcting relative price distortion between the traded and non-traded goods, which would avoid over-flow of resources to tradable sectors and ease the economic structure imbalance. It shall be pointed out that trade surplus is the most important factor among various economic fundamentals that support the RMB appreciation expectations, while the origin of trade surplus lies in the overflow of domestic resources to tradable sector. Therefore, the most fundamental goal that exchange rate reform shall achieve is to establish a rational incentive mechanism to direct reasonable allocation of resources between tradable and nontradable sectors.

Of course exchange rate reform is not the only instrument to adjust resource allocation between tradable and nontradable sectors. The establishments of clear property rights of production factors, market-oriented price formation mechanism and reducing monopoly in China's service sectors are also important.

However, reforms on factor prices cannot substitute for exchange rate reform. For example, under distorted exchange rate, even if China have implemented market-oriented reforms of energy prices, energy prices are still distorted since undervaluation of exchange rate would correspondingly result in overvaluation of domestic energy price. Therefore there is complementary relationship between factor price reforms and exchange rate reform, and both of them are important. If one important price is distorted, the other price will be distorted too. Distorted resource allocation follows.

If we have to sort out which one is more important, exchange rate reform may stand out. There are several reasons. First of all, exchange rate reform is more on target to reduce RMB appreciation expectations and international community pressures, which are crucial to maintaining near term macroeconomic stability. Second, it is more convenient to use and more effective in improving the distorted allocation of resources. Third, taking into the current inflation expectations account, exchange rate price reform also helps to curb inflation.

Benefits

It helps guide reasonable allocation of resources among various sectors, reduce the trade surplus, and alleviate many other related economic structural imbalances.

Shortcomings

(1) In the short term, there will be a negative impact on both output and employment in traded goods sector. The real exchange rate appreciation caused by either the nominal exchange rate appreciation (a drop in demand) or general increases in price levels (rising costs) mean profit losses of traded goods sectors, which are associated with structural adjustment of output and decline in employment.

(2) It is hard to achieve only a moderate level of inflation and hence monetary policy would face a very difficult situation in the reforms of factor prices. In particular when the initial inflation level is high, the effects of inflation expectations are hard to manage and the risks of serious inflation increase.
(3) Inflation may erode the real purchasing power of residents' wealth, and deteriorate the pattern of income distribution.
(4) Inflation increases uncertainties that enterprises and residents face in future investment consumption, and hence brought about the loss of output.

Policy option four: A coordinated basket peg system in East Asia or other regional exchange rate cooperation plans

In addition to the aforementioned policy options, many other options have been put forward by the international community for China to refer to. Some are based on regional exchange rate cooperation. Among them, the plan of "Common Currency Basket Peg" proposed by Williamson (1999) has been paid much attention. Another representative come from Eiji Ogawa, who advocates the ASEAN+3 (Japan, China, and Korea) to establish a Asian Currency Unit (ACU) as a weighted average of East Asian currencies and to maintain the exchange rate stability within the region by managing its own currency within the reasonable band around the ACU (Ogawa and Shimizu, 2005). Ogawa and Ito (2002) have also suggested that East Asian economies shall move to a basket currency regime based on their own traded weights. Wyplosz (2001) argues that East Asia may adopt a similar approach to that of the current European Monetary System (EMS) to build an Asian Monetary System (AMS). The common feature of these proposals is to maintain the stability of the regional exchange rate. For China, their benefits and shortcomings are quite similar to those of the second policy option discussed above, namely being pegged to a basket of currencies. For more discussions, please refer to Zhang (2006).

A MIDDLE GROUND SOLUTION TO THE REFORM OF RMB EXCHANGE RATE

The content of the middle ground solution

The middle ground solution to RMB exchange rate reform is detailed as the following two major points: (1) the yuan exchange rate against the US dollar is appreciated 10% one time; (2) after this 10% appreciation, the exchange rate fluctuate within an annual floating band of ± 3% against the US dollar.

A middle ground adjustment of exchange rate

(i) Due to the fast and immense structural change of the Chinese economy, it is very difficult to estimate a proper level of equilibrium RMB exchange rate. Several regular methods of computing equilibrium exchange rate as listed in Montiel and Hinkle (1999) are confronting substantial challenges in the application for estimation for equilibrium RMB exchange rate. The most commonly adopted method is the single equation model due to its simplicity. However, the issues of how to choose a proper real RMB exchange rate and how to choose analytical determinants according to specific patterns in Chinese economy, have not been sufficiently addressed in the literature so far. The empirical results are quite mixed as well. Besides, some partial equilibrium or general equilibrium models based on multiple equations encounter many challenges in data collection, model specification, and robustness of models, and it is quite difficult to reach convincing and agreed conclusions based on such models.

(ii) However, imbalances in the balance of international payments, supply and demand in the foreign exchange markets, and domestic economic structure suggest that the current exchange rate has departed from its reasonable level.

(iii) Appropriate RMB exchange rate adjustments should make the exchange rate move closer to its equilibrium level on the one hand, and should not produce too huge negative impacts on the macroeconomic stability in the short term.

(iv) The one-time 10% appreciation against the US dollar is able to achieve the goal of approaching to the equilibrium exchange rate,[4] but will not produce immense negative impact. There are a large quantity of studies on the impacts of exchange rate on GDP growth, imports and exports, employment, inflations and other important macroeconomic variables. But most of them have defects in data collections, model specification and reliability tests. Recent studies of Yao *et al.* (2009) and Cui and Su (2009) are among the most convincing ones. The former focuses on examining the relationship between export prices and exports, and concludes that export price elasticity is approximately –0.65, namely 1% raise in the export prices yields 0.65% decrease in export. The latter calculates the pass-through effects exchange rate and obtains a estimate of around 50%, namely 10% increase in the RMB trade-weighted exchange rate usually generate a 5% raise of export prices averagely.[5] If we combine the key findings of these two studies, we may conclude that if the RMB appreciates against the US dollar 10%, supposing that all other conditions remain unchanged, the nominal effective exchange rate will appreciate 10% too, and it will make export growth rate drop 3.3%. A scenario which is much closer to the reality is that when the RMB appreciates 10%, the currencies of most competing export countries, namely East Asian countries, may appreciate more or less. Hence the appreciation of the nominal effective exchange rate of RMB may be lower than 10% and the actual fall in China's export growth rate may be less than 3.3%.

A one-time 10% appreciation of the RMB against the dollar will not only produce shocks to exports, but also decrease import substitution. It will also decrease short-term investment,[6] slow down national economic growth, and lower domestic price levels. China did some kind of "stress test" and found that many firms would fail because their profit margins are very small. Even a 5% appreciation was said to eliminate many firms. The Chinese economy is forced to make structural adjustment after the global financial crisis. In the period of structural adjustment, it is unavoidable to have more bankruptcies and structural unemployment. For the sustainability of economic development, Chinese authority should make subtle balance between stability and development. Based on both international and domestic experiences, a fluctuation of 3–4% in export growth is not rare and will not make immense losses in term of job opportunities. If the economy remains at a normal level, such an export impact will not affect the growth of national economy, prices and employment seriously.

The market generally holds a relatively optimistic view of China's economic performance in 2010. The whole-year GDP growth rate forecasts made by the IMF and the World Bank are 9% and 8.7%, respectively. The estimates from other academic and financial institutions are generally between 9% and 11%. It indicates that China's economic growth has been back to the normal track or even confronted the danger of overheating. If we take other governmental supporting measures into consideration, it is concluded that China is capable of dealing with the shocks coming from exchange rate adjustment.

A trade-off solution to RMB exchange rate formation mechanism

(i) By introducing an annual floating band of ± 3% after one-off appreciation, the RMB exchange rate system transits to a "managed floating regime", which lies in between the two extremes, namely the fixed and freely floating exchange rate regimes. There are several aims for the ± 3% fluctuation band to achieve. The first one is to promote awareness of exchange rate risks of enterprises and residents, and hence prepares for further expansion in fluctuation band. The second is that such a fluctuation band may be employed to move closer to the equilibrium exchange rate. Based on international experiences and our calculations, a rapid growing economy like China's usually needs 3% appreciation in its real effective exchange rate per year. The third is to manage expectations. By permitting a ±3% fluctuation band, monetary authorities are able to curb excessive expectation on appreciation and hence to avoid their negative shock on economic stability.

(ii) A band of ±3% fluctuation, managed by monetary authorities, can be based on pegging to a basket of currencies. Given increasing importance of regional trade and investment in East Asia, monetary authorities may take consideration of some form of regional exchange rate cooperation in ASEAN+3 economies.

An evaluation of the middle ground solution to RMB exchange rate reform

"Middle ground" has two meanings. Firstly, it is a middle ground between 30–40% appreciation against the US dollar as was proposed by Bergsten (2010) and very limited appreciation against the US dollar or keeping existing rate unchanged which were proposed by many Chinese economists. Secondly, it is a middle ground between holdings to US dollar peg regime which we thought is not fit for existing economic situation and free floating regime which we thought will be associated with too much volatility and can hardly be introduced in the near future.

Benefits

(1) Through a one-time RMB appreciation against the dollar, it achieves an appropriate level of effective exchange rate which is closer to the equilibrium one. It helps to reallocate domestic resources between tradable and nontradable sectors, to reduce trade surplus and to adjust economic structural imbalances.

(2) To eliminate unilateral RMB appreciation expectations more thoroughly and to reduce the negative impact of speculative capital inflows.

(3) To respond positively to the challenges posed by the international community, and to help avoid trade wars.
(4) In the context of inflation, it helps to bring down inflation expectations as well as actual inflation.
(5) To introduce fluctuations in the RMB exchange rate against the US dollar, to promote awareness of exchange rate risks of enterprises and residents, and to promote the developments of relevant financial products and markets for hedging exchange rate risks.
(6) To increase the international community's demand for the RMB, and to increase the usage of yuan in the neighbouring countries and regions.

Shortcomings

(1) In the short run, it will produce negative shocks on exports, investment in tradable sectors, and short-term economic growth, which may also be accompanied by a small amount of frictional unemployment.

The timing of the compromise plan

Based on a number of reasons, we believe that now is a very good time for implementing the compromise plan of the RMB exchange rate reform.

(1) Due to maintaining a relatively loose monetary policy, the risk of asset price bubbles may be one of main negative shocks for the Chinese macroeconomy in 2010. Monetary authorities need to pay much effort to stop the RMB appreciation expectations and the corresponding shocks on monetary supply and adjustments of domestic assets prices.
(2) As international pressures on trade wars and RMB appreciations increase, to keep a friendly international economic environment and the global free trade system, China needs to take measures actively and positively.

(3) By adopting an expansionary fiscal policy and loose monetary policy, China has successfully spurred its economic growth. China has rebounded from the global slump with vigour and its GDP growth target in 2009, namely 8%, has been achieved. Besides, there is no deflation pressure in the near future. Therefore China is capable of dealing with adjustments in economic structure brought by the RMB appreciation. Negative shocks of a one time 10% RMB appreciation shall be limited and the macroeconomy will fluctuate in its normal range.
(4) The negative effects on potential economic growth of distortions in economic structure have intensified gradually. A series of reforms including exchange rate reform shall be conducted to adjust the domestic economic structure as soon as possible. Such reforms will lay a firm foundation for a healthy and sustainable economic growth.

SUMMARY AND CONCLUSIONS

Exchange rate policy plays a key role in protecting macroeconomics stability and adjusting economic structure in the current China. It differs from other policy measures in one crucial respect: it addresses simultaneously internal balance and external balance. In this chapter we evaluate benefits and shortcomings of China's current *de facto* dollar peg system and many policy options available for the RMB exchange rate reform.

We find that all things considered, a one time 10% RMB appreciation accompanied by an annual ± 3% band against the US dollar is better than the alternatives. It has many benefits, such as to reallocate domestic resources between tradable and nontradable sectors, to reduce trade surplus, to adjust economic structural imbalances, to eliminate unilateral RMB appreciation expectations more thoroughly, and to reduce the negative impact of speculative capital inflows, and so on. It has shortcomings as well. In the short run, it will produce negative shocks on exports, investment in tradable sector, and short-term economic growth, which may also be accompanied by a small amount of frictional unemployment.

We also conclude that now is a very good time for implementing the middle ground solution of the RMB exchange rate reform. The negative effects on potential economic growth of distortions in economic structure have intensified gradually. A series of reforms including exchange rate reform shall be conducted to adjust the domestic economic structure as soon as possible. Such reforms will lay a firm foundation for a sound economic recovery and sustainable economic growth.

REFERENCES

Bernanke, B., Gertler, M. and Gilchrist, S. (2000). "The Financial Accelerator in a Quantitative Business Cycle Framework." In J. Taylor and M. Woodford (Eds.), *Handbook of Macroeconomics.* Amsterdam: North-Holland, pp. 1341–1393.

Bi, Y. and Zhu, Z. (2007). "Pass-Through Effect of RMB Exchange Rate Movements on Export Prices of Chinese Goods." *World Economy* (Chinese), 5.

Chen, Y., Pan, J. and Xie, L. (2008). "The Energy Content of China's Import and Export Commodities and Their Policy Implications." *Economic Research* (Chinese), 7.

Cheung, Y.-W., Menzie, D. C. and Eiji, F. (2009). "China's Current Account and Exchange Rate." NBER Working Paper, No. 14673.

Cui, L., Chang, S. and Jian, C. (2009). "Exchange Rate Pass-through and Currency Invoicing in China's Exports." *China Economic Issues,* July, Hong Kong Monetary Authority.

Bergsten, F. (2010). "Correcting the Chinese Exchange Rate: An Action Plan." Testimony before the Committee on Ways and Means, US House of Representatives, March 24.

Gao, S. (2009). "Trends and Risks of Inflation." Round-Table Seminar No. 13 (Chinese), China Finance 40 Forum, September 29.

Montiel, P. J. and Hinkle, L. E. (1999). "Exchange Rate Misalignment: An Overview." In E. H. Lawrance and J. M. Peter (Eds.), *Exchange Rate Misalignment: Concepts and Measurement for Developing Countries.* New York: The World Bank, pp. 1–32.

Ogawa, E. and Junko, S. (2005). "A Deviation Measurement for Coordinated Exchange Rate Policies in East Asia." RIETI Discussion Paper Series, No. 17.

Ogawa, E. and Ito, T. (2002). "On the Desirability of a Regional Basket Currency Arrangement." *Journal of the Japanese and International Economies,* 16, 3, pp. 317–334.

Shi, J., Fu, X. and Xu, W. (2008). "Pass Through of the RMB Exchange Rate Movement on China's Price Level." *Economic Research* (Chinese), 7.

Williamson, O. (1999). "The Case for a Common Basket Peg for East Asian Currencies." In S. Collignon, J. Pisani-Ferry and Y. C. Park (Eds.), *Exchange Rate Policies in the Emerging Asian Countries.* London and New York: Routledge.

Wyplosz, C. (2001). "A Monetary Union in Asia? Some European Lessons." In D. Gruen and J. Simon (Eds.), *Future Directions for Monetary Policies in East Asia.* Reserve Bank of Australia.

Yao, Z., Tian, F. and Su, Q. (2009). "The Income Elasticity of China's Exports and Price Elasticity." working paper, International Finance Research Center at Institute of World Economic and Politics, Chinese Academy of Social Sciences (Chinese).

Zhang, B. (2006). "Exchange Rate Cooperation in East Asia: A Chinese Perspective." *World Economy* (Chinese), 5.

Zhang, M. (2010). "China Faced Short-Term Capital Flows in 2009." RCIF Working Papers (Chinese), No. 2010004.

NOTES

* Bin Zhang, Institute of World Economics and Politics at Chinese Academy of Social Sciences; China Finance 40 Forum; Email: bjzhangbin@gmail.com. Xiuping Hua, Management School at University of Sheffield; China Finance 40 Forum; Email: huaxiuping@gmail.com.

1. Though not necessarily in net value-added terms.
2. Even though this generally reflects largely the forces of domestic politics.
3. The scarcity in the service industry cannot fully be attributed to the distorted exchange rate, the administrative monopoly existing in many service sectors and insufficient supply of relevant public goods are among other important reasons for underdevelopment of service sectors.
4. The most recent study of Cheung *et al.* (2009) argues that the current exchange rate is undervalued around 10%.
5. The pass-though effect of exchange rate has been extensively studied in the literature, for instance Bi and Zhu (2007), Shi *et al.* (2009), and

so on. However, the model of Cui *et al.* (2009) does well in its robustness test. In general, most studies conclude that the pass-through effect coefficient lie between 30% and 70%, and it differs across different industries as well. In the surveys conducted by the author in Jiangsu Province, most representatives from export enterprises mentioned that 50% concession in prices has been a usually acceptable number for both sides of exporters and importers in negotiations since 2008.

6. The RMB appreciation will affect investments and employment in both directions. For the traded goods sector, the effects are negative, while for the non-traded goods sector, the effects are positive.

Part IV

The Future of APEC

9

Continuing the APEC Agenda and the Evolving Regional Institutional Architecture in the Context of an Emerging Asia

Khee Giap Tan & Shu Wen Chiang*

Singapore National Committee for Pacific Economic Cooperation

ABSTRACT

After the global financial tsunami of 2008 and economic recession of major developed economies in 2009, the growth engines of Asia, especially China and India, have recovered strongly. Mounting sovereign debts and national budget deficits in the west continued, however, to threaten the fragile global growth. Trans-Pacific trade imbalances, the role of the greenback as the principal reserve currency in the wake of a weakening Euro continued to draw attention and concern. Over the longer term, however, the focus of Asian policy makers should be inclusive growth and sustainable advancement and not economic growth per se. Rather, quality of life with attention to environmental protection and equitable progress through balanced regional development should carry more and more weight. Asian societies must ensure an adequate non-welfare type comprehensive social safety net and capacity building. In terms of evolving regional institutional architecture, the APEC-PECC nexus would continue to serve as the accepted, relevant and useful platform for pushing further the agenda for greater globalization in trade and deliberation on various reforms. At least half of the APEC-PECC members are also member of the G-20 Group. The former should reflect the voices and aspirations of those economies which are not members of G-20. The Global Governance Group which was initiated by Singapore in 2009 will help to strengthen governance for governments globally, especially for the smaller economies.

Keywords: Protectionism; APEC Agenda; Regional Institutional Architecture; Trans-Pacific imbalances; US dollar; export-oriented growth; managed float; world reserves; reserve currency; civil society; governance; corporate social responsibility; regional institutional architecture; G-2; G-20; PECC; inclusive growth; comprehensive social safety nets.

INTRODUCTION

The ongoing global economic restructuring has thrown open wide and deep dislocations with new opportunities and challenges in the rapidly growing Asia. This paper examines both newly identified trends and development in Asia, it also discusses the pertinent discontents about globalisation that have caused considerable imbalances within Asian economies and significant dissatisfaction amongst Asian workers.[1] On one hand, globalisation has undoubtedly led to massive wealth creation and reduced poverty in Asian economies, in particular China. However, there is also a strong urgency to promote "inclusive growth and development" in Asia that will allow a large part of its labour force to contribute — and benefit accordingly — from greater globalisation. This is essential in overcoming the widening income disparity and potential structural unemployment caused by rapid technological advancement.

The first section of this chapter addresses the following broad observations on pertinent issues in consideration for continuing the APEC agenda. These observations include the changing relative share of global gross domestic product (GDP) for major economies, the potential risks and challenges East Asian economies may face in the future. Recent macroeconomic policy initiatives such as the impact of massive fiscal stimulus, the escalating foreign exchange surpluses in East Asia which underscores the increasing trade imbalance between East and West and the role of the US dollar as a major reserves currency. The second section of this chapter considers an integrated approach that promotes balance, inclusive growth, balance and sustainable development for East Asian economies. This section examines the increasing need to study how the environment and globalisation share a symbiotic relationship in order to better understand the vision of sustainable growth. In particular, how East Asians could work to strengthen resiliency of their societies by further enhancing quality of life with the "correct" role of the government. Finally, the last section addresses the evolving regional financial architecture in the context of rising China with emphasis paid to the Asia Pacific context including the Pacific Economic Council of Cooperation (PECC), Asian Pacific Economic Council (APEC), Association of South East Asian Nations Plus (ASEAN+3/+6/+8), East Asian Community (EAC), Asia Pacific Community (APC), Group of 20 and the newly proposed global Governance Groups (3G).

Recent global economic recovery, the shift of economic dominance from East to West and developed economies' rising protectionism

In the wake of recovery from the 2008–2009 global financial tsunami, it was recently announced by the World Bank that the developing economies of East Asia will grow by 8.7% in 2010, a sharp rise in its forecast growth reflecting healthy recovery of global demand, facilitated by simultaneous and sustained fiscal and monetary stimulus in the region. This optimism was also further echoed in International Monetary Fund's (IMF) recent GDP forecast — it expects emerging Asian nations such as China and India to lead growth at around 10%, in contrast to an estimated expansion of 2.6% growth of the American economy.

It is observed that there has been a steady shift of economic power from the Western hemisphere to Eastern economies, especially since the new millennium. This trend is witnessed in Table 1 which shows the relative share of global GDP for major economies between the East and West. In terms of purchasing power parity (PPP) using GDP of the world as 100, it is observed that the share of global GDP by the East (i.e. 36% by summing up China, Japan and India) would be exceeding those of the West (i.e. 33.9% by summing up Europe and the US) for the first time by 2015 since the Second World War. In fact, the 21 members of PECC/APEC would account for up to 60% of the global GDP by 2015, according to estimates by the Asian Macroeconomic Studies Unit at the Lee Kuan Yew School of Public Policy at the National University of Singapore.

Despite Asia's growing relative share of GDP in comparison to the West, it is crucial to note that Asian economies were not spared during the 2008–09 global financial tsunami. Afterall, the global crisis had caused high levels of unemployment and led to business failures of many major corporations in the East Asian economies. Studies by the Asian Development Bank in 2009 has revealed that while there is decoupling of growth trends between East Asian and western developed economies, there is however no decoupling in terms of growth turning points, demonstrating substantial interdependency in international trade. In the midst of coping with this global financial tsunami, there appears the imminent risk of protectionism rearing its ugly head.

Although America is one of the leading champions of globalisation, she is preoccupied and is coping with domestic financial and economic difficulties as the Obama government stays committed to resist pressure of protectionism from within. Clearly trade protectionism has to be resisted as exports of the US to the Asia-Pacific

Table 1. Relative Shares of Global Gross Domestic Product for Major Economies

	1	1000	1500	1600	1700	1820	1870	1913	1950	1978	1995	2003	2015
China	25.4	22.1	24.9	29.0	22.3	32.9	17.1	8.8	4.6	5.0	10.9	15.1	23.1
India	32.0	28.1	24.4	22.4	24.4	16.0	12.1	7.5	4.2	3.4	4.6	5.5	7.2
Japan	1.1	2.7	3.1	2.9	4.1	3.0	2.3	2.6	3.0	7.7	8.4	6.6	6.0
	58.5	52.9	52.4	54.3	50.8	51.9	31.5	18.9	11.8	16.1	23.9	27.2	36.3
Europe	13.7	9.1	11.8	19.8	21.9	23.0	33.1	33.0	26.2	27.9	23.8	19.2	15.4
USA	0.3	0.4	0.3	0.2	0.1	1.8	8.9	18.9	27.3	21.8	20.9	20.6	18.5
Russia	1.5	2.4	3.4	3.4	4.4	5.4	7.5	8.5	9.6	9.2	2.2	3.8	5.2
	15.5	11.9	15.5	23.4	26.4	30.2	49.5	60.4	63.1	58.9	46.9	43.6	39.1

Source: Maddison 2007 & 2015 estimates are by Asian Macroeconomic Studies Unit at the Lee Kuan Yew School of Public Policy, National University of Singapore, Using PPP with the world as 100

region are based on high value-added goods and services such as electrical machinery, aircraft, medical equipment and knowledge-based businesses. As such, it is strongly reiterated in the 2009 APEC meetings in Singapore by Prime Minister Lee Hsien Loong that regional economic integration has to be at the core of the APEC agenda to further advance free trade and to open up markets in the Asia Pacific region. Therefore APEC's continued role and responsibility must be to uphold its core mission which is to accelerate free trade, promote investment liberalisation and enhance regional integration in human and natural resources among its members.

Besides the threat of protectionism, developing nations in Asia have encountered head on with unintended consequences of globalisation and undesirable outcomes of international integration such as the worsening income disparity, sector-base economic instability being exacerbated by lowly paid jobs, rapid appreciation of land prices and property assets bubbles. This unbalanced and unsustainable growth strategy between urban and rural areas exposes the longstanding social vulnerability especially for China and India, as this is further exacerbated by a mismatch of technical skill sets. Additionally, social safety nets in Asia remain somewhat unsatisfactory due to poor retirement benefits systems, increasingly expensive education and healthcare as public goods — these issues signal for urgent public policies that requires a proactive role from the government. It is therefore crucial to increase investment expenditures in social protection and safety programmes in Asia before it potentially compounds further the structural unemployment problem in the region.

Implications of massive fiscal stimulus, mounting sovereign debts and national budget deficits in the West

In the wake of the global financial meltdown, aggressive fiscal stimulus measures have been implemented to restore economic growth and increase aggregate demand. For instance, the US has spent US$292 billion in a massive fiscal stimulus with the latest sovereign debt now ballooning and reached in excess of 90% of her GDP in a massive fiscal stimulus package. However, this is simply not sustainable in the long–run unless there is a strong commitment to exercise strict discipline from major economies to gradually reduce the size of fiscal deficits. Such concerns are especially evident for European economies as we are being reminded the explosive consequences of such concerned situations in Iceland, Greece, Spain and Portugal.

Moreover, there is a potential threat of medium term global inflationary pressure due to the substantial amount of fiscal and monetary stimulus as proposed by major economies in the world. It has been estimated that the US budget deficit would hit US$1.5 trillion or bigger than 10% of the GDP in 2010. President Obama has announced his commitment to steadily reduce the budget deficit to US$533 million or 3% of the GDP by 2013 when his term ends. We may similarly expect governments of other major economies to begin exercising fiscal discipline. If not, it is expected that public debt will continue to rise steadily in advanced economies. More specifically, G-20 economies debt levels are expected to increase to close to 120% of GDP — up from about 80% of GDP before the crisis as revealed by IMF in July 2009. This increase in deficits and debt may lead to complicated tradeoffs in the future as policymakers try to balance two competing risks: on one hand, a quick withdrawal of fiscal stimulus may prove to be insufficient in restoring economic growth. On the other hand, a delayed withdrawal may cause investors' concerns of sustainability and undermine the recovery instead.

Additionally, recent losses incurred by sovereign wealth funds (SWFs) in the aftermath of the 2009 global financial meltdown do have serious implications on international financial institutions, corporate trade financing and the pace of economic recovery due to the limited resources of the IMF as demand for assistance by troubled economies continue to rise. Hence, it is suggested that cross-country direct investments in infrastructure and commitments in longer-term financial resources by SWFs to emerging economies to release production bottlenecks may be a win-win solution in terms of financial returns and growth sustainability.

Is the export-oriented external demand-driven East Asian growth model obsolete?

Due to the simultaneous economic contractions in Europe, North America and Japan's export markets, high growth East Asian economies such as China, Hong Kong, Chinese Taipei, Malaysia, Korea, Singapore and Thailand have experienced serious economic repercussions and unemployment disruptions. As a result, there are increasing concerns on, and some quarters even questioned, the continued relevance of the East Asia's export-oriented and external demand-driven growth strategy. The argument that the resiliency of East Asian exports is due to its undervalued local currency is increasingly less valid as exchange rate regimes in East Asia have substantially moved towards a more managed-floating system as determined by the market, and that is linked to a trade-weighted basket of currencies, with the exception of Hong Kong.

Moreover, in the absence of a viable international financial architecture, East Asian governments may have built up foreign exchange reserves since 1997 as an insurance against potential currency speculative attacks. This second-best strategy or experience is further reinforced in the wake of the 2009 global financial meltdown. East Asian economies have to be extra cautious with their management of foreign reserves. As such, the correct external demand-driven export-oriented growth strategy practiced by East Asian economies primary serves to reduce prevailing poverty, raise standard of living through improved education, lay down a strong economic foundation and strengthen sustained purchasing power for her people in order to meet challenges in the competitive globalisation environment. In the aftermath of the 2009 global financial meltdown, it is evident that the ensuing East Asian strategy must be rebalanced and be fine-tuned for longer-term model sustainability and be viewed as an interim means to achieve the ultimate end of stimulating the consumption-driven domestic demand which would serve to enhance greater intra-Asian trade.

We are thus convinced that East Asian export-oriented growth strategy is consistent with trade globalisation and wealth creation.

However, it may require urgent and major fine-tuning. This refers to the need to correct trade over-dependence, enhance social resiliency and the quality of life for its people. The ability to efficiently organise factors of production, significantly improve infrastructure such as transportation, telecommunications, logistics and ports will ensure East Asia's competitive advantage in its export sector.

Hence, there is a pertinent need to consider both push and pull factors in reviewing the growth model, instead of re-inventing or re-formulating a new growth model. More specifically, in order to improve resiliency of East Asian's export-oriented growth model, trans-pacific trade imbalances have to be addressed which were brought about by nations pursuing often conflicted policies. Accordingly, there must be a strong desire to stimulate domestic consumption through enhancing resiliency of Asian societies and quality of life for her hard working people which would be deliberated in the next section.

Trans-Pacific imbalances and the role of the greenback as a major reserves currency in the wake of weakening euro

There has been an increasing trans-Pacific global imbalance in terms of accumulated foreign exchange reserves and national savings with no wealth creation by US households whose household debts have outstripped personnel income. As it can be seen in Table 2, all these Asian economies hold a total of more than $3300 billion, half of the world total foreign exchange reserves! Such imbalances are not healthy and clearly unsustainable in the long-run especially as ability to absorb East Asian exports by the US and European counterparts are unlikely to be robust as these economies attempt to continue or struggle with reducing their national debts in a big way. Recent trends, however, indicate that overseas public and private investors are showing nervousness by switching from US longer-term government bonds to safer short term US treasury bills

Table 2. Foreign Exchange Reserves in East Asia

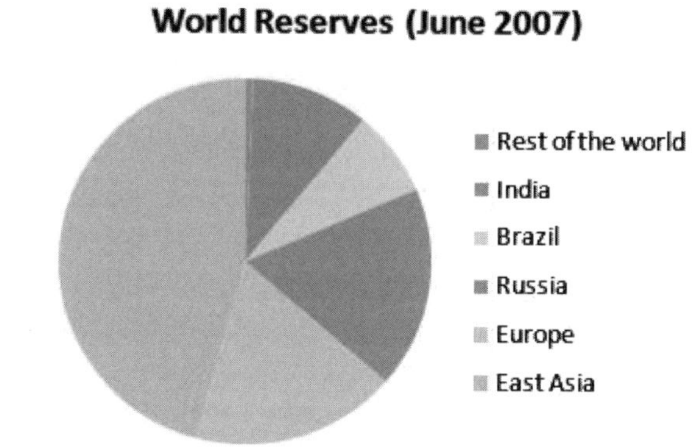

Rank	Country	Reserves (millions of USD)
—	World (Sum of all countries)	$6, 561, 594
1	Mainland China	$1, 433, 600
2	Japan	$954, 480
5	Taiwan	$265, 920
6	South Korea	$257, 290
8	Singapore	$152, 450
9	Hong Kong	$140, 800
12	Malaysia	$98, 230
16	Thailand	$82, 600
33	Philippines	$32, 400
48	Vietnam	$20, 000
62	Macau	$11, 100
110	Cambodia	$1, 385
122	Myanmar	$932
136	Laos	$317

Source: IMF International Financial Statistics

due to uncertainty in the recent mounting debt crisis in quite a few European economies.

As summarised in Table 3, the position of the greenback as the top reserve currency has been steadily challenged by the rise of the euro and that of the Japanese Yen. However, moving forward, such

Table 3. The Role of USD, USD as a Natural Monopoly

Currency	1999 (%)	2000 (%)	2001 (%)	2002 (%)	2003 (%)	2004 (%)	2005 (%)	2006 (%)	2007 (%)
USD dollar	70.9	70.5	70.7	66.5	65.8	65.9	66.4	65.7	63.9
Euro	17.9	18.8	19.8	24.2	25.3	24.9	24.3	25.2	26.5
Sterling pound	2.9	2.8	2.7	2.9	2.6	3.3	3.6	4.2	4.7
Japanese yen	6.4	6.3	5.2	4.5	4.1	3.9	3.7	3.2	2.9
Swiss franc	0.2	0.3	0.3	0.4	0.2	0.2	0.1	0.2	0.2
Other	1.6	1.4	1.2	1.4	1.9	1.8	1.9	1.5	1.8

Source: IMF International Financial Statistics

trends may now be halted or reversed, given the recent 2009 economic debacles of the UK and European economies, and continued economic stagnation of the Japanese economy. As larger amount of the greenback is aggressively made available to the global economy since 2009, the global demand for the dollar is ironically not reduced given that there is no good alternative, notwithstanding her own domestic financial and economic difficulties! Hence, it appears that the status of the greenback as a natural monopoly as the world's top reserve currency has not changed at least for the time being, although China has begun since 2009 to build the foundation for the regionalisation of the RMB. China's capital account is unlikely to be liberalised in the medium term, and we believe that it will take a few decades before the RMB currency is be considered and fully accepted as an international reserve currency.

Following, cash-rich Asian SWFs may well be persuaded to purchase sovereign and corporate bonds from economies and companies in financial difficulties — as this could be guaranteed by international agencies such as the IMF and ADB potentially with Japan and Singapore playing a leading role. In fact this approach had been adopted in a smaller scale during the 1997 Asian financial crisis, and perhaps should be explored and considered on a bigger scale.

Inclusive growth and sustainable development for East Asia: Quantitative, quality and equitable progress

There has been substantial literature published on the increasing pollution to the environment which has impacted on the quality of air and water due to the rapid economic growth witnessed in emerging economies in East Asia. Accordingly, it is crucial for quantitative measures of performance such as GDPs to be balanced by qualitative measures in order to preserve our common environment. The explosive growth for poorer economies and declining population amongst wealthy economies in Asia would not be beneficial to economic integration and cross-generation tax burden either. This would lead to the deterioration of quality of life and worsen the income disparity in East Asia.

As such, on a regional level, the vision of inclusive growth with income equity and quality of life could only be effectively achieved through experience-sharing and peer reviews. A more focused and coordinated regional discourse to adapt structural reforms and harmoniously integrate East Asian economies is on the agenda. On the national level, East Asians can enjoy a better quality of life with the presence of an established comprehensive social security system that is sensitive to its peoples' needs and must also cover affordable retirement benefits, health care, public housing, quality education and skills upgrading.

The symbiotic relationship between environment and globalisation: How Do They Interact?

We now turn to the question of how the environment and globalisation interact through three different means of influences — the economy, knowledge and governance. More specifically, this integrated framework reveals all aspects of the climate change problem interact mutually. Figure 1 depicts the cycle from the "underlying driving forces of population, economy, technology and governance through greenhouse gas and other emissions, changes in the physical climate system to adaptation and mitigation, and back to the driving

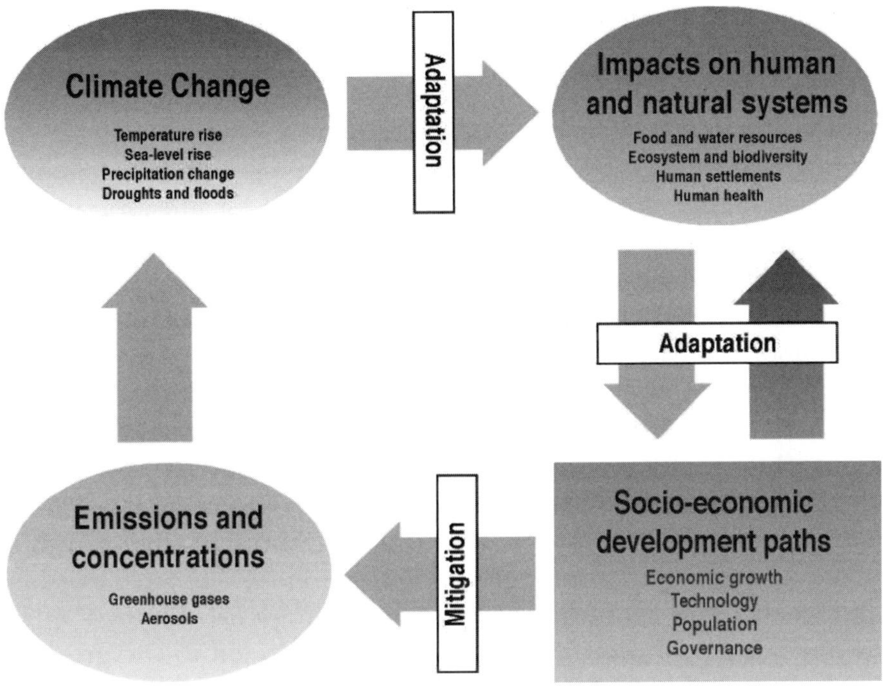

Figure 1. How Do Environment and Globalisation Interact? Climate Change — An Integrated Framework

Source: International Panel on Climate Change, www.ipcc.ch

forces". In other words, changes in one part of the cycle influence other components in a "dynamic manner, through multiple paths".

Firstly, the economy as a means of influence serves as a development pathway to reveal how globalisation affects the environment. For instance, the scale of economic activities and consumption will increase the allowance for more dispersed externalities. Newly developed or developing countries can benefit from globalisation and rely on limited energetic resources to grow, especially in China and India. Technological advancement on techniques to extract more from nature can assist countries in becoming cleaner. On the other hand, the environment also affects globalisation — for example, natural resources scarcity and/or abundance are drivers for globalisation as they incite supply and demand forces in global markets. Next, the need for environmental amelioration can extract costs from economy and siphon resources away from development goals.

The second means of influence is "knowledge" in which globalisation affects the environment in the following ways. For instance, through knowledge transfer and sharing among nations, globalisation has helped spread and encourage quality of life aspirations. Global interactions also facilitate exchange of environmental knowledge and best practices. Next, civil society movements help increase awareness of climate change. On the other hand, information about environmental stress and environmentally friendly technology now travel rapidly in a compressed world, and environmentally degraded locations are marginalised. There is a rising demand for material pursuits and for alternative energy.

The third means of influence is through "governance" — globalisation has impacted the environment through the growing demand and need for a global regulation to enforce existing agreements and build upon countries' synergies to improve environmental performance. Globalisation has also led to the growing involvement of a diverse group of participants from all over the world which has in turn stimulated the quality of environmental discourse. On the other hand, the environment has also affected globalisation as environmental standards influence patterns of trade and investments nationally and internationally. Secondly, stakeholders' participation in environmental governance such as various NGOs and civil society has led to a demand for greater corporate social responsibility (CSR).

Potential reform measures for a non-welfare base comprehensive social safety net and capacity building in knowledge-based economies for Asia

One of the major factors that accounted for the relatively higher private sector savings amongst Asians as compared to their Western counterparts is the lack of basic and adequate social safety nets available to them. Hence, there is a strong need for Asians to have sufficient savings for affordable healthcares or other welfare services by bailing in the private sector. In the same vein, it is important to note that East Asian economies must avoid the slippery road of welfare states such as the model Japan has embarked upon which has now proven to be a heavy burden to the state and could be politically irreversible.

There are successful examples of functioning non-state sponsored or co-payment systems between employers and employees for healthcare services, unemployment insurance and wage-based tax credit schemes in Asia, such as those being practiced in Singapore, Malaysia and South Korea, could well be examined and can be adapted to reflect local needs. Once basic and adequate social security system are being adequately taken care of and mature over time, private consumption can expect to rise steadily as those advanced economies which constitutes to at least 60% of their GDP. This rise in private consumption would then mitigate the vulnerability of the external-demand driven and overly export-dependent East Asian model.

The strength and competitiveness of a society can only be achieved through the resiliency of its people, and a comprehensive affordable quality education system that enhances individuals' capability is a pre-requisite for an innovation-led development and knowledge based-economy. Affordable quality education has thus emerged in the forefront of the continuing APEC agenda, especially for China as a leverage means for upward social mobility and meritocracy. In rapidly growing East Asian economies with swift property appreciation, one effective way to ensure equitable growth is through the introduction of affordable public housing scheme which could see its value appreciate in conjunction with consistent expansion of the economic pie over time.

Affordability is the key word, and the overriding agenda for APEC in the coming decade must be a study of relevant experiences in search of a better model of comprehensive social coverage in terms of bailing in private sector for healthcare services for elderly care, decent welfare supports for those who have lost the ability to compete, providing affordable education to reduce illiteracy and up-skill technical contents in preparation for intensifying globalisation. Finally affordable public housing for the majority would mitigate the income disparity brought about by rapid economic growth and imbalance rural-urban development.

Evolving regional institutional architecture: PECC, APEC, East Asian Community & Asia Pacific Community

Japanese Prime Minister Masayoshi, who apparently owed his idea to Pacific Basin Economic Council (PBEC) by businessmen grouping and Pacific Trade Development Conference (PAFTAD) led by academic economists, first proposed the Pacific Basin Cooperation in his inaugural speech in 1978. Together with his Foreign Minister Saburo Ohkita, he visited Australia and New Zealand and obtained eager support from Prime Minister Malcolm Fraser.

Such pioneer effort led to the formation of the Pacific Economic Cooperation Council (PECC) consisting of a tripartite effort including academics, private sector businessmen and bureaucrats. This eventually led to the first inter-government organisation of Asia Pacific Economics Council (APEC) in 1989 with twelve members all from PECC.

APEC's momentum was then enhanced by the 1994 Bogor Declaration, 1995 Osaka Action Agenda and 1996 Manila Action Plan that saw its membership increased to 21 nations by 1998. However, APEC's momentum was severely disrupted by the 1997–98 Asian financial crisis.

Following this, the East Asian Community (EAC) was first proposed by Japan's Prime Minister Hatoyama in October 2009 in which he stressed on the necessity of strengthening the ASEAN Plus-Three cooperation. The willingness of the Japanese to take adequate initiative and provide support towards the East Asian Summit (EAS) is significant with affirmation that such move would not damage the Japan-US alliance. However, the US was displeased that she was excluded from EAC and preferred further promotion of liberalisation within APEC instead. However, Prime Minister Abhisit Vejiajira of Thailand , the host of ASEAN Summit 2009, expressed concerns about a strong non-ASEAN initiative that may exclude ASEAN from the driver's seat for EAC.

Australian Prime Minister Kevin Rudd contested Prime Minister Hatoyama's proposition of EAC during the East Asia Summit (EAS) by reiterating his proposal of the Asia Pacific Community (APC) which includes US and India. Cleary most economies of APEC/PECC would still prefer to work within the existing APEC framework, as the non-binding regional institution has indeed served members well and has since facilitated regional trade and economic integration. Smaller economies such as New Zealand, Singapore, Chinese Taipei, Hong Kong, Malaysia, the Philippines and Vietnam which have benefited and are at the forefront of free trade would find APC unattractive as they naturally prefer their legitimate voices to be heard directly through APEC instead of being voiced through proxies in APC.

ASEAN 10+3, ASEAN 10+6, or ASEAN 10+8 or the G-2 process?

The Association of South East Asian Nations (ASEAN) consist of ten countries namely Brunei, Cambodia, Indonesia, Laos, Malaysia, Myanmar, the Philippines, Singapore, Thailand and Vietnam. Additionally, ASEAN-10 has adopted the ASEAN Charter and announced its ASEAN Economic Community blueprint which aims to achieve an ASEAN Free Trade Area (AFTA) by 2015.

The ASEAN Free-Trade Agreement (FTA) has proceeded since 1992, but various bilateral FTAs and regional FTAs such as ASEAN 10+1 FTAs have mushroomed only in the recent decade. Recent concluded RFTAs include the China-ASEAN FTA, Japan-ASEAN FTA, Korea-ASEAN FTA, and India-ASEAN FTA. It appears that ASEAN-10 is not quick in merging towards further integration of ASEAN 10+3 (i.e. China, Japan and South Korea) or ASEAN 10+6 (i.e. Australia, India and New Zealand) partly due to remaining gaps in the readiness amongst its ten members as they are quite satisfied with their status quo, and they are quite insistence to remain in the driving seat under ASEAN 10+1 arrangement in order to underscore ASEAN-10's importance.

Following President Obama's first 2009 ASEAN 10-USA dialogue held in Singapore, there has been recent talks of an ASEAN 10+8, first mooted by Singapore and gaining attention, to further include Russia and the US. Since the late 1990s, the rapid emergence of China as one of the responsible international stake holders has taken shape and it is no doubt that China's core economic and political interests would reflect and shape the future evolution of the regional institutional architecture (RIA). The evolution of RIA would be determined by the evolving challenges and opportunities that commonly confront Asian economies. China seems to favour a strong push for regional integration, institutional and capacity building in Asia broadly and seems to have down played the G-2 process with the US by emphasising her common interests and commitments especially with her Asian neighbours. In fact China has of late articulated publicly the paramount importance of forming an Asian consensus pertaining to political, economic and social reforms and liberalisation, which includes respect for diversity, pragmatism, gradualism and open-mindedness.

PECC/APEC, G-20 and G-2 Nexus and the newly proposed 3G Group

Following the 2009 global financial tsunami and the emerging presence of China, India, Russia and Brazil, the G-20 was formed in November 2008 in Washington and is fast becoming the most important — if not, the premium — platform in replacing G-8 in which the world's leading industrialised and developing countries are effectively represented and address pertinent agendas. The urgent agenda may include the excesses brought about by inadequate regulation of financial institutions, the worsening climate change, and the rising global trade imbalances.

On the other hand, there are mounting concerns that G-20 is not adequately reflecting concerns of the smaller economies which are currently not G-20 members despite the fact that they also face similar financial, trade and climate challenges. Insufficient representation is also underscored by the fact that only slightly less than half of the G-20 members are from APEC.

With regard to PECC — a sister-institution of APEC — it has been playing a relevant Track-II role in terms of floating pertinent issues, consensus seeking and shaping agenda amongst the existing 21 economies since 2005 by convening annual meetings back-to-back with annual APEC meetings.

In an attempt to promote effective global governance, Singapore has proposed the Global Governance Groups or the 3G Group at the United Nations Headquarters in New York. Singapore also hosted and convened an informal meeting of ministers during the 2010 World Economic Forum's annual meeting. The informal coalition consisting of ministers and representatives from 28 countries will help to ensure the views of economies of all sizes can be taken on board the G-20 group in the meetings held in Canada and South Korea 2010.

The 3G members are drawn from all continents and include the following 28 countries: Bahrain, Bahamas, Barbados, Belgium, Botswana, Brunei, Chile, Costa Rica, Guatemala, Ireland, Jamaica, Liechtenstein, Luxembourg, Malaysia, Monaco, New Zealand, Panama, the Philippines, Qatar, San Marino, Rwanda, Senegal, Singapore, Sweden, Switzerland, United Arab Emirates, Uruguay, and Vietnam.

There is a need for inclusive and broad base participation of countries based on the concept of variable geometry, as it is often adopted in global negotiations where all countries regardless of their size are called to participate in issues in which they have significant interests. For instance, Liechtenstein, which has a huge stake in global financial regulation, convened a meeting of experts from 3G countries in April 2010.

NOTES

* Dr. Khee Ghiap Tan, Chair, Singapore National Committee for Pacific Economic Cooperation (SINCPEC) & Associate Professor of Public

Policy, Lee Kuan Yew School of Public Policy, National University of Singapore. Dr. Shu Wen Chiang is a Research Associate at SINCPEC.

1. Paper prepared for presentation at the Conference on "APEC at 20 and the Rise of China", organised by Hong Kong APEC Study Centre, Lingnan University in conjunction with East Asian Institute, National University of Singapore, Asia Pacific Economic Association and Hong Kong Baptist University.

Index